CRACKING CASES

DR. HENRY C. LEE

with **thomas w. o'neil**

CRACKING CASES

the science of
solving crimes

Prometheus Books

59 John Glenn Drive
Amherst, New York 14228-2197

Published 2002 by Prometheus Books

Inquiries should be addressed to
Prometheus Books
59 John Glenn Drive
Amherst, New York 14228–2197
VOICE: 716–691–0133, ext. 207
FAX: 716–564–2711
WWW.PROMETHEUSBOOKS.COM

06 05 04 03 02   5 4 3 2 1

Photos used courtesy Dr. Henry C. Lee

Library of Congress Cataloging-in-Publication Data

Lee, Henry C.
    Cracking cases : the science of solving crimes / Henry C. Lee with Thomas W. O'Neil.
        p. cm.
    Includes bibliographical references and index.
    ISBN 1–57392–985–9 (alk. paper)
    1. Criminal investigation. 2. Forensic sciences. I. O'Neil, Thomas. II. Title.
HV8073 .L44 2002
363.25—dc21

2002020819

Printed in Canada on acid-free paper

CONTENTS

ACKNOWLEDGMENTS

Upon completing this book, I am very humbly indebted to a number of persons who have assisted me in the five cases we have covered. Please let me state my deep and abiding gratitude to the following individuals. First and foremost, I want to thank my co-author Tom O'Neil. His hard work and cooperation make this project possible.

Prometheus Books has been extremely professional throughout this entire project. Most important Linda Greenspan Regan is an outstanding editor and has provided this project with her excellent insights since its inception. Chris Kramer, Peggy Deemer, Jill Maxick and others at Prometheus have given this book their considerable professionalism and expertise, along with Transcontinental Printing.

I want to thank the prosecutors who worked on those cases. This very sincere gratitude extends to their assistants and staff as well. Kurt Spohn was an old friend of mine prior to the Mathison case, yet he outdid himself with his outstanding work on that case. Walter Flanagan, another old friend, did a wonderful job prosecuting the Woodchipper case, seeing that matter through long and complex trials. Another old friend, Robert Satti, who was aided most ably by Kevin Kane, steered the Sherman case through to its successful conclusion, after conducting a long and arduous investigation. Susan Dannelly was tenacious and extremely dedicated in the way she prosecuted the

MacArthur case. The American public, as well as myself, owes a great deal of gratitude to the way these prosecutors do their jobs in achieving a just outcome to terrible crimes.

I want to thank the countless professionals on the state and local police departments who worked so diligently to solve these murders. Many put in countless extra hours, working far into the night and without any extra compensation other than their being part of a great team. These knowledgeable and experienced detectives and police officers are so essential in protecting us all from the crimes and barbarities, which lie in wait for us all. Specifically, I want to thank the members of the Connecticut State Police Forensic Laboratory in Meriden. These individuals are most professional and I have been privileged to work with them for years. Thus, I am thanking Major Palmbach, Sergeant Sudol, Sergeant Mills, E. Pagliaro, K. Zercie, D. Howard, J. Hubbell, F. Kwok, C. Ladd, K. Lamy, D. Messina, R. O'Brien, P. Penders, M. Raffin, J. Reho, K. Settachatgul, M. Supple, D. Tramontozzi, J. Weronik, and all of the other fine individuals who do such wonderful work there. A special thank you to the administrative staff, V. Shook, J. Schneider, V. Kazlowski, and J. Cooper, who diligently support us each and every day. I also want to thank Mickey Gura for his special photographic assistance to me. There are countless others in the court systems who have brought their dedication and expertise to the task of prosecuting these cases. The individuals are too numerous to single out, yet I would be remiss if I failed to mention Gail Schor and Mary Simoneau, who did an excellent job as court reporters on the Sherman Case.

I am also very grateful to Dr. Lawrence J. DeNardis, the president of the University of New Haven, for his continued support and friendship as well as Dr. T. Johnson, Dr. H. Harris, and Dr. A. Harper. My continued association with that university, after twenty-five years, remains a great source of pride for me.

Finally, I want to thank those closest to me for their wonderful support and assistance on this project as well as the other challenges which confront me on a daily basis. Judge Anthony DiMaio and his wife Elaine are high on this list. Thanks to Dr. Jacob Loke, Dr. Mary Tse, Dr. Effie Chang, Lily Chuang, Dr. Frank Chuang, Dr. Romeo Vidone, and Joseph and Flore Ko, who have all provided me with encouragement and support.

My mother, An-Fu Lee, is foremost among those family members who have nurtured and assisted me. Now 105 years old, she has spent a lifetime in assisting my twelve siblings and myself find a good life for ourselves. I also must thank my son, Dr. Stanley Lee, and my daughter, Sherry Lee, for their love and support. Margaret, my wife of thirty-nine years, has been the mainstay of my world since I first met her back in China. As I have pointed out in this work, she has also been able to assist me through many difficult investigations as well as being my loving companion and the mother of my two children.

I would like to thank Governor John Rowland and his wife Mrs. Patty Rowland, Lt. Governor M. Jodi Rell, and Mama Jo McKenzie for their friendship and support. I would also like to thank Commissioner Arthur Spada, Colonel Timothy Barry, and my many fine sworn and civilian friends in the Department of Public Safety for their years of friendship and support.

In conclusion, I have a great many wonderful friends in this world. Many are prosecutors, police officers, forensic investigators, educators, and public office holders. I have to acknowledge their wonderful contributions toward making this complex world a safer and better place.

Tom O'Neil would like to thank his wife of thirty-six years, Emily Rosensteel O'Neil who heads up his list, followed closely by his daughter, Meg, and his son, Tom (a former student of mine at the University of New Haven), and his two living brothers Rory and Terry, as well as his late brother Jack. Tom has received outstanding help from many of his colleagues at Gateway Community College in New Haven, including the excellent staff at the College Library, including Bonnie Pease, Carol Boulay, Nora Bird, Patty Costello, Martha Lipowski, Michele Cone, and Bob Reilly. Tom also wants to single out Dr. Kerin Kelsey of the Humanities Department for her continued leadership and support.

Tom would also like to thank his old friend Tom Klute, Assistant Manager for Photo Services at Yale University, and Carl Kaufman of the same department as well as his old friend John Schilke, Manager of Audio Visual at Yale University. In Guilford, Connecticut, Tom's hometown community, he would like to extend a special word of thanks to Patricia Widlitz a member of the Connecticut General Assembly.

FOREWORD

In fall 1979, I was about to start my first serious trial as the new public defender for rural Litchfield, Connecticut. The case involved two men who had been charged with the gang rape of a woman. The case did not look good for the defense. The woman's statement was pretty scary for the defendants. She said she had been abducted from a bar, driven to a secluded road, and raped repeatedly by both men. She related that the men took her underpants after the rape and threw them up in a tree. She was dropped back at the bar and promptly reported the kidnapping and rape to the police.

The police followed her directions to the secluded spot and, lo and behold, her underpants were still hanging in the tree. They were seized as evidence and were the prosecution's prize exhibit at the trial.

After the underpants were marked as a full exhibit and shown to the jury, the defense seemed doomed. Even Judge Luke Martin, a mild-mannered sweetheart of a judge, was duly impressed. He called the lawyers to his bench and whispered, "How the heck are you going to get those underpants out of the tree, Charlie?" I didn't know the answer at the time. Also, I didn't know Dr. Henry Lee at the time either.

One of my public defender colleagues and mentor was attorney Tony DeMayo of New Haven. I called Tony and mentioned my problem in retrieving the panties from the tree. He said, "Call Henry Lee at the University of New Haven." I called Henry and he arrived at my office the very next day, huge briefcase in hand.

He said "All right, what your client tell you?" (Henry was still working on his English back then.) I told him that my client and the codefendant were knock-around bar guys. They claimed they knew the woman and that when they left the bar that night, she was sleeping in their car. They thought she might have had some company in the car earlier. She woke up and seemed in a party mood. They readily admitted that they all had plenty to drink before they drove off to park on a country lane. They both had sexual intercourse with her at least twice and ejaculated each time inside her. They were adamant that the sex was voluntary and freely admitted tossing her underpants in the tree.

Henry asked if he could examine the underpants. Once an object is officially in evidence, it is rarely let out of the courthouse. In this case, the combination of an easygoing judge and a fair-minded prosecutor allowed me to take the celebrity underpants to Henry's lab. He examined them on a Saturday, which I learned later was the Chinese New Year, and Henry's wife and children were waiting for Henry to drive them to Chinatown for a parade that he was to lead!

When the trial reconvened, I called my next witness, Dr. Henry Lee. Henry strode through the courtroom in what was to be his trademark entrance in every case. He nodded to Judge Martin and said, "Good morning, your honor." He then turned to the jury and said, "Good morning, ladies and gentlemen."

When I started to question him, he would turn and face the jury directly to give his answers personally to them. His testimony was fantastic for the defense. He detected a number of different seminal stains in the underpants, none of which belonged to the defendants. And, as he pointed out, they were made before the underpants were removed and placed in the tree! The victim's credibility was slipping. He testified that there were a number of tests that the hospital might have done on the victim to link the defendants to her. The state tried to rebut the latter testimony by presenting the hospital's pharmacist, who testified that the testing materials were too expensive and had a short shelf life. Hearing this, Henry said to me "Put me back on the stand and ask me same questions." I did. Henry said the testing materials cost fifty cents and had a shelf life of fifty years! The judge dismissed the kidnapping charges. The jury found both defendants not guilty, and I found a new hero, and a friend.

After the verdict the young prosecutor, now Appellate Court Judge Anne C. Dranginis, leaned over to her investigator and said, "I'll never try another case again without that guy Lee on my side." She was true to her word and never lost a case using Henry Lee.

I should emphasize that the "underpants in the tree" case is a rarity in domestic violence cases. It has been my experience in the vast majority of domestic violence cases that women are telling the truth. Furthermore, it has also been my experience that many women will fail to report the violence that is brutally perpetuated against them for a variety of reasons, one of which is the well-documented "battered women's syndrome."

Henry has three dangerous weapons: knowledge, experience, and common sense. Perhaps his best attribute is his sense of humor. Once at a luncheon at his house, a medical doctor friend seated next to me was chiding a graduate student as to why she was researching a certain medical fact when it already was proven true beyond all doubt. To make his point, the doctor said the fact was as sure as if he dropped his chopsticks, they would fall to the floor. Henry said quietly, "not if they were in a vacuum!"

I observed Henry at another trial where he was testifying about a double homicide. Henry, through blood spatters and other evidence, methodically walked the court through each step the killer took during the murders. When he finished, the defendant was heard to whisper, "How the hell did he know?" He knew because he is perhaps the brightest criminologist in the world.

This book will bring you into his world of expertise. He will walk you through five of the most difficult type murders to solve. These murders are difficult because the defendants were all respected members of their communities and extremely clever. Their stories show the true face of the total reality of domestic violence in America.

Dr. Henry Lee does their unmasking in a way that would make Sherlock Holmes extremely jealous.

Judge Charles D. Gill
Connecticut Superior Court

A PROLOGUE

It was a ghastly sight to look upon. The murderer staggering backward to the wall, and shutting out the sight with his hand, seized a heavy club and struck her down. ... Of all bad deeds that, under cover of darkness, had been committed within wide London's bounds since night hung over it, that was the worst. Of all the horrors that rose with a foul scent upon the morning air, that was the foulest and most cruel.

—Charles Dickens, *Oliver Twist*

At the outset, permit me to define the term *forensics* as the direct application of scientific knowledge and techniques to matters of law. The study of modern forensic investigations is similar to navigating the high seas, in that this subject is both an art and a science. The seafarer may have taken his sun line correctly and fine-tuned his position on his chart for the effects of tide and current, but if his senses are telling him his vessel is in another spot on the sea, then he must combine his findings with his intuition and common sense to adjust for a proper course. This is especially important to remember today, since, just like navigation, technology is making great strides in providing the forensic scientist with ever improving data. Still, even with all of this precise information, the wise forensic investigator will always remember that he must bring all of his life experiences and logic to find the truth. This means common sense, informed intuition, and the courage to see things as they are. Then he must speak honestly about what it all adds up to.

The five cases presented in this book are instances where scientific findings merged with informed intuition to help achieve justice. How can a man have possibly strangled his wife in her master bedroom and yet be able to prove he was sailing with friends at the time of her death? If a wife and the mother of three children has disappeared five weeks earlier, should her husband be dogged by police inquiries, and should his home be searched? What if no one has been able to find any direct evidence of a crime, let alone a body? How could three law enforcement officers actually murder their wives?

The quotation from Charles Dickens that introduces this book seems particularly poignant to me in light of the five cases we recount and the gender of the spousal abusers and the murder victims. Spousal abuse is one of the most underreported crimes in America today. Nationally, the vast majority of these cases presents a male perpetrator and a female victim. And in the minority of cases where a wife has assaulted her husband, this attack has often been precipitated by prior male-to-female spousal abuse. We have made progress, even since the mid-eighties, in responding to this national problem, but our society still has a long way to go in curtailing this menace.

Spousal abuse can be physical or psychological, or a combination, as most often happens. Control is a common element in both forms. You will see that abusive men want to control their spouses' finances, their minds and, ultimately, their bodies. In a marital context, the problem can involve a codependency that inhibits the victim from facing the brutish reality as well as from breaking away. If you happen to meet a victim of spousal abuse in a public place, as a friend of mine recently did, and the victim seems ambivalent about prosecuting her spouse, impress upon this woman the importance of putting any ambivalence aside and prosecuting, no matter her fear of being killed or her mistaken sense of loyalty to her abusive husband. Incidentally, while we are on the subject of domestic abuse, it's interesting to note that criminologists have found that spousal crimes are seasonal. During the holiday seasons, for instance, more homicides and domestic assaults are committed. The causes for this are rather simple: stress, pressures, alcohol consumption, and confrontations all result in these tragedies.

Overall, today's rapidly advancing forensic technology is grounded on centuries of steady progress in the field. Each advance we make is the product of many experiments and an algebraic sum of all the other efforts put forth by our ancestors in forensics. The very first paper known to have been written on forensics dealt with legal medicine, which I will define as the application of the medical sciences to the legal fields of crime and punishment. According to the world's scholars, it was written by a Chinese doctor (fortuitously for me), Hsu Chich 'Ts' si, in the sixth century C.E. However, this work is known only through subsequent citations and references since there is no known copy of it in existence today. I was fortunate to receive a copy of one of the later works, written by an unknown author in China in 1247, that alluded to the earlier landmark book. Legal medicine began to flourish around the sixteenth century, concurrent with the development of modern-day medicine and related sciences.

The end of the eighteenth century marked the true beginning of chemistry. This opened the way for the birth of toxicology. *Toxicology* is defined as a science that deals with poisons and their effect on living organisms, and also with substances otherwise harmless which interact with organisms in a harmful manner.[1] M. J. B. Orfila (1787–1853), a Spaniard, is considered the father of modern-day toxicology. At twenty, Dr. Orfila moved to Paris, where he eventually rose to great prominence in the field of medical research. His work established toxicology as an accepted science. Dr. Orfila also became the earliest known medical authority to present evidence at a criminal trial. His most famous expert testimony involved a murder victim named Lafarge who had traveled to Paris on a business trip and mysteriously died. Lafarge had taken ill after eating a cake that his wife had prepared and sent to him. Madame Lafarge, it was established, was known to be unhappy in her marriage and had recently purchased arsenic. Because of his illness, Monsieur Lafarge left Paris and returned home, where he died. Police tests for arsenic proved inconclusive, and Lafarge was buried. A month later, Orfila had the body exhumed and found traces of arsenic in the dead man's system. In his testimony, Dr. Orfila also established for the jury that the equipment used for the tests, as well as the earth around the burial site, was free of any arsenic contamination. Madame Lafarge was convicted of murder and was sentenced to jail. Orfila performed many other historic tests, including one that showed that it was impossible to pull intact spermatozoa from a seminal stain and that microscopic tests were the preferred method for identifying sperm cells.

A Frenchman, Alphonse Bertillon (1853–1914) pioneered a system of measurements which was designed to establish criminal records to define one individual as distinct from all others. Though rudimentary and later replaced by fingerprint techniques and other breakthrough sciences, Bertillon's system gave birth to *anthropometry*, which I will define as the science of measuring the human body and its parts and functional capacities.[2] These early attempts to discern the identifiable and distinguishing characteristics of an individual contributed to all the technology and effort put forth today to accomplish the same goal: To determine scientifically the exact identity of a human being.

In the 1870s, the use of fingerprints for personal identification came out of the work of William Herschel, who was a British civil servant stationed in India, and Henry Faulds, a Scottish physician who worked in Japan. The first person to propose publicly that fingerprinting be used as a means for identifying someone was an American, Thomas Taylor, a microscopist with the U.S. Department of Agriculture in Washington, D.C. Taylor's ideas were published in the July 1877 issue of the *American Journal of Microscopy*. In 1894, Mark Twain, the renowned American author, published a novella, *Puddn'-head Wilson and those extraordinary twins*, in which a murder is solved by using fingerprint evidence. Then, another British civil servant in India, Edward Henry, became the first to devise a fingerprint classification system, so that sets of individual fingerprints could be catalogued and easily retrieved. Meanwhile, in Austria, Hans Gross wrote about what he foresaw as a new field, that of criminalistics, though he only put his thoughts on paper and did not apply his concepts in the field. In Paris, after the turn of the century, Victor Balthazard and Edmond Locard carried forward and added to Gross's theories. Balthazard, medical examiner for the city of Paris, studied probability models pertaining to fingerprints, bullet comparisons, animal hairs, and blood-spatter patterns. In 1910 Locard set up the first police crime laboratory in Lyons; he is known for his postulate that any two surfaces coming into contact leave trace evidence behind. Today this is known as the *Locard Exchange Principle*.

In 1907, August Vollmer was chief of police in Berkeley, California, where he reached out to enlist the services of a University of California chemistry professor to identify a suspect. The evidence was then presented to a grand jury, though it was later ruled out because it was improperly handled prior to the laboratory findings. Vollmer then established clear and precise controls for processing such evidence and went to great lengths to train his personnel in their use. Vollmer would subsequently serve as chief of the Los Angeles police for one year and was responsible for setting up a crime laboratory there. Others quickly followed his lead. Finally, the British author Arthur Conan Doyle stirred wide public interest in the use of the sciences to solve crimes. His hero, Sherlock Holmes, along with his sidekick, Dr. Watson, did much to inform and excite a worldwide audience on the possibilities that forensic science had to offer law enforcement in the investigative process and in solving crimes.

I have briefly traced the earliest background of forensics as a way to whet the reader's appetite for the five case studies that are set forth in this book. In today's complex world of criminology and forensics, many new sciences can be brought to bear in a criminal investigation. The cases we cover should provide a collective insight to many of these forensic fields. To assist the reader, each case is broken down into a statement of its facts, its investigation, the case's court proceedings and trials, and a final and in-depth analysis of the actual forensic sciences used in solving the crime. Wherever possible, we have used pseudonyms for individuals not directly involved in the details of the case. (I believe less is more here.) I've denoted this by using an asterisk following these names.

Each of the five cases presents the opportunity, through its respective facts, investigation, and legal resolution, to study particular aspects of forensic investigation and how the forensic work fits in with the rest of the criminal justice system. No one person, in any of these cases, is responsible for the guilty being found out and successfully prosecuted before the bar of justice. The algebraic sum of the whole effort in these cases is far more than the sum of the individual parts. This is how the criminal justice system should work, and I want to humbly say that I've been privileged to play a part in these five human dramas. And now, please allow me to present the cases.

chapter ONE

THE MATHISON MURDER CASE

And the Lord said to Cain, where is thy brother
Abel. . . . And He said to him: What hast thou
done? The voice of thy brother's blood cries to me
from the earth.

Gen. 4: 9–10

The human being is both very complicated and very simple. As
we go through life, our goals and ambitions may change, but
our basic nature does not. If we have a sound grasp of what we want,
balanced against what is both good and attainable, we may live a
moral life despite whatever competing demands are placed on us.
Unfortunately, not all of us adhere to these sound principles.

In this chapter we look at a situation in which a man, Kenneth
Mathison, was able to win the genuine respect of a wide number of
officers and men in the Hilo Police Department. The setting for this
case is tropical and lush Hawaii and Sergeant Mathison, a veteran of
twenty-five years on the Hilo force, has reached a crossroads in his life.
Through determination, some good luck, and a lot of hard work, Mathison is at the brink of becoming a very successful player in the island's
real estate field. His wife, Yvonne, loves her husband and their two
children. Mrs. Mathison is also a very respected maternity nursing professional at Hilo Medical Center, located on Big Island. However, the

bond between this dynamic pair of professionals is about to be strained because of a paternity suit filed against Mathison and the fact that he has also incurred substantial debt to build his real estate empire.

The Mathison case is one that shines light down onto another dark question: Can police officers be expected to thoroughly investigate a fellow member of the force? Especially one who is well thought of and one with whom many police professionals have worked? The answers to these questions are critical to the very essence of successful police investigation. The sole objective of any investigation must be, and always must be, the search for the truth. No matter where the trail of evidence leads and no matter who, if anyone, is ultimately held responsible for the breaking of the law, investigations ultimately get back to that one objective: the truth.

THE FACTS OF THE CASE

On the Friday evening after Thanksgiving, November 27, 1992, the Hilo area of the Hawaiian Islands saw a torrential rainstorm hit the mountainous region. Yvonne and Sergeant Kenneth Mathison were driving that night in their tan 1988 Ford van along Route 131, known as Volcano Highway. Sergeant Mathison was a veteran police officer with the Hilo force, one who was respected by his fellow officers and was forty-two years old on the last night of his wife's life. Yvonne, who was a well-respected maternity nurse at Hilo Medical Center, had a daughter, Tina Marie, by a prior marriage, as well as a son, Michael, with Mathison. Yvonne was ten years older than her husband.

Mathison, in addition to his police work, had established himself as a highly successful contractor, and he had assets that totaled $1.6 million. In his police career, he had first made his professional reputation doing undercover work in the island's narcotics squad. Balanced against this financial success was the fact that Mathison and a partner owed $800,000 on a smallish shopping center they owned. Mathison had also recently purchased a good deal of life, accidental death, and mortgage insurance for his wife and himself. The net breakdown of the policies was that if Yvonne Mathison were to die, her husband would receive $400,000; if she died by accident, then he would get $595,000, and if Yvonne died in an automobile-related accident, her husband would receive $675,000. He had two policies on himself that added up to $700,000.

The Mathisons were not strangers to upheavals in their relationship. The couple had married each other twice; their first marriage had ended in a divorce several years earlier. By the Thanksgiving weekend of 1992, the couple had again been experiencing some stormy moments in their second union. In October Mathison had been named in a paternity suit. On this Friday night of the Thanksgiving weekend, when the Pacific rain pounded down in sheets, according to Mathison, he was about to break the news to his wife that a long-anticipated vacation trip would have to wait, since he was about to be named as a party in another paternity suit.

At about 8:40 P.M., just after her husband had made this startling report to her, Yvonne, in Mathison's words, "turned white." Mrs. Mathison was driving and, according to her husband, she leapt out of the vehicle before he was even aware of her intentions. He then had difficulty moving over to the driver's seat to regain control of the van. He said he had only become aware of Yvonne's erratic behavior when he felt a burst of cool air in the van.

Bill and Gisela McGuire of Hawaiian Acres in Puna said that they, indeed, saw a woman jump out in front of their vehicle in the rain that night on Volcano Highway. Bill, a retired truck driver, was behind the wheel of the family's Jeep pickup, as he, his wife, and their twelve-year-old son were approaching the Mountain View section of the road. The woman in the road had suddenly emerged from out of a clump of trees near the roadway and had darted into the Hilo-bound traffic lane. The McGuire pickup almost struck her, and the couple said they had only one or two seconds to react, particularly since the coastal storm had made the wet night particularly black.

"She deliberately stepped right out in front of me and turned her back, just like she was trying to get someone hurt. If I'd delayed [turning the wheel] one-thousandth of a second, I'd have hit her," Bill McGuire would later recall. Bill and Gisela McGuire would also say that the woman "had dark hair and could have been Caucasian." Bill would say that she "basically" looked like Yvonne Mathison, based on photos of her he was shown. When he was asked what was meant by his observation that this woman appeared to be trying to get hurt, Bill McGuire characterized her behavior as reckless and self-destructive. He said that the woman was "not acting normally," and that "she did not appear to be walking in a normal fashion."

When asked if the woman in the wind- and rainswept highway that evening was acting punch-drunk, Bill McGuire responded, "basically, something like that." Gisela McGuire recalled that the woman appeared "disoriented." She also said that she remembered that the woman in the roadway was wearing light-colored clothing. Following this strange and close call, the McGuire family proceeded to their destination, the Kubio Mall in Hilo, arriving just before 9 P.M.

Several other passersby reported a bizarre scene being played out on that stretch of Volcano Highway, one that was very close to the road's fifteen-mile Mountain View marker. Susan Albein was driving along the highway and was taken aback at the sight of a man wrestling with what appeared to be a spare tire in a van. Albein thought that the individual was trying to change a flat and that he might need assistance, but she decided against stopping because this man appeared angry and she had only her young son with her. Driving by a second time, Albein observed a purple-clad woman in the vehicle. Another motorist, Roy Ah Chin, said that when he stopped to offer help, a man shined a flashlight into his eyes, blinding him, and said that no one had been hurt and assistance was not needed.

Ironically, two occupants of a passing car were able to sketch in the dark night's gruesome details most professionally. These two witnesses were both veteran police officers. Douglas Gibb was the retired Honolulu police chief, and in the five years since leaving the force, he had become chief of security for the First Bank of Hawaii. Bernard

Ching, also a retired Honolulu policeman who was now a security manager for Sears in Hawaii, rode in the passenger's seat of Gibb's car as they traveled toward Gibb's vacation home. At about 9:30 P.M. the pair of retired officers saw a tan van on the side of the road, facing the wrong way, with a man holding the body of a woman, rocking her back and forth, in the rear of the vehicle. The van was pointed in the wrong direction, and its driver's side was tilted against some bushes at about a forty-five-degree angle. As he approached this scene, Gibb recalled that the vehicle's headlights were in his eyes but that they were flicked off as he got closer. Ching had a better view of this surreal scene since he did not have to contend with driving through the rain. He could see that the turned-around vehicle was flush up against the embankment and roadside bushes. As they moved past the van, Ching said to Gibb, "It's a Code 1," police jargon for an automobile accident. Ching thought he saw lights from a nearby house above a driveway adjacent to the spot where the van sat, and the incident looked under control. Ching, it developed, was mistaken, since there was no house on higher ground. Ching then said to Gibb that there was no need to stop, since "there's help there."

At about this time, Sharon Forsythe and her husband were also driving on that stretch of Volcano Highway, and a man approached through the driving rain toward the couple. Via the passenger's side window, this pedestrian, who was later identified as Sergeant Mathison, asked the couple to telephone the police. Mathison would later explain that he had no police radio on him to call for help himself. The Forsythes then drove directly to a store in Mountain View and made the call. The dispatcher advised them that a call on the incident had already been made. This initial 911 call could have come from Roy Ah Chin, the motorist who said that he stopped at this scene and asked a man if help was needed. Chin said that the individual told him two times that no one had been hurt and that no help was needed. When he arrived home a few minutes later, Chin called the police dispatcher, anyway.

By now Mr. and Mrs. Forsythe had returned to the scene and then set off a warning flare. At this time, Sharon Forsythe looked into the back of the van and saw blood running down an arm and someone holding a body. "He [the man she had seen earlier] was just rocking her," she would later recall. The Forsythes left the scene after the police arrived, but were not asked their names or for any kind of statement. Sharon said that she had become "nosy" during this strange episode and had wondered about what could have caused such serious injuries. Thus, she had looked around as much as possible.

Help arrived soon afterward. Paramedic Daren Rosario was one of the first on the scene. He said that Kenneth Mathison was sobbing and, after a brief examination of Yvonne Mathison, he quickly determined that she was dead. When he reported this to Mathison, Rosario said, the police sergeant became very distraught. Rosario also recalled that he had not been prepared for the lethally serious nature of Yvonne's injuries since he had seen very little damage to the van as he had approached the scene. Later on, paramedics would use tape to constrain Yvonne's arms as they transported her body to an ambulance which would then take her remains to the Hilo Medical Center.

Officer Richard Sherlock of the Hilo police was the first policeman to arrive at the scene. In another ironic twist in this series of events, Officer Sherlock, it turned out, had personal ties to both Yvonne and Kenneth Mathison. Sherlock had first met Yvonne in August of 1992 when his wife had given birth to their child at Hilo Medical Center and Mrs. Mathison had served as the attending maternity nurse. "She helped us out a lot," Sherlock said. He was impressed by the competent and caring assistance Yvonne had rendered the couple. And Sherlock knew and respected fellow policeman Kenneth Mathison since he had been his supervising sergeant in Puna for an entire year, shortly after Sherlock had joined the force. Sherlock said that when he had initially looked into the van he had found Mathison cradling his wife's bloodied body in his arms in the rear of the vehicle, with Yvonne covered by a blanket.

Officer Martin Ellazar was the other Hilo policeman who was initially at the scene. "There was a lot of blood" in the van and on Yvonne and Kenneth Mathison, he would say. He also recalled that he found

Yvonne's "extensively damaged eyeglasses" in the rear of the van. One lens from these eyeglasses was discovered in the front of the vehicle, under the passenger's seat. Police investigators also found Yvonne's very badly damaged Seiko watch hanging from the turn signal switch, on the left side of the steering wheel shaft. The watch initially showed evidence of "forced contact" caused by friction against concrete or some other very hard surface. A later report from the FBI crime labs would indicate that the Seiko was damaged in close proximity to Yvonne's head, since fragments of her hair were discovered trapped in its cracked crystal. Strangely, the damaged watch's time and date were askew, showing 8:56, Saturday, November 26.

Kenneth Mathison appeared to be in a highly emotional state as he began to talk to the medical assistance personnel, police, and others who began to arrive at the scene. He explained that Yvonne's erratic behavior, a result of their family fight, had caused her death. His wife had leaped into the dark night, and he had been forced to turn the van around and to desperately search for her. While reacting this way in the black and rainy night, he had accidentally struck Yvonne, inflicting the injuries which caused her death.

Totally panicked, Kenneth Mathison said he had forced the van around in the opposite direction and had swerved it up into the muddy ditch and embankment. Mathison had then found his wife lying in the road at the foot of a driveway, and he immediately saw that she was very badly injured. Contrary to his police and medical first-assistance training (the standard procedure: a victim with possible neck, head, or back injuries should not be moved, if at all possible), Mathison had then picked his wife up and tried to reenter the van from the back, but found the rear door locked. He then was able to reenter the vehicle from the driver's side, with no problem. This sharply conflicted with eyewitness accounts which had the van's driver's side flush against the embankment and its bushes, tilting at a forty-five-degree angle. Mathison said he next tried to get the van out of the ditch to go for help, but was unable to do so. The veteran policeman then tried to move his wife from the front seat to the rear of the van, but he could not. He said he then took his wife's body out of the van, placed her on the ground, unlocked the rear door, and carried her into the van from the back. There, Mathison said, he tied a fifteen-foot length of yellow crime scene line around Yvonne, to secure her while he again tried to free the van and drive for help. When he was again unable to regain the highway, he said he returned to the rear of the van where he was finally found sobbing, cradling his wife's body in his arms.

Mathison told the investigators that earlier that Friday, Yvonne and he had driven down to her family's home in Puna to leave some building supplies from his business for them to use. As they drove homeward through the storm, the couple had decided to take some time and spend the night in the Volcano area. And then to have things end like this.

Yvonne Mathison's body was taken that evening to the Hilo Medical Center, and an autopsy was soon performed. At Mathison's request, his wife's remains were then cremated. Dr. Charles Reinhold, the top Hilo Medical Center pathologist, conducted the autopsy. Yvonne Mathison, among her many other injuries, was found to have a badly broken jaw, two broken fingers on her left hand, multiple wounds on her head and arms, and indications of a variety of other blows to her person. Dr. Reinhold also noted abrasions on her arms which could have "quite easily" been caused by a rope, distinctly different from any marks left by medical tape placed around her by paramedics. Based on the information from the police report and the injuries found on her body, Yvonne Mathison's death was ruled accidental.

Laurie Raquel was a Hilo neighbor of the Mathisons who had observed a wild and bitter dispute between the two of them a month earlier. Much of this horrific fight had played itself out in the rain and darkness right in front of Raquel's home. During the weeks following Yvonne's death, others in their neighborhood were questioned by Hilo police investigators, but not Raquel. Even though she had called the police that night, "No one came, during or after the incident," she would later comment to others.

But we're now getting ahead of ourselves. Suffice it to say, in January of 1993 the Hilo police completed their investigation of what had happened the night of November 27, 1992, and forwarded their results to the prosecutor's office. Their recommendation: Yvonne Mathison's death should be prosecuted as third-degree negligent homicide, a misdemeanor to be tried as a traffic offense.

THE INVESTIGATION OF THE CASE

As the 1992 holiday season folded into January of 1993, the Hilo police made public that Sergeant Mathison would officially be charged with a traffic misdemeanor. Laurie Raquel was not the only individual to question the limited scope of the investigation into the untimely and strange death of Yvonne Mathison. The media and other influential individuals began to speak out, wondering if a police cover-up was impeding this homicide investigation. Public pressure began to mount for a widening of the probe of what had really happened to Yvonne Mathison on that Friday night after Thanksgiving of 1992. This pressure was particularly directed at the Hilo police investigators, who, some suspected, were glossing over facts in a very problematic case to protect Kenneth Mathison, one of their own.

Then, on January 15, 1993, Assistant District Attorney Kurt W. Spohn in the county prosecutor's office called on the Hilo police to conduct additional investigative work on the Mathison case. Spohn specifically asked that I be consulted about the bloodstain evidence found inside the van. Soon afterward, the media discovered this development, and the case became big news. Kurt Spohn said his request was made due to "inconsistencies in the case," leading his investigators and him to suspect that much more had happened than was announced and that the facts could lead to a far more serious charge than a misdemeanor.

Lieutenant Francis Rodillas and Detective Paul Ferreira were two of the police investigators assigned to conduct a more in-depth investigation. Rodillas, Ferreira, and some of their other colleagues were taking a harder look into the evidence in the Mathison death. Ferreira first telephoned me on March 11, 1993, at my office in the Connecticut State Forensics Laboratory in Meriden.

My office reflects the kind of work we forensic professionals do. I have three tiers of bookshelves that contain a large number of case files I've been requested to work on. If a messy desk is the sign of a good mind, then I must be alright in that category. Besides the computer behind my desk, which I use for everything from scheduling to developing policy to reconstructing cases, I am surrounded with crime scene photos, mixed in with mementoes, medals, and plaques. Chiefs from police departments around the world have presented mementos to me. My days are as crowded as my desk. Often, I have more than a dozen task force meetings to attend, a couple of crime scenes to investigate, and three dinners where I'm asked to speak. I am an advisor or consultant on a number of state, regional, and national police matters and often work with agents of the Federal Bureau of Investigation and area police departments. At times I have to prepare to receive police officials from Singapore or England or from a nearby jurisdiction.

When Paul Ferreira first called me from Hilo that day, he had said that there were "inconsistencies" in the physical evidence that they had

A view of Mathison's Ford van in the Hilo police garage.

observed and that these considerations were leading his colleagues and him to believe that a murder may have been committed. This type of call for assistance was not a very unusual occurrence for me. Every week I receive hundreds of requests from around this country and abroad, asking for my assistance in case investigations. I had long since decided that, with my limitations of time and resources, I have to be most careful in promising when and where I can actually render assistance to other law enforcement agencies in their investigations. I told Paul this and, based on what little I had heard, I regretted that, with several hundred major case investigations waiting for me, I would probably be "too busy" to be of much help to him. I suggested to him that he should contact Dr. Alvin Omori, the chief medical examiner in Honolulu, or other local forensic experts. Paul was very persuasive, and his concerns changed my mind. I told him that I would take a look at some of the crime scene photographs he and the other investigators had taken. I suggested to him that he should not send me the entire file, but just a few, selected photographs and investigation reports which depicted those areas of "inconsistencies." However, when I put the phone down and checked my schedule that day, I was convinced that, most likely, I would not be looking into the Mathison case any further.

As I have emphasized, one of the absolute rules of the forensic professional is that the investigator must keep an open mind on any and all scientific evidence. This approach must be dispassionate and as totally objective as possible. Thus, when I had received the investigative reports, the autopsy report, and a set of crime scene photographs sent by Paul Ferreira and had studied them, I was able to see rather quickly that there was much more to this case than what Sergeant Mathison had alleged. This was particularly true of the photos taken of the blood evidence from the interior of the Mathisons' Ford van. So, on March 21, I wrote to Paul that there were very serious inconsistencies in what the patterns of the blood spatters showed and what Mathison had told the police who first arrived on the scene the night of his wife's death. I concluded in my letter to Detective Ferreira that I was "in agreement" with Paul on these points. I now had the distinct feeling that I would be studying this case a great deal more thoroughly than I had originally thought when Paul called me ten days earlier.

Initially, Paul Ferreira had sent me a set of 175 photos which had been taken by members of the Hilo Police Department over a period of three months, starting with fourteen taken by Detective S. Guillermo of the Hilo Police Department on the night of Yvonne's death and twenty-five autopsy photos taken at Hilo Hospital. The majority of Detective Guillermo's photos depict a variety of exterior views of the Mathisons' van. There were another six shots taken which showed the bloodstains found at various locations inside the van. Since most of these were views of the vehicle from a distance, no detailed analysis of the blood-spatter patterns could be made from them.

Another grouping of photos was taken by Officers Steve Guillermo and Larry Webber, who were also among the first at the scene. Officer Martin Ellazar was subsequently assigned to the case a week after Yvonne Mathison's death. He executed a search warrant for the van and took photos between December 9 and 12. Ellazar did an excellent job in documenting the crime scene. His series of eleven photos depict much closer views of the bloodstains in the interior of the vehicle, which was useful to me. What appear to be bloodstains can be clearly seen in the cargo area in the rear of the van, on the middle console and the roof area near the dome light, on the plastic cover of the speedometer, on the steering wheel, and on the driver's side door and window. Some of these bloodstains are consistent with contact-transfer smears, such as when bloody hair or clothing brushes against a surface. Still others are similar to medium-velocity impact types of spatters, meaning that the blood actually flew through the air from the point of origin to the receiving surface where it spattered due to an impact force. I quickly examined these photos in my study at home, working in the middle of the night. I closed my eyes and my mind began to churn through the possibilities. Nothing in Sergeant Mathison's narrative of the events could account for the types of blood spatters that had been photographically documented inside the van.

Paul Ferreira took the next batch of thirty-two photos, on February 23. He did this after obtaining a second search warrant for the van.

Prosecutor Spohn was moving very cautiously and insisted on the second warrant, especially since he felt the vehicle's chain of custody had been questionable. With the exception of three shots of the exterior of the van, all of these photos contained compelling blood evidence. These patterns can be summarized into four subgroupings:

1. Blood-like stains are seen on the drywall panel and the spare tire in the cargo area which consist of low-velocity passive blood drops, meaning that the blood had dripped from above, downward, propelled only by the force of gravity. Also, there were a number of contact-type blood smears, and medium-velocity, cast-off blood spatter, meaning that some movement of a bloody object caused the blood to be cast off and to land on that particular surface.

2. There were stains found on the roof near the dome light, sun visor, and steering wheel and on the side of the driver's seat which were consistent with contact-transfer patterns. Some of these were indicative of a transfer pattern caused by hair swipe.

3. Blood stains were found on the driver's inside door, window, and door frame areas. These were mainly contact-dripping patterns, meaning that blood had dripped from a bloody source onto these surfaces. Still others in this area were caused by medium-velocity impact blood spatters, indicating a force had caused the blood to move in that direction from its source.

4. Bloodstains were shown on the plastic cover of the instrument panel which were consistent with medium-velocity impact blood spatters. These blood spatters could have been produced only by external, medium-velocity impact forces.

Two days later, Paul Ferreira took another eighty-seven photographs. These can also be organized into four subgroupings:

1. Twenty-two of these show exterior views of the van. They show that the clearance between the bumper of the vehicle and the ground is about fourteen inches.

2. Thirty-one pictures are additional views of the van's interior. These, more or less, duplicate the blood-grouping photos taken by him on February 23.

3. Twenty-six of these photos are views of the undercarriage of the vehicle. Blood and tissue-like substances appear at several locations on the passenger's side of the van's undercarriage. The clearance between the lowest portion of the undercarriage and the ground appears to be between ten and fourteen inches.

4. Eight of the photographs show the evidence seized by the Hilo Police Department, which included clothing items and other objects.

Finally, twenty-five photos were taken by Dr. Reinhold at the Hilo Hospital autopsy. They depicted facial injuries, a tire-like impression on Yvonne Mathison's left chest area, and other injuries apparent on her left hand, left arm, and her head.

Now the Mathison investigation was gathering momentum. Any implication that members of the Hilo Police Department were performing their duties in an indifferent or even counterproductive fashion had been completely put to rest. Indeed, the Hilo police had done an outstanding job of preserving all of the blood evidence in the van, keeping the vehicle in a secured storage area. They made sure that there was no chance of anyone getting to it to remove any physical evidence, such as incriminating bloodstains. Unfortunately, photographs are a two-dimensional representation of things and very often lack a three-dimensional portrayal of the crime scene and evidence. Photographs are highly valuable but provide only a selective representation. Thus, I can only study the crime scene through the limitations of the camera's optic and the photographer's point of view. After studying these photographs, it was crystal clear to me that I would be going to Hawaii to conduct a further examination. But the first available weekend would be May 13 the following spring (1993). I would have to wait until then to closely examine the van and the other evidence which had been collected by the Hilo detectives.

At about this time several other investigative efforts were being launched which would bear fruit in this complicated investigation. Though she was never called or questioned, the eyewitness account of Hilo neighbor Laurie Raquel would come into play, laying the evidentiary groundwork for the fact that Yvonne and Kenneth Mathison were experiencing severe tensions in their marriage.

A month before Yvonne Mathison died in her family van, she and her husband had a bitter dispute on an evening which also saw a heavy rainfall, a dispute that erupted into an extremely loud and volatile fight. The couple's argument climaxed with Yvonne leaving her home and running down the street, away from her husband. Mathison proceeded to get into a family car and followed his wife down their rain-swept street, directly in front of Laurie Raquel's house. Mathison drove his "sliding" car toward his wife in a way which deeply alarmed Raquel, who later said, "He almost hit her right in front of our house." When Mathison had finally stopped alongside his wife, he screamed at her, "Get the hell into the car." The incident was so disquieting that Raquel called the police, even though she knew that Mathison was on the force. In fact, Sergeant Mathison was an influential member of the Hilo Police Department and had, perhaps, discouraged other witnesses from coming forward. But his wall was beginning to crumble.

Kurt Spohn was originally with the Hawaii County Prosecutor's office when he took over this case. In late October 1993, Spohn accepted a job offer to join the attorney general's office for the state of Hawaii. The county prosecutor and the attorney general quickly agreed that the case would be best served if Spohn took the case with him, which he did. This decision assured a continuity in the investigation. Through all of this, county detectives and members of the state prosecutor's office were uncovering more evidence of Mathison's heavy-handed treatment of his wife. Yvonne had exclusive ownership of a house on Kuulei Street in Hilo, after the couple's divorce. Following their remarriage, Mathison had refinanced Yvonne's home in his own name, coming out of that deal with 100 percent of the ownership, and $140,000. This raised investigators' eyebrows.

Now deputy attorney general, Kurt Spohn was an excellent selection to head up this high-profile prosecution. A Yale graduate, Spohn is a meticulous individual and a brilliant lawyer. With Spohn's support, George Kruse took on the role of chief state investigator. There were solid reasons for the prosecutors to be concerned about Mathison's continuing presence on the Hilo police establishment. It later developed that Mathison had had some form of contact with at least two individuals who would become witnesses in this case.

During the spring of 1993, the forensic laboratory at the Federal Bureau of Investigation was analyzing the fifteen-foot, yellow synthetic rope (the kind also used on small boats) which carried a substantial number of human hair specimens. The FBI lab scientists discovered dozens of hairs that were similar to Yvonne's, embedded in the rope. Nearly all of these hair strands had been broken off in the middle and were not pulled out of Mrs. Mathison's head by the roots, according to the FBI report. This indicated, the bureau's scientists concluded, that the rope had been "tightened up considerably" once it had become entangled with Yvonne's hair. These hair strands were a match for the hair taken from Yvonne during the autopsy, prior to her remains being cremated. Special Agent Michael Malone of the FBI laboratory found that this rope had been tightened with such intense force that it broke the individual strands. This conclusion conflicted with Mathison's claim that he had simply secured his wife's body as he prepared to look for assistance.

However, the Reverend Orville Mathison, Kenneth Mathison's father, would tell of Yvonne's coming into contact with a similar yellow rope on the day before her death. On the morning of Thanksgiving day, the family had been loading a motorcycle into the cargo bay of the van, and some of the line had become entangled in Yvonne's hair. The FBI report, however, concluded that a substantial amount of force had been applied to Mrs. Mathison's brown hair, enough to break the strands.

On May 7 I flew to Hawaii. I had been able to move my original departure date forward six days. The entire trip from Hartford to a stopover in Chicago, then on to Hawaii, and finally to Hilo took a total of seventeen hours. Detective Paul Ferreira was waiting at the Hilo airport. Kurt Spohn was away attending a homicide seminar in Honolulu, and Paul had broken away from the training. Later on, Spohn told me that he'd asked Detective Ferreira how my investigation of the van had gone. I'm flattered that the prosecutor quoted Paul as saying he'd learned more in the few hours he'd observed me than in the entire two-week seminar. Because of the seminar, I would not get the opportunity to meet Spohn in person until the following December when I would arrive to testify at the case's preliminary hearing.

Although I have been to Hawaii many times to work on cases and to testify, this was my first trip to Hilo. My trips there have always been limited to Honolulu. Over the years, I have made many good friends, such as the former District Attorney Keith Kaneshiro and his principal assistant, Carol Sunaga. This list also includes former Crime Lab Director Gilbert Chang and current Director Joanne Fruyo, Dr. Lee Goff, Chief Medical Examiner Dr. Kanti VonGuluthner, former Major Wilson Sullivan, Tracy Tanaka, Curtis Kubo from the Honolulu Police Department, and Sergeant Brian Kaya and John Wilt from Maui. In most of my trips, my wife, Margaret S. Lee, accompanies me, often working with me as my loyal assistant. Margaret helps me pack the wide array of equipment I need to bring along. This equipment list includes laser lights, a large magnifier, microscopes, chemicals, and reagents. My first impression of Big Island, Hawaii, where Hilo is located, was dominated by its extreme beauty and its immensity. Margaret and I checked into our hotel and went to our room. We had a gorgeous view of a tropical rock garden, and in the distance I can still see, in my mind's eye, the greenish and blue Pacific Ocean, which sent a stream of white-tipped breakers up against the black volcanic rocks below our windows. Standing there I could take in all of the bay area, dominated by palm trees and the deep blue waters. I could have simply enjoyed this experience for days, except for the fact that I was there to answer the call to assist and to seek answers for what events led to a very tragic and untimely death.

Early the following day, Paul Ferreira and I got to work and mapped out our schedule for the next few days. We would first visit the scene. We planned to walk through the entire roadside crime scene to reconstruct the possible sequence of events and then settle in to examine the Mathisons' van to search for evidence and to reconstruct the blood-spatter evidence.

Although the van had considerable rust on its exterior, it was in good shape. It had been housed in the Hilo police garage. Camera and magnifying glass in hand, I spent nearly ten hours examining the van. I examined every inch of the van's exterior. I could find no fresh damage areas, no visible bloodstains, no tissue-like material, and no fabric impressions on the exterior surface of the van. Usually, in traffic accidents involving a vehicle hitting a person, we find damage to the vehicle and exchanges of trace evidence due to the force of impact. Those are the clues which a forensic scientist would often find if a vehicle has been in an accident. What I did find was a purplish-colored stain on the exterior of the van, behind the driver's side door. Chemical testing for the presence of blood here proved negative, and the stain appeared to have come from some kind of fruit or berry. Some dried vegetation was noted on the lower part of the driver's doorjamb.

With the assistance of Margaret, Paul Ferreira, and Francis Rodillas, the van was then placed on a lift so I could inspect its undercarriage. I

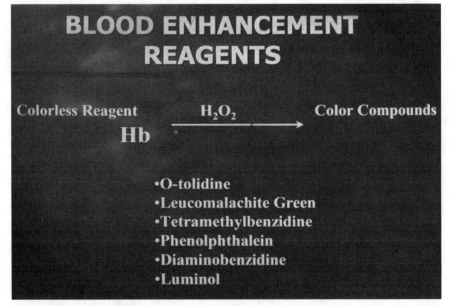

Reagents for the detection of blood.

must admit to some apprehension, if not downright fear, each time I climb under a heavy vehicle with one end suspended in space, directly above me. Once I actually get to work, I'm able to put this anxiety aside, but until then I sometimes have to wonder about the old, rusty suspension devices in the police garage slipping and what it would feel like to be crushed underneath. A hazard of the forensics trade. Lying on my back, I quickly got to work. Several recently damaged areas were found and photographed. These undercarriage damages contained contact-type smears of a substance later identified as human blood. Hair-like fibers, soil residue, and vegetative matter were also found in several areas under the passenger's side of the van. These items of evidence were also photographed before samples were collected. Chemical testing for the presence of blood was positive for specimens from the axle and muffler. Hair and fiber-like materials were found on the passenger's side of the axle area. These materials were also collected and transferred to the Hilo Police Department for future testing.

Moving into the vehicle, a fracture mark in the windshield was noticed. This fracture was consistent with a linear, radial fracture pattern. No blood or hair-like matter could be found. Some reddish, blood-like stains were discovered on several areas on and around the driver's seat, on the roof area of its driver's side, and on the interior of the driver's door. These stains were all collected and later tested for human blood and all proved positive.

Next, we moved our examination to the interior of the vehicle. We started from the front midportion of the van, the area between the driver's and passenger's seats. A bloodstain was observed on the side of the back support of the driver's seat. This stain measured three inches by five inches and was consistent with a contact-transfer type of smear. Also, stains were found on the plastic cover in front of the instrument panel. These bloodstains were consistent with medium-velocity impact types of blood spatters, meaning that the source of the blood, or its point of origin, was not in direct contact with the surface, but blood was projected by a force which propelled the blood droplets onto the receiving surface. It is possible to trace the direction from which blood spatters originate, as well as assess their path through the air. These blood droplets came down to the plastic surface from above, hitting the plastic cover at an angle of approximately ten to twenty degrees.

Moving upward, now, we inspected the roof portion of the vehicle, where a large bloodstain on the sun visor of the driver's side and another on the roof near the dome light were found. The visor stain measured five by three inches and was consistent with a transfer-swipe type of pattern. The direction of the swipe was in a right to left motion, using the driver's seat, looking forward, as a frame of reference. The stain, when chemically enhanced, resembled a hair-swipe type of pattern. In addition, medium-velocity impact blood spatters were also observed in this area. The bloodstain found near the dome light was long and crusty. This stain measured eleven inches in length and consisted of four distinct but connected blood patterns. It was also consistent with a typical contact-swipe pattern. Human hair was also found in this area and was collected. After testing, these hair findings were identified as similar to Yvonne Mathison's head hair. Several other bloodstains were also found on the roof of the vehicle, on the driver's side, which were also similar to contact-transfer patterns.

Blood-like stains were found on the middle top portion of the driver's metal door frame. One stain was heavy and crusty and was approximately two by three inches. This bloodstain was consistent with a combination of a direct-contact and a transfer type of pattern. This stain also indicated that at one time the blood source had had direct contact with this metal surface, and that this blood source then moved away from the metal surface and thus caused a transfer type of blood pattern to be left behind. Blood-like crusts were found on the screw and nut above that bloodstain. In addition, hairs which were consistent with human head hair were also found, and these hairs and hair fragments were collected for further examination.

We basically followed a zone search method to examine the van. In other words, the van was divided up into zones, and we systematically searched each zone for clues. Next, blood-like stains were observed on the interior surface of the driver's window. These consisted of a group of approximately thirty individual small blood spatters. The size of these blood spatters was approximately one to three millimeters in diameter. The pattern of these stains was consistent with medium-velocity impact spatters. This finding suggested that the driver's window was raised at the time these blood spatters were deposited. Approximately fifteen bloodstains were found on the interior surface of the driver's door. Some of these bloodstains were consistent with smear patterns. These smears appear to show a motion from right to left and downward. Other bloodstains were consistent with vertical blood drops which impacted the surface of the door at an acute angle of approximately ten to twenty degrees.

Bloodstains were also found on the interior surface of the driver's door frame. A four-inch-long bloodstain was located on the upper right corner of the frame. This stain is consistent with a contact-transfer type of pattern. A bloodstain approximately two inches wide and thirty inches long was next found on the left side of the door frame. This stain was consistent with a contact dripping and running pattern. The direction of this blood flow was clearly from the top, downward.

After a break for lunch, we moved our attention to the next zone, the instep area next to the driver's door. There we discovered dry, vegetative materials, a cigarette butt, soil-like debris, hair-like matter, and bloodstains in the form of spatters. These blood spatters consisted of approximately twenty small bloodstains, about one to three millimeters in size. With the aid of forensic light sources, we found a bundle of hairs in the shadow of the corner of the instep. This bundle of hairs consisted of approximately twenty strands. These hairs were microscopically similar to Yvonne's head hair. Blood-like crusts were also found caked on these hair remains. Most important, the hairs had crushed, cut ends. This suggested that these hair strands had gone through a traumatic impact as they were separated from Yvonne's head.

The next search area was the van's steering wheel and shaft. We found blood smears on the steering wheel which were multiple deposits, meaning that some of the bloodstains were left on top of other bloodstains. As previously stated, Yvonne's watch was found hanging on the turn signal lever on the left side of the steering wheel. Bloodstains were then observed on the plastic surface adjacent to the left side of the steering wheel column. Now we moved from the steering wheel column to the odometer, where we discovered another striking finding. There were approximately one hundred or more blood spatters on the right side of the odometer cover. These blood spatters were consistent with medium-velocity impact spatters. The direction of these spatters was from the upper left toward the lower right and impacted the odometer cover at a ten- to twenty-degree angle. This finding suggests that Yvonne was hit repeatedly by a blunt object while she was sitting on the driver's side.

We now moved our attention to the rear of the van. We found a large number of bloodstains in the area in and around the spare tire. Most of these bloodstains were consistent with contact-transfer smears. A bloody imprint pattern was discovered on the top interior panel of this area. However, this pattern was not totally visible. In 1976, when I was a professor at the University of New Haven, we did some research to develop techniques to enhance bloody imprints. One of the chemicals that we discovered worked well was Ortho-Tolidine. Ortho-Tolidine, in reduced form, is colorless. However, in the presence of heme (a molecule attached to hemoglobin) and hydrogen peroxide, Ortho-Tolidine will turn blue. We then applied this chemical reagent to the surface containing this imprint pattern. The top portion of the pattern appeared to consist of two contact handprints. Both of these imprints were left by an individual's hand which was covered with blood. The bloodied handprint to the left, as one looked toward the rear of the van, appeared to have been made with a partially closed fist, in motion. The direction of this motion is from left to right, again looking toward the rear, and downward, at a forty-five degree angle. The other bloody handprint, the one to the right, was made by a twisting motion, from left to right, and downward. This bloody handprint also continued in a downward motion, toward the left, as one again looks to the back. These imprints showed that someone's hand, covered with blood, had contact with this area and caused these pattern transfers.

Finally, we found a large amount of blood spatters on the interior roof, near the middle portion of the van. Approximately one hundred blood spatters were established, consistent with medium-velocity spatters. Some of these one hundred spatters appeared to be moving from right to left facing forward, and others appeared to be moving from the van's back to its front. Some of these spatters could have been caused by a casting-off type of motion. Others were similar to medium-velocity impact patterns.

During this investigation I took sixty-six photos and many pages of notes. While I continued my work, I was ably assisted by Detective Ferreira and Peter Alona, an experienced investigator from the county prosecutor's office. After spending a considerable amount of time in Hilo, I returned to my office and wrote a reconstruction report, complete with the photos and a fourteen-point evidentiary summary. In this summation I was able to make the point that, with the blood, hair, and fiber evidence collected, it was clear that the victim had made contact with the passenger's side undercarriage. The tire-like impression on Yvonne Mathison's left chest area furthered this finding. No tire marks, I noted, were found on Yvonne's face or the rest of her body. Along with the findings in the autopsy report, the sum of the evidence showed that there was "clearly a lack of typical automobile injury patterns on the lower extremities of the victim's body, and there was no damage found on the exterior of the van." This would also suggest that Yvonne Mathison was not struck by any vehicle while in an upright position. Also, in the autopsy report eventually issued by Dr. Alvin Omori of the Honolulu Medical Center, he concluded that "the injuries found on the victim's head could not be explained by an auto accident."

In my summarization, I noted that the medium-velocity blood spatter found on the plastic cover of the instrument panel, with its amount and distribution, suggested that the blood was deposited, from the driver's perspective, in a left to right and downward direction, "with an energetic source." I continued on this critical point: "These patterns could have been produced by arterial or venous gushing from the victim's wounds." Again, this type of blood pattern could not be explained by a vehicle running over the victim. I added that the large amount of the medium-velocity blood spatters found on the driver's instrument cover indicated that "these blood spatters were produced by multiple impact sources." The contact-transfer smears with hair-swipe patterns found on the sun visor and on the roof area near the dome light indicated that at "one time a blood source was in contact with this area, causing a transfer. The hair swipe patterns could have been caused by hair soaked with blood. The pattern indicates movement from left to right, which is also inconsistent with the theory that the victim was run over by a vehicle."

As I continued, I noted that "the heavy, crusty stain found near the nut above the window frame" indicated that there had been "heavy contact between a blood source and this particular area. Hair and tissue-like materials observed in this area could suggest that the victim's head had impacted this particular location at one point in time." Of course, I again noted that these patterns were also inconsistent with "a simple traffic accident." I went on to conclude that "a large amount of medium-velocity blood spatter was found on the roof of the cargo bay and on the interior wall of the passenger's side near the spare wheel. The patterns, amount, and distribution of these suggested that at one point in time multiple medium-velocity impacts were applied to a blood source, thus causing some of the deposits."

Finally, I reported that the enhanced blood imprints "found on the interior wall of the passenger's side of the cargo bay [indicated] that an individual's hand covered with blood [had] contacted the wall surface with two separate motions in a downward direction." Following my investigation of all the blood spatters and other samples, I summed up my findings with two points:

1. The bloodstains found on the undercarriage of the passenger's side of the vehicle are consistent with contact-transfer smears from a blood source. These could have resulted from an incident in which the victim was run over.
2. The blood-spatter patterns inside the van are inconsistent with a traffic accident. These patterns are consistent with that which

would result from multiple impact forces being exerted on the left side of Yvonne's face and her head.

I sent my findings on June 20, 1993, to Police Chief Victor V. Vierra of the Hilo Police Department and, of course, to Deputy Attorney General Kurt Spohn. More was happening on the investigative front, and the circle of profoundly damaging evidence continued to tighten around Sergeant Kenneth Mathison. All of this culminated in an arrest warrant for Mathison being issued on December 6, 1993, on one count of second-degree murder and one count of kidnapping. He would be arrested the next day, December 7, a little over a year after Yvonne's tragic death. Chief Vierra placed the defendant on administrative leave that day, and Mathison's bail was set at $105,000. His father, Orville Mathison, quickly produced that amount, resulting in his son's release from custody.

Hawaii District Court Judge William Chillingworth held four days of public evidentiary hearings which started on December 16 in his Keaau courtroom. Prosecutor Spohn produced the evidence he had gathered against Mathison. Of course, by now the case had attracted wide media interest, with some reporters covering the proceedings from news media based on the mainland. A total of eighteen witnesses testified. George Kruse read into the record a statement of findings from special agent Michael Malone, the hair expert from the FBI laboratory.[1] Several other prosecution expert witnesses testified, including me. These hearings concluded on December 21, and, on that day, the suspended Sergeant Mathison was formally discharged from the Hilo Police.[2]

Almost two more years would pass before this murder case would come to trial. During this time the defense team gathered as attorneys for Kenneth Mathison vigorously attempted to block my testimony. Mathison's lawyers also filed a motion for a change of venue because of the vast of media coverage the case had attracted. Both of these defense efforts failed. In still another irony that occurred in this terrible case, the actual trial would take place during the Thanksgiving season of 1995, the same time of year as the original tragedy in 1992. Of course, I had to cancel quite a few meetings and postpone several other testimonies to clear my calendar for a return trip for the trial.

THE MATHISON TRIAL

The trial of Kenneth Mathison for the murder of his wife, Yvonne, took place in the Keaau courtroom of Judge Greg Nakamura. This murder case had taken on a life of its own, becoming one of the most sensational murder trials in the history of the Hawaiian Islands. When the final verdict by the jury of seven men and five women would be rendered five weeks after the trial's start, three extra police officers would have to be called into the courtroom by Judge Nakamura, as a precaution. Members of the families, friends, and many other supporters were there, including Yvonne's brother, Robert Martins, and her daughter, Tina Marie Cawagas. In addition, the Reverend Orville Mathison, Kenneth's father, and some of Mathison's friends were present. The tension and friction could be felt in the air.

Prosecutor Kurt Spohn had headed up a very sound team effort during the almost three years the case was pursued. He would introduce, in addition to my forensic testimony, the expert testimony of Dr. Werner Spitz, of Wayne County, Michigan, an internationally respected forensic pathologist. One of the Hawaiian papers called Dr. Spitz "the author of the bible on forensic pathology."[3] Herbert Mac-Donnell, a professor from Corning Community College in New York and director of a forensic laboratory, would also appear for the prosecution. Later on, my credentials on blood-pattern analysis would be attacked by a defense expert, retired Captain Tom Bevel of the Oklahoma City Police Department, a former student of MacDonnell's. The local media said MacDonnell was considered "the modern day father in the field of blood-spatter stain analysis."[4] MacDonnell would refute Tom Bevel on my credentials, saying that my expertise was "unimpeachable" and way beyond what the defense witness had said in

Prosecutor Kurt Spohn and Dr. Lee in the Hawaii courtroom.

court. Though the trial judge limited MacDonnell's testimony, Kurt Spohn later told me MacDonnell was prepared to support every conclusion I had drawn in the case.

The Mathison team was headed by attorney Michael Weight, a well-known and highly respected defense attorney from Honolulu, and they would assemble and call their own experts to rebut the prosecution's case. In addition, the defense also contacted Dr. Michael Baden, a world-renowned medical examiner from New York. However, Dr. Baden informed the defense, after he had reviewed all of the record, that he agreed with my conclusions and findings. Dr. Baden was not called by the defense to testify during the trial.

Much was made during the trial about what kind of payment each of us received. I had agreed, after being contacted by Detective Ferreira and taking my first close look at the inside of the Mathisons' van, to participate in the case for my expenses. MacDonnell was receiving a flat sum of $5,000, plus expenses, for his services. The defense's key blood expert, Tom Bevel, would be paid $125 per hour, not to exceed $1,500 per day for his testimony, plus reimbursement for expenses. MacDonnell also explained that working on the case provided him with a three-day chance to get away from his laboratory. If the scientist is true to his professional calling, the amount of money he receives for his work seems irrelevant, doesn't it? Like the honest umpire, the expert has to call the facts the way he sees them.

Most of the facts in this case had stayed substantially in place since the time of Yvonne Mathison's death in late November 1992. However, there was one significant change in the defendant's accounting of what had happened that Friday night. Contrary to what he had told the first police officers arriving on the scene, Sergeant Kenneth Mathison was now claiming that he had not run over his wife while he was searching for her in the heavy rains on Volcano Highway. Instead, he now remembered, he had found Yvonne's body after she had been struck by another motorist, a hit-and-run driver. Mathison would insist that he had found Yvonne lying, mortally wounded, at the foot of the driveway that was below the lighted property which Chief Gibb and his companion Bernard Ching had taken as assurance that help was on the way. But more on that later in the trial.

Prosecutor Spohn moved straight ahead with his effort to prove his charges that Mathison had beaten his wife to death, after tying her up with that length of yellow synthetic cord. Spohn would introduce evidence of Mathison buying $675,000 worth of life insurance on Yvonne, adding that he would be entitled to an additional $1,000,000 rider should she become the victim of a hit-and-run driver. He would also show that Mathison had financial troubles with the $800,000 he and his partner owed on their shopping center. And Spohn would zero in on Mathison's reputation, calling him a "professional liar." He cited a life insurance policy Mathison had purchased which awarded the insured a better rate if he was a nonsmoker. Mathison not only smoked, but had signed the insurance document's smoking disclaimer. In another formal contradiction, in the earlier paternity suit Mathison had initially claimed that he had had a vasectomy performed, then denied that, and finally went back to his original version, that he'd had the procedure performed. Spohn would say that Mathison first learned his trade as a liar when he became an undercover narcotics officer in his earlier years in the Hilo Police Department, a charge Mathison would deny, saying he had never resorted to lying in that job assignment.

I was called to the witness stand on October 30, fairly early in the five-week trial. To make my points understandable to the court and members of the jury, I used red ink to demonstrate the science of blood spatter and showed sixty-nine slides of crime scene photographs of the bloodstains which were found inside the van. In the Mathison case, Prosecutor Spohn enabled me to get to the very heart of what I had to offer. I testified that the blood evidence and its patterns which we found in the Mathison van were caused by "impact," by someone being struck by the hands or by a blunt object, such as a pipe or a flashlight. These patterns indicated "vigorous activity within the van." On the stand I emphasized what I had found, six critical types of bloodstain patterns in the van, and I was able to make the following points:

1. A "swipe" of blood on the driver's side visor showed that blood on Yvonne's hair "had direct contact with that surface."
2. There were hairs and heavily crusted blood found in the area of the metal nut above the driver's side door, indicating that Yvonne's head and face were hitting against that area of the van.
3. A portion of a rope and a bunch of hairs with damaged ends were found on the step-up below the driver's side door. This showed that a bundle of head hair had been separated from Yvonne's skull by blunt force and subsequently fell into the van's step-up area.
4. Bloody imprints of a hand and fingers were found on the wall next to the van's cargo door, which indicated that Yvonne's hands, covered with large amounts of blood, were against the wall next to the cargo door.
5. Medium-velocity impact blood spatters were found on the instrument panel cover, which suggested that the victim received repeated blows while she was sitting in the driver's side of the van.

6. There was one section of floor in the back of the van where soil was deposited on top of the blood, which led to the determination that the bloodstain preceded the soil. At one point in my cross examination, I expressed the opinion that, "Simply holding a dead body in the front seat could not explain all of those different types of bloodstain patterns found in that area."

When the defense's blood-spatter experts took the stand, the blood-spatter evidence which I had found in the van had proven very difficult for the defense to refute. Tom Bevel used a dashboard taken from a similar Ford van to show where the blood was found on the instrument panel. He said it was possible that the blood was sprayed there when Mathison tried to move his wife's body into the van's rear and her head struck the steering wheel in that process. Upon cross examination, Bevel could not say which version of his accounting of the blood-spatter facts was more likely to be true, the prosecution's or

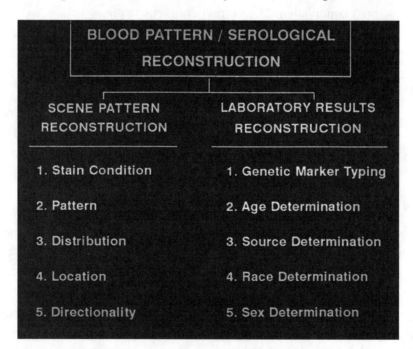

A flowchart for reconstruction of blood evidence.

defense's. As noted before, Tom Bevel, in his direct examination, was trying to imply that I was not as highly respected in professional circles as some would lead them to believe. Herbert MacDonnell's refutation of Tom's charge and his testimony had spoken for themselves. As an aside, let me refer to the old adage of trial law which holds that the lawyer with the strongest case will argue the facts, one with less strength will argue the law, and the one with the weakest case will use *ad hominems*, that is, go after personalities.

The defense spent a lot of time trying to refute the hair evidence. Dr. Jeffrey Herten, an assistant professor at the University of California at Irving, was called to address the question of the strength and condition of Yvonne Mathison's hair. Dr. Herten was introduced as an expert in the field of dermapathology, the study of abnormal skin.[5] The FBI laboratory's slides of the hair, he said, showed abnormalities, pointing out tapered areas called "Pohle's marks." These indicated weakened areas of the hair caused by dietary or other physical problems which occurred when the hair was growing. These areas showed what was termed a "bulbous enlargement," meaning that Yvonne's hair was fragile and more prone to fracture or breakage. He said, in answering a question from defense counsel, that it was "possible" that simply brushing up against a rope could result in the abundance of hair left behind. He also said that "a fair amount" of hair could become entangled if a rope came in contact with the hair. The jagged plastic edges of the synthetic rope could, Dr. Herten testified, snag hair strands because the hair strands were "sticking out, a lot like Velcro."

On the prosecution's side of the case, Dr. Spitz testified on the overall nature of the wounds to Yvonne's head. He had found that there was a severe wound, from a blow by an instrument, which tore the skin on the side of her head and caused a severe skull fracture. This was not a wound which could have been caused by a car, he told the court. He then made a very critical observation: "This was a perpendicular blow." This meant that the blow came down on Mrs. Mathison's head from directly above, at an angle of ninety degrees. A car, Dr. Spitz underscored, would have caused a "grazing blow." He also added that there were no traces of any "burn marks" to the opposite side of the victim's head, ones that would have been consistent with her being struck by a car. Dr. Spitz went on to testify that this terrible and lethal blow appeared to have come from a weapon like a pipe, one with a threaded end, similar to something found at a construction site.

Referring to a fracture in the ulna in Yvonne's left arm, Dr. Spitz said that this was consistent with a sharp blow and represented a defensive wound, with the victim raising her arm to protect herself from her assailant. It was not, he said, due to a wound from being hit by a car. Dr. Spitz also testified that a grouping of wounds seen on the victim's head would have come from a repeated and rapid series of blows by her attacker. Those wounds were there, he said, "Simply because they were inflicted in rapid succession." As a result of this attack and because of its intensity, Dr. Spitz continued, Yvonne Mathison's brain began to swell. He concluded that Yvonne's brain showed mild to moderate swelling, which meant that she lived about fifteen minutes after being attacked.[6]

The defense team called Dr. Charles Petty, a top forensic pathologist from Texas, to refute the testimony of Dr. Spitz. Dr. Petty said the severity of the blow to Mrs. Mathison's head was such that it must have come from a force at least equivalent to a "fifteen-pound sledgehammer." Spitz, during redirect testimony, said, "I've seen many such injuries [from smaller weapons]" as severe as the one in question, and it would be a "vast exaggeration" to say at least "a fifteen-pound sledgehammer" would be needed to cause such damage to a person's skull. On the fracture to Yvonne's ulna, Dr. Spitz concluded that "the ulna could not, and I emphasize, could not have been broken by [being run] over by a vehicle."

There had been a good deal of speculation on whether the defense would put Kenneth Mathison on the stand. The former police sergeant finally spent four hours in the witness chair.[7] During his cross-examination by Kurt Spohn, Mathison had to use the words "I do not remember" several times, particularly in reference to why he had initially said he had run over his wife himself. While he testified, Mathison would not look directly at the jury, preferring to lean in the opposite direction. It was at this time that Spohn drove home the point about Mathison telling lies in the past, such as about the vasectomy and his applying for insurance as a nonsmoker when he smoked heavily.

The closing arguments in this trial seem to reflect the relative strengths of each side's case. Prosecutor Spohn told the jurors to "use common sense" in assessing the evidence. He hit away at the conflicting nature of the defendant's accounts of what had happened on the night of his wife's death. He also counted out the financial facts in the case which gave Mathison a strong motive to kill his wife. In the two hours allotted him, Spohn drove home the testimony of Spitz and myself, laying out the scientific facts as they had earlier been presented to the jury. He summed up by reminding the jurors that the assault had ended with Yvonne Mathison lying on a road, bound, with her husband driving a car over her.

Michael Weight argued that the prosecution had not been able to remove reasonable doubt on what had actually killed Yvonne since police did not find the murder weapon. He attempted to create for the jury a series of events involving another driver, one who struck Mrs. Mathison after she had leaped from the van in response to news of the paternity suit. This individual saw Yvonne walking in the roadway, after it was too late. "The hand follows the eye," so this driver turned the steering wheel in Yvonne's direction. He didn't even know he'd struck her and was able to swerve back onto the highway and continue. Weight added that this other driver "may have been sleepy, had a bit to drink, who knows?" Weight explained that Mathison's garbled story about running over his wife himself was due to his client's being "near hysteria." He emphasized Mathison's strong financial situation, meaning life insurance would not have been important to him and was thus not a sound motive. "There's a veritable cornucopia of reasonable doubt, a bucketful," he argued. Weight concluded his closing statement by declaring that the prosecution had failed to establish two keys to its case's evidence: There were no marks from a weapon on the van's interior roof or other surfaces where a weapon would have struck; and, there was a lack of any blood trails from a weapon as it was swung in the van.

Judge Nakamura gave his final instructions to the jury, and the twelve began their deliberations at 7:00 P.M., Wednesday, November 22. Within three hours the jury returned with a guilty verdict on both counts, murder in the second degree and kidnapping.[8] A loud outcry came from those in the courtroom, with Yvonne Mathison's family calling out, "Praise God. Thank you, Jesus." Robert Martins, Yvonne's brother, said, "We're just glad the family doesn't have to go through this anymore. I'm going to go up to the cemetery right now, and I'm going to sit down and let my sister go." Her daughter, Tina Marie Cawagas, said, "It was a long struggle, but it's over, and she can finally rest in peace now." Kenneth Mathison was immediately incarcerated that evening, and the judge set the sentencing portion of this trial for March 15, 1996.[9] Mathison eventually received a sentence of life in prison, with parole, which means that he faces a minimum of twenty-five-years incarceration for what he did to his wife that terrible night. As one newspaper covering the trial ruefully noted, Mathison would be spending those years with many individuals he had helped bring to justice. Again, in another savage irony of the kind this case provided, Mathison's conviction came almost three years to the night of the murder he committed, and the jurors completed their work just in time to return home and enjoy their Thanksgiving holiday.

This conviction proved a victory for more than Yvonne Mathison's family and the prosecution team. The case, which had received its share of national attention, was also a signal victory for the cause of forensic evidence. In a news analysis under the headline, "A Happier Anniversary" published the Sunday after the verdict, writer Dave Smith of the *Hawaii Tribune-Herald* declared that, "When push comes to shove, expert witnesses working on the people's side proved far more convincing than those for the defense." Smith also wondered how many other assailants there "are out there," besides Kenneth Mathison, who may have been able to get away with their crimes, for a lack of solid scientific evidence.[10]

Prosecutor Spohn made it clear that other factors helped convict Mathison. The defendant himself, Spohn told a reporter, "made it a much more simple case by testifying. The most powerful evidence the state could have," would be a jury's negative assessment of a defendant's credibility. Reporters summing up the trial gave credit to several of the state's witnesses, especially two women, neighbor Laurie Raquel, who witnessed the earlier and bitter fight between the Mathisons, and Susan Albein's "obvious distress while telling of a man wrestling in a van where she saw a purple-clad woman." Spohn, though, underscored the importance of the scientific facts presented in this case. "The scientific evidence was relatively compelling. Whenever I pushed their [the defense's] experts, none could exclude the prosecution's case."

The clash of expert witnesses from each side drew a substantial amount of analysis. In fact, in his closing argument, defense counsel Michael Weight had attempted to discredit the entire nature of expert testimony. He told the jury that the experts' approaches were, in effect, "I'm an expert, and I can see it, therefore, it is so." Smith concluded that "In the face of a particularly damaging prosecution expert, Weight was able to do little more than try to impress upon jurors the expert's opinion was just that." However, as Smith wrote in his wrap-up, "It was scientific 'facts' depicted in reports and hundreds of photographs that took center stage for most of the trial. And it was the prosecution experts' manner and apparent conviction in their conclusions, that told by far the most convincing portrayal." On a personal note, let me add that, given the relatively short amount of time the jury was out, the defense attorney's attempts to discredit the scientific testimony did not seem to work.

Still, Kurt Spohn did note that jurors can become fed up with expert witnesses whose findings are in conflict, especially when combined with an attack on another's credibility. "The 'he's wrong,' 'no, he's wrong,' or, 'I am a better expert than he is,' all sounds like little kids." However, continuing in Dave Smith's excellent analysis, Spohn said that expert analysis "can be crucial. Forensic experts can really steer you in the right direction, pointing out things, without their expertise, [we] might miss." Smith uses a state-of-the-art nickname for the expert witness in his conclusion: "For attorneys, these tailored microscope-slingers appear a necessary evil, praised or condemned depending on which way the evidence tide turns." My reaction to that would be that, even if the expert witness shows up in the courtroom wearing overalls, but his scientific facts and conclusions are based on a correct scientific foundation, then so be it. Let the facts fall where they may.

In the week after this conviction, Hawaii Attorney General Marjery S. Bronster told a news conference that her office took over the prosecution "to dispel the perception that Mathison had been accorded preferential treatment during the investigation because of his status as a police officer." She also called the conviction "a major victory" and said that it showed that Mathison "received no such preferential treatment." She concluded that "Yvonne Mathison and others like her should not have to die for people to understand the seriousness of the need for services to prevent it [spousal abuse]." Considering the dreadful nature of the cases covered in this book, Attorney General Bronster's words have the absolute ring of truth to them.

THE SCIENTIFIC FACTS
OF THE MATHISON CASE

The Mathison murder is a case where a number of critically important questions were answered by forensic science. From my first close look at the photos sent to me by Detective Paul Ferreira of the Hilo police, I realized any trained investigator could see that something very different from what was alleged had actually happened inside the Mathison van on the evening of November 27, 1992. The vast majority of what I would later spend many hours studying would be blood-spatter evidence, along with the related analysis of other specimens which I found in and on the vehicle, such as hairs, fiber, rope, and tissue.

However, before going into an analysis of the makeup of blood as evidence itself and other aspects of the forensics from this case, I again need to emphasize the critical importance of the Hilo Police

Department's work—the photographs, the documentation of the evidence, and the preservation of the crime scene and the van itself—and how that crime scene integrity enabled me to do my job as a scientist. There is no substitute for a well-preserved crime scene, absolutely none. And there are many ways for well-intentioned investigators to compromise the physical integrity of a crime scene. One of the most onerous of these is what I like to call "the wagon train procedures." This occurs when a number of inessential and untrained individuals step through, into, or around the crime scene. Just like one of those camp fire scenes in a western movie. Each extra person who moves into the crime scene may further disturb and disrupt the original ecology of that location where a crime may or may not have been committed. In the Mathison case, specifically, it would have been quite easy, it seems to me, for the murderer himself to get into the van and remove bloodstains and other physical evidence. But this did not happen, and I want to tip my hat to the department for its fine work in keeping things inside the van as close to what they were like when paramedics and police first arrived on that rainy night.

Of course, the single most important evidence was the blood pattern itself. Before getting into a discussion of how blood does spatter and how one is able to determine, with a great deal of accuracy, the type and angle from which the blood has originated from a particular source, I think it would be useful to understand what blood is. Let's look at exactly how a blood drop forms, its velocity as it moves through the air, what its other aerodynamics are, and how the blood drop reacts when it hits a hard surface, either a flat one or one that is sloped at an angle.

Blood is a very complicated mixture of different kinds of cells dissolved in liquid substances. Understanding something about blood's composition helps in appreciating the kinds of analyses that forensic serologists can do and the kind of information that can be deduced from the results of these tests. Blood consists of two phases, or parts: the *cellular* portion and the *liquid* portion. The liquid portion is called plasma.

The cellular portion of the blood contains three kinds of cells: *red blood cells* (or *erythrocytes*), *white blood cells* (or *leucocytes*), and *platelets* (or *thrombocytes*). Red cells are by far the most numerous. Blood from a healthy person has about 4 to 6 million of these donut-shaped cells in every microliter of blood (about one-fiftieth of a drop). Thus, a drop of blood contains about 200 million red cells. A red blood cell is about 7.5 mm in diameter and 2mm in thickness. White blood cells are less numerous; there are also different kinds of them. Normal blood has 4,000 to 10,000 white cells per microliter of blood. These play a role mainly in fighting infections and in defense against diseases. Platelets, which are involved in blood clotting, are the third kind of cell-like element in blood. Plasma, the liquid part of blood, contains a large number of chemical substances. These include nutrients, antibodies, proteins, and enzymes. Some of the proteins are needed for blood clotting, as in healing or the scabbing over of a wound. If the clotting proteins are removed from the plasma, the resulting fluid is called *serum*.

Blood cells are suspended in plasma and circulate in our body through a network of blood vessels, arteries, veins, and capillaries. This network of circulation provides a vital function of human life. Once this circulation is interrupted by an injury, through a gun shot, sharp instrument, or blunt force, bleeding will occur. Depending on the type of injury, its location, the force involved, the severity of the injury, and the environmental factors, a different type of bleeding will result. Once the blood leaves the human body and is deposited on a surface, it will eventually become a bloodstain. Bloodstains provide extremely valuable information to the forensic investigator.

Since there was no real doubt about who was in the Mathisons' vehicle on the night of Yvonne's tragic death, there is no need to review the steps which were taken to determine that Mrs. Mathison was the source of the bloodstains. However, in other chapters in this book, we will delve more deeply into the makeup of human blood, especially as this is applicable to finding a match from a particular blood specimen with a specific person. This process is called *individualization*, and, with recent developments in the field of DNA, the science has led us to very specific analyses on the identity of a blood source. We will also, in those chapters, trace the history and evolution of the science of blood analysis. I think it is useful now to focus our scientific review on the nature of the blood drop itself, how it moves through the air, and how the pattern was produced and, as I mentioned before, how the investigator is able to evaluate where the blood source was at the time of the blood's becoming airborne. We will confine this analysis to the blood drop's impact effect on hard surfaces, as were found in the Mathisons' van, and on the variations in blood spatter caused by the fact that some of these van surfaces were struck by the blood at other than a perpendicular angle.

Blood is a fluid and, as such, will follow the laws of physics. The blood fluid is not affected by the gender, age, or race of the donor. Nor does blood with some amounts of alcohol or drugs move through the air differently from normal human blood. As blood gathers on a surface in sufficient quantity, it will begin to form a drop. As this drop gets heavy enough, it will detach itself from that surface. As this happens, the drop will form a spherical shape. Contrary to the popular belief, the blood droplet will not take on a teardrop shape, but will remain spherical in space until it drops onto a surface. Once a blood drop impacts the surface, a bloodstain will be formed. Every drop falling from the same height, striking this same surface at the same angle of contact, will produce a stain of the same basic shape. Change any of these factors, and the shape of the bloodstain will change.

It has been determined that the volume of a blood drop is approximately 0.05 cc. While we may say that this is the average volume of a blood drop, not all blood drops are the same volume. The volume of a blood drop is naturally dependent on the surface or orifice from which it originates. Should all drops of blood come from an eyedropper held in the same position, we would be able to gauge their volume and thus make estimates such as the distance traveled. However, this ideal is not the case in the real world. Each drop of blood is released from its own surface, and we do not always know the nature of that surface. For example, a blood drop released from the point of a knife will be much smaller than a drop coming from the tip of a finger, elbow, or the side of an axe.

The volume of a simple blood drop can be as small as 0.03 ml and as large as 0.15 cc. For that reason we cannot simply measure the size of a stain and determine the exact distance that it has traveled, unless we know the original drop's volume. Another critical factor is the velocity at which the blood drop left the originating surface. A blood drop falling from a height of twenty-four inches with only the simple force of gravity influencing it will produce a different pattern from the blood spatter produced by a drop that is the result of vigorous thrust originating from the same height. Thus, the velocity at which the blood travels through the air becomes another critical factor for analysis. The velocity of a free-falling drop of blood is limited by gravitational forces. This terminal velocity of the drop has been determined at about twenty-five feet per second. In free fall, the blood drop will reach this terminal velocity after traveling a distance from about twenty feet.

Since blood drops form consistent stains under identical conditions and the distance the blood drop falls will determine the size of the stain on impact with the same impact surface, the nature of the surface where the blood drop lands will affect the size and shape of the bloodstain. This impact area is called the target. In fact, the angle of the target has more effect on the shape of the stain than the distance fallen or the drop's velocity of flight. If the blood drop hits the surface at a straight perpendicular angle, that is at ninety degrees, the drop will produce a round stain. Conversely, if the target surface is struck at a thirty-degree angle, the stain will be elliptical. This is, of course, only logical. These shapes will remain consistent in width and length for a given impact angle if all other factors remain the same. We can, through careful observation, then determine the angle at which the blood drop hits the surface. In the Mathison case, the shape of those impact blood spatters found on the instrument panel indicated to us those blood drops impacted the target surface from several different directions at approximately ten- to twenty-degree angles.

The texture of the target surface will also have an effect on the shape of the bloodstain. A blood drop impacting clean glass or plastic will produce a blood drop with smooth outside edges. The drop will maintain its surface tension, flatten out on the surface, and produce a circular and even stain. A blood drop impacting a rough surface, such as coarse paper, will cause the surface tension to break. This will produce what is called "scalloping" on the edges of the stain, since the edges of the stain's final outline will bear a resemblance to that of a mollusk's shell, meaning the outer edges will not be smooth, but uneven and pointed.

Since all of the surfaces inside the Mathisons' van were not the same, it was important to explore how other surface textures affected the shape of the bloodstain and whether or not we could glean critical information from rough surfaces. Shag carpeting is an example of a surface which is so rough, uneven, and malleable that it is difficult for the investigator to determine the specific direction of blood travel prior to impact. However, the general direction of travel may be established by closely examining the carpet fibers. The blood drop will contact one side of a fiber and break up. Perhaps the back side of this fiber has had no contact with the blood drop and will remain intact. When conducting an investigation on this kind of uneven surface, the investigator must use great patience in the crime scene work and should conduct experiments before coming to any kind of definitive conclusion.

There are numerous blood drops that impacted the instrument panel cover at approximately ten- to twenty-degree angles in the Mathisons' van. The angle cited above is, of course, an acute angle. The more acute the angle of a bloodstain's impact, the more elongated the stain will appear. At an eighty-degree impact angle, the stain will begin to lose the roundness of the ninety-degree, or perpendicular, blood impact angle. The eighty-degree angled droplet will begin to take on an elliptical shape. This elongation of the stain will become more pronounced as the angle is decreased. At about thirty degrees the stain will begin to produce a very noticeable "tail." Upon impact this tail may actually depart from the original drop and will form a line leading away from the host drop, while still remaining in an even line. One important rule of thumb: The more acute the angle, the easier it is to determine the direction of travel. Stains with scalloped edges will also indicate the horizontal direction of travel of the drop. As the angle becomes more acute, that is increases, the scalloped edges will be longer on one side. The longer edges will point in the direction in which the drop was traveling. As the angle of impact becomes even more acute, one side of the drop may contain no scalloping at all, while the opposite side will have very long scallops. Some of these longish scallops may actually depart from the parent blood drop, but will still be traceable back to the originating drop. Likewise, as with the rounder blood drops, the more acute the angle of impact, the easier it is to determine the horizontal direction of the drop's travel.

In the interpretation of bloodstain patterns, it is critical that one be able to determine, if possible, the direction from which the blood has actually traveled. This can lead to the determination of points of origin. Much of the forensic investigator's job is to provide the detectives with data on what actually happened at a crime scene and how these events played themselves out. This information also can prove or disprove a suspect's account. The bloodstain patterns found in the van proved that Mathison's story about Yvonne's jumping out of a moving vehicle was a lie.

The basic technique for determining stain angle, and one that permits the investigator to determine the point of origin, relies on measuring the stain and putting data through a geometric formula, using preprinted tables, a calculator, or laptop computer. Great care must be taken when measuring the stains. Even a small error will result in a mistaken set of findings. The width measurement is almost always the easier of the two measurements to make because the drop's edges are usually well defined. The length measurement can be more difficult to obtain, and patience mixed with experience has to be applied. Stains in the ninety- to forty-degree range are usually easier to measure because the blood drop's tail is rounded, causing fairly defined edges. When the stain is from thirty to less than ten degrees, sometimes the measurement of length becomes problematic due to the separation of the tail. Careful examination of the edge will show where the end of the blood drop is and where the tail begins. With these measurements and the use of a working investigative formula, the investigator can, with excellent precision, determine the angles of impact for several drops and be in a position to find the point of origin of the blood source.

The reconstruction of the two dimensional point from which a bloodstain pattern originated is called the point of convergence. This can show the general direction of force that produced the stain by indicating the possible location from which the blood drop may have originated. Conversely, this point of convergence will rule out certain locations as not possibly the point of origin, thus narrowing down the scope of the investigation. This can, of course, prove to be invaluable information in ruling out allegations by certain witnesses, and in providing support for other statements. For example, the blood spatter found on the driver's side of the Mathison van indicated that Yvonne was hit repeatedly where she was sitting, in the driver's seat. Mathison administered in rapid succession a series of blows to his wife Yvonne's head, using a blunt object as the murder weapon. The forensic scientist does not normally have to use all of the stains available in finding the point of convergence for a bloodstain. However, one will need to use a number of stains. Practically speaking, under normal conditions the forensic scientist can choose several representative stains, perhaps eight. He will then be able to determine the point of convergence.

Once the point of convergence has been determined, the forensic scientist is now ready to move on to finding the three-dimensional point of origin of a bloodstain pattern, which includes the elevation above the target surface that coincides with the point of convergence. Again, one should select a sampling of the best represented stains. Now the investigator can find the angle of impact of each selected stain, and record this angle with each of the stains. Developing the point of origin, which shows the elevation of the blood source as well as its horizontal locations, can become very critical in a case such as the Mathison murder.

By studying the bloodstains and other types of physical evidence at the crime scene, the forensic scientist can also see where one blood drop has overlapped another. By determining which stain came first, along with the point of origin, one can actually begin to develop the "sequence of events." This means placing the victim, suspect, and witnesses in given areas at given times, in relation to each stain. By analyzing the bloodstains and the soil found on the floor of the back of the Mathison van, we were able to show how Kenneth Mathison, after he attacked Yvonne at the back of the van, threw her body out of the van and ran over the body with the van. Finally, he carried her back into the van. That is why bloodstains were found under the soil. One rule which bears noting at this time: In general, the first blow administered will not usually produce a bloodstain pattern. Therefore, if an investigator finds three of the cast-off type of bloodstain patterns at a crime scene, he can deduce that at least four blows were struck.

Finally, let's conclude the scientific review of the Mathison case with a description of the several kinds of bloodstain patterns we commonly find, along with a breakdown of the different energy with which blood can be spattered. *Mist* is the term used to describe the high-velocity type of bloodstain. These tiny droplets are 1 mm or less in diameter. Though this blood residue is most commonly found as a result of a gunshot wound, mist can be caused by other high-energy impact sources. *Fine drops* are 3 mm or less in diameter. These can be produced in a number of ways, but are usually produced by forces greater than gravity. *Medium* blood drops are 3 mm to 6 mm in diameter and can be produced in a variety of ways, either by gravity alone or through other kinds of forces. *Large* blood drops are 6 mm in diameter or larger and, again, result from a wide variety of causes. The medium- to large-size blood drops are commonly the result of blood naturally falling out of a wound or from a weapon due to simple gravitational forces. They are also referred to as low-velocity blood drops.

Of the blood spatters found in the Mathison van, some were consistent with medium-velocity impact spatters. Others were similar to low-velocity blood drops. Another critical element in this investigation was the determination of the impact of the blow which caused the blood spatters found in several sites within the vehicle. Low-velocity impact spatter is created by a force at a speed of less than twenty-five feet per second. Blood which is affected only by gravity falls into this category, such as blood dripping from a wound onto a surface. Medium-velocity impact spatter is that which is impacted with a force greater than twenty-five feet per second, but less than one hundred feet per second. Spatter created by this force is commonly associated with a beating. This type of spatter found in the Mathison van resulted in my finding that a substantial amount of force must have caused that blood spatter deposited on the instrument cover in the front of the vehicle. High-velocity impact is created by an impact greater than one hundred feet per second and is usually associated with but not confined to gunshot wounds. In the Mathison case, we did not observe any high-velocity type of blood spatters. Therefore, we know that a gunshot was not the cause of death. The Zapruder film of the gunshot which hit President John F. Kennedy in the head in Dallas on November 22, 1963, showed a high-velocity impact wound, which created the blood mist as defined above.

The blood smears found in the Mathison investigation were indicative of a struggle being fought in the close confines of the couple's van that evening. A blood smear is caused by an object which carries blood coming into contact with another surface, such as the interior of the Ford van. It was possible by studying the contours of a blood smear to trace the direction of the thrust which caused it. It was also possible to discern that blood-covered hairs were in contact with the surface and caused the smear.

We can also note voids in blood evidence, meaning the absence of blood where it logically should be found. As the investigator goes through the exacting scientific procedures essential to a careful investigation, his deductive and inductive logical reasoning should be taking into account these voids. At some crime scenes, the absence of evidence itself can be a most telling indicator of the nature and scope of a crime.

THE SUMMARY OF THE CASE

The Mathison case presented a number of critical points of analysis and also taught us several important lessons. First and foremost among these is the importance of protecting the integrity of the scene of the crime. Even though I looked at my first photos of the inside of the Mathisons' tan Ford van a good four months after the murder had been committed, the Hilo Police Department had conscientiously maintained the integrity of the vehicle's interior. Bloodstains and blood patterns, fortunately for the cause of justice, do not disappear rapidly, and we were able to deduce what had actually happened on the night of November 27, 1992.

Once alerted to the possibility that Kenneth Mathison was lying to cover up his murdering Yvonne, the Hilo police also put aside any misplaced sense of loyalty to a brother officer and pursued their investigation in a stellar manner. The force was, of course, further motivated by the prosecutor's office. Kurt Spohn, in particular, played a pivotal role in successfully bringing a murderer to justice in this case. In short, there was no "blue wall of silence" established among the rank and file.

The Hawaii media also played a constructive role in helping to gather the facts and in bringing a complicated, three-year investigation to a successful conclusion. Some will argue that the media tend to sensationalize a situation like this one for their own selfish purposes. However, the facts in this case themselves wove together to form a very dramatic tableau. The media like to remind us that a plane landing successfully at a busy airport is not a news story. And here we have a veteran and respected police officer, one who had also become a very successful businessman, betraying the trust placed in him by his wife, their families, and the community at large. If that is not newsworthy, then what is?

The forensic science which Dr. Spitz, Herb MacDonnell, myself, and others on the prosecution team were able to use comes down to us over centuries of careful and painstaking development. This news coverage of a successful prosecution, as complex as it can sometimes be, helps to further educate the general public and opinion leaders on what is available to the modern criminal investigator. However, with all of these technological advances, the people's side in a criminal case must still rely on the daily work and dedication of the police investigator. If Detective Paul Ferreira and fellow officers on the Hilo police force had not been so dogged in pursuing the original blood-evidence leads, perhaps we would not be looking back at this prosecution as a success, and a man who ruthlessly murdered his wife would still be at large.

It is essential for me to single out Kurt Spohn for his outstanding work on this difficult case. I am happy to report that Mr. Spohn has been permanently assigned to the Hawaii Attorney General's office where he performs as one of its very ablest deputy Attorney Generals. From the very outset, I became convinced that the prosecution team was peopled at all levels by dedicated and selfless individuals, such as Kurt Spohn. However, any great man always has a greater lady behind him. To this end, the charming force behind Kurt is his smart and lovely wife, June. She must be the true force behind Kurt Spohn, just like my wife, Margaret, is the force behind me. We have been married thirty-nine years. Without her support, I don't know if I could spend that many hours a day working in my laboratory or at the crime scene attempting, through physical evidence, to find out the scientific truth of each case. Detective Paul Ferreira of the Hilo Police Department is now a lieutenant and Lt. Francis Rodillas has been promoted to captain. Like Kurt, they are continuing to do great work, and their reputations are growing. In addition, a number of other officers and investigators have received well-earned commendations for their work on this case.

Let's conclude this chapter with the hope that Yvonne Mathison's terrible final ordeal and death are not totally in vain. Quite obviously, the entire tragedy speaks to the need to end family and domestic violence. The Mathison case should also send a message to people both in Hawaii and everywhere else around the world: The murderer cannot commit a perfect crime. The proper investigation of the scientific facts and discovering the crucial pieces of physical evidence will mean that the villain will be brought to justice. And it is up to those of us in the fields of forensic science and criminal justice to bring these facts to light, no matter what our conclusions show.

chapter
two

THE WOODCHIPPER MURDER

If something happens to me, don't think it was an accident.

—Helle Crafts

The so-called Woodchipper Case is one which contributed to a change in the American criminal justice system. The old English court system and our common law roots, even up until the 1980s, depended on the police discovering a body as categorical proof that a homicide had been committed. The time-honored term *corpus delicti* springs from this tradition. This ancient concept, expressed in Latin, literally means "the body of the crime." Throughout American history this concept seemed to dominate the thinking of our courts and law enforcement.

By 1985, however, this ironclad insistence on the existence of an identifiable body had begun to change. As the American population was becoming larger and more transient with both women and men taking on job opportunities that meant relocation, a new need arose. If someone disappeared, yet there was limited physical proof of a crime, and a network of family and friends kept in touch on the situation, a police investigation would be demanded. What was critical was that the potential victim's family and friends continued to communicate with one another. The country's police departments and court systems were simply responding to these changing times.

65

As with one other case presented here, a European young woman, Helle Crafts, was born a long way from her final home, and this fact played a role in the investigation. Helle lived in a suburban home set on a wooded lot in Newtown, Connecticut, with her husband, Richard Crafts, and their three children. Danish by birth, Helle was the ideal old-fashioned and forbearing wife to her pilot husband and the devoted mother of her two boys and one girl. She had no close family members here in this country. Fortuitously, Helle also had a circle of close and devoted friends who seriously cared about her. In the last few months of 1986, I was busy teaching, in addition to confronting my burgeoning daily case workload as chief of the state of Connecticut State Police Forensic Laboratory in Meriden. What had occurred in Newtown did not come to my attention until well after Thanksgiving of that year. When the first news of a potential homicide reached me, I quickly knew that this case would mean that my family would not be seeing much of me for the coming Christmas holidays. Here is this story.

THE FACTS OF THE CASE

Helle Crafts made the prophetic statement quoted at the opening of the chapter to several close friends of hers. These friends were mainly other young flight attendants, like Helle, who worked for Pan American Airlines, one of the more highly respected carriers of its day and one that attracted a cosmopolitan, even glamorous, workforce. Helle had worked for Pan Am for seventeen years as of November 1986. Helle Lorck Nielsen was born in Denmark on July 7, 1947, to middle-class parents, Elisabeth Fredericksen Lorck Nielsen and Ib Nielsen. She was the couple's only child, and the family lived in Charlottenlund, a small town north of Copenhagen.

Helle's mother doted on her daughter, and the two became very close, a bond which would last a lifetime. During her early years in school, Helle thrived, making friends with her classmates and winning the respect of her teachers. She projected a sunny and reasonable disposition, doing well in all of her subjects. Later, Helle would display particular ability in languages, mastering English and French, and having the facility to converse in Swedish, Norwegian, and German. When she was seven, Ib and Lis Nielsen separated. Ib, who owned a gas station, had become involved with another woman, which led to divorce. Lis had always worked, believing that a woman's role did not have to be confined to only raising her child, so she did well as a secretary in a nearby school. Growing up, Helle also became accustomed to seeing weapons in her home since Ib had been active in the Danish Resistance during Nazi Germany's occupation in World War II. Later Ib would keep guns in the house, as a member of the Home Guard. Helle was not only used to seeing weapons in her home but also learned to handle them. She successfully completed her ten years of public schooling at the age of sixteen, which is customary in Denmark for those not choosing to go into a profession such as medicine, law, or science. Ib and Lis reunited and eventually remarried when Helle was a young adult, but the second formal ceremony was only a formality, to simplify the couple's estate.

After her Danish schooling was completed, Helle studied in England, also working as an *au pair*. She later worked as an *au pair* in France, which improved her fluency in that language as well, and studied to become an interpreter in Copenhagen. Helle's love of travel and flying increased, which at the age of twenty, culminated in her taking her first airline job as a stewardess for Capital Airways. In this new life, she flew for Air Congo out of Brussels and Frankfurt as part of a turnkey-plane and crew-leasing arrangement Capital had established. All of this heightened Helle's desire to see the world in a career in the airline industry.

Helle matured into a tallish and thin, ash blond young woman, one who continued to make friends effortlessly. The other young women Helle met soon grew to trust her for her sincerity and her discretion. She was very private about her own relationships and had no interest in gossiping. Her excellent posture, high cheek bones, a pronounced dimple in her chin, and broad smile made her, without any single feature standing out, a very attractive young lady. In the words of a neighbor and mother of two who once sat across a lunch table from Helle, "She was quiet, even modest, yet with her charm and good looks she reminded you a little of someone like Blythe Danner, the actress. Helle also showed that she was an excellent mother. In other words, she was fun, yet a very serious person."

Alyce Smith* was one of the new and very close friends Helle made in the late sixties and one who remained close to her after they both emigrated to America. Alyce, who was Helle's age, also blonde and quite good-looking, was more outgoing and vivacious than her best friend. In 1969 Helle and Alyce responded to a Pan Am recruiting ad and were among the eight Danish applicants accepted for training as stewardesses with the airline. Pan Am training would be in Miami, so they both arrived in America, where they would eventually set down roots. While they were in their training class, the Pan Am trainees lived at Lennie's Hideaway, which had a large and very popular swimming pool. Flight crews from all of the major airlines would drop by poolside and chat with the newest recruits. In late May, just before the Memorial Day weekend of that year, Helle Nielsen met another single young adult, an American service veteran with a past that seemed to intrigue Helle, a man who wanted to make piloting a commercial airliner his own professional career. (Much of the information in this chapter, particularly the early backgrounds on Helle Nielsen and Richard Crafts, come from Arthur Herzog's excellent 1989 detailed work, *The Woodchipper Murder*. Material on Crafts's background also comes from two personal interviews with Crafts conducted by my coauthor, Tom O'Neil, and from his correspondence with him.)

Richard Bunel Crafts was born in New York City on December 20, 1937. John Andrew and Lucretia Bunel Crafts later had two more children, two girls, Suzanne and Karen. Mr. Crafts, known as Andy, became the very successful founder of an accounting firm on Park Avenue. In his earlier years, Andy Crafts had piloted a plane during

---

*denotes pseudonyms

World War I and had played football in college. Perhaps foreshadowing his son Richard's later penchant for secrecy, Andy Crafts never revealed to his three children his earlier marriage which had ended in divorce. This was only brought to light by daughter Karen when she was an adult, and then by accident.

As a successful businessman, Andy Crafts moved his family into a large house in one of the wealthiest areas of Darien, Connecticut, a posh suburb less than an hour's train ride to New York's Grand Central Station. Andy was known as a strict and aloof father given to furious bursts of temper, especially if he had had too much to drink. He was also proud of his success, joining the exclusive Wee Burn Country Club in Darien, which then boasted fewer than one hundred members. In the 1950s, his wife Lucretia opened a children's clothing shop in town, called Fashions for the Young.

For his elementary schooling, Richard attended a private school. He was not a particularly good student, but was not a discipline problem either. At about this time, Richard got into some typical adolescent trouble when he was caught using a BB gun to shoot out the windows of a house being built across the street. During his high school years, Richard Crafts did not distinguish himself in the classroom. His graduation photo in the 1955 Darien High School yearbook shows Crafts was one of the few pictured who did not smile. Neither a scholar nor an athlete, the five foot, eight inch, slightly built, quiet Crafts did not stand out in any way. He seemed just another face in the white, suburban crowd.

After graduation, however, Crafts's ordinary childhood and early manhood seemed to move off track. Though his father was financially comfortable, Crafts ended up paying for his own college education, working at a convenience store and carrying a full course-load at the same time. After one semester at the University of Connecticut in Storrs, studying agriculture, the nineteen-year-old found the grind too demanding and, dissatisfied with his grades, he left school. In August 1956, Richard startled his family by joining the Marine Corps, a dinnertime announcement that threw his father into a rage and disappointed his mother.

Not a great deal is known about Crafts's four years in the Marine Corps. Crafts did say in one interview with Tom O'Neil that he learned to fly "117 types of aircraft" in the Corps. Becoming a flyer meant that Crafts was following in his father's footsteps. The new recruit had thrived at boot camp at Parris Island, making private first class before any of the others in his platoon. He then became a member of an elite marine drill team which took him around the country. Crafts became a pilot by being accepted into the U.S. Naval Air Training Station at Pensacola, Florida, and eventually specialized in flying helicopters. Because of his status as a pilot, winning his wings also meant that he was commissioned a second lieutenant. After a year's service at an air station in North Carolina, he was transferred to a section of the world that would soon prove very important to both the young officer and millions of other American servicemen, the Far East. He was stationed in Korea and Japan and made three sea tours with his squadron, duty which meant he became proficient in landing and taking off from the flight decks of aircraft carriers. Promoted to first lieutenant after eighteen months, Crafts's duties, like those of many other junior officers, also included prosecuting and defending marines and sailors in courts-martial. At about this time, he served with Malcolm Bird, who would later meet, court, and marry Suzanne Crafts, his younger sister. Crafts would eventually decide to leave the Marine Corps, though he loved to fly, after being denied a transfer to a shore station billet that he felt should have been his.

During his marine years in the Far East, Crafts had volunteered for assignment to Air America, the air arm of the Central Intelligence Agency which was conducting clandestine military operations in Laos, Cambodia, and Vietnam. He would later deny that he had ever worked for the CIA, but admitted to Tom O'Neil that Air America was exclusively funded by that agency. Prior to the Geneva Accord which was signed to end French fighting in Vietnam, Air America could boast a huge commitment of men and munitions, but its operations had to be scaled back after that treaty was signed. So, after leaving active military service, Crafts was hired directly by Air America, though his new duties would officially be under the umbrella of the U.S. Agency for International Development.

This was obviously work which Crafts felt most suited to perform. He was, for the first and only time in his life, in a combat theater of war, though hardly anyone in America appreciated the extent of the country's involvement in Southeast Asia. He would fly fixed-wing aircraft to deliver rice and munitions to friendly forces in Laos. On one mission, he was actually wounded in the leg by ground fire. Later on, Crafts would also talk at intimate dinner parties about other types of assignments, such as the beheading of a native chief who was allied with the Communist side in the Laotian civil war. Away from the Mickey Mouse monotony of daily military life, Crafts was now a well-paid and well-respected employee of the CIA, mixing his devotion to duty and patriotic motives with the life of a mercenary in the Far East. His Darien boyhood must now have been a distant memory.

After four years at Air America, Crafts in the summer of 1966 left his life in the CIA and the Far East and returned to the United States. Back home, he bounced around for eighteen months, taking odd jobs flying planes wherever and whenever he could, to pay his bills. In his early thirties, he knew that he loved flying and could boast about more harrowing experiences than most combat veterans. Yet, Crafts also must have realized that he had very little success in formal education, no college degree, so flying was all he could really think about doing for his future. A return to college, as kids on campuses began protesting the Vietnam War, was out of the question. After flying helicopters over New York City and other stopgap work around the country, Crafts finally caught his major break: Eastern Airlines hired him in early 1968. His more than five thousand hours of flight experience must have been a strong consideration in his being hired.

His new employer sent Crafts to Miami in May 1969 to recertify on several of their aircraft. It was only natural that the thirty-one-year-old bachelor would drop over to Lennie's Hideaway to meet Pan Am's latest class of stewardess trainees. Though an aviator, Crafts must not have stood out among the other pilots and flight engineers (his first job was that of an engineer) as he sat poolside. Slight of build and on the small side, Crafts liked to dress down, wearing clothes which might have identified him as coming from rural America. His dark hair, beginning to show the first traces of gray, was always a little unkempt. His was not the studied L.L. Bean look, but was simply scruffy. Yet, Crafts had always been able to attract members of the opposite sex, according to buddies in the service and others who had gotten to know him well. Indeed, he was very interested in meeting new young women. He led a picaresque lifestyle. In this pursuit of new and romantic individuals, Crafts had a knack for being direct in a manner which appealed to women.

At their first encounter Helle Nielsen seemed to see things in Richard Crafts which her companions were missing. Helle had a few romantic interests in her life, but the nontraditional Crafts quickly established himself as someone she thought was special. When Helle and Alyce completed their flight attendant training in Miami, they found themselves assigned to the New York area, along with a number of their classmates. Helle asked Crafts for his help in finding an apartment in Queens, where he had a place. Queens was reasonable and close to the airports. She and a half dozen of the girls moved into a three-bedroom place which was adequate, since several of the girls always seemed to be on the road.

Crafts would later tell police that he was engaged to another woman during the next several years, a time which saw Helle and Richard go through an on-again, off-again romance. Rather than break up with Crafts for his seemingly effortless ability to attract women, Helle just accepted it. Yet, the two went through some stormy times. Crafts was reassigned to Miami by Eastern for a year or so in the early seventies, and both Helle and he had an understanding that each would see others. When Crafts was reassigned to New York in 1973, these two very different individuals began to talk about marriage and finally settling down. In the fall a couple of years later, Helle found out she was expecting her lover's child; Crafts and she decided it was time to marry. The ceremony was scheduled for a short time later, so short a timespan that Helle's parents were unable to attend. On November 29, 1975, just after Thanksgiving, in a modest ceremony at the New Hampshire home of Fredric and Ursula Etten,* the couple became Mr. and Mrs. Richard Crafts. Helle had befriended the Dutch Etten, meeting her through her husband, who was a pilot at Eastern. Alyce Smith and her fiancée, Arthur Bennett,* a businessman, were in attendance that day, as well as Lucretia Crafts, the groom's mother, who had been a widow for more than ten years. Crafts's youngest sister, Karen, and her husband, David Rodgers, also bore witness to the new union.

It is important to take a moment here to analyze the background and factors which went into this marriage. This emphasis on the character of the relationship between Richard and Helle Crafts becomes very critical in light of the later disappearance of Helle and how this void created a furor among her closest friends. So, a close look at when and how Richard and Helle Crafts first met and later married is essential to gaining an understanding of this case. It is equally important to note that the Federal Bureau of Investigation established a special unit in its ranks devoted to *profiling* individuals who have committed crimes. All good police work has to be concerned with the motives behind why individuals commit a crime. This case would be one that would eventually become a multidisciplinary forensic investigation, one that would include many specialized fields, including: odontology (the study of the structure and comparison, along with abnormalities, of the teeth), anthropology, blood pattern analysis, trace evidence, and forensic medicine.

This investigation required the participation of all these fields since, until this case and several similar to it, traditional police work called for the proof of corpus delicti, in essence, a body. A homicide would require the finding of a body which was swiftly identifiable as that of the murder victim. However, with advances in forensic science, this traditional requirement for an intact corpse was placed in the ancient past, and now the human identification process is grounded in DNA profiling, serological typing, dental records, and fingerprints.

The character and behaviors which Richard and Helle Crafts

brought to their marriage become very important, the husband's, in particular. Very few who knew Crafts while he was growing up in Darien and those with whom he served and later worked could have guessed at his enormous intelligence. Contrary to being an early strength for him, though, this strong intellect must have served as a deep frustration for a young man who could not last more than one semester at the University of Connecticut. There is also more than a hint of tension here between Crafts and his successful and wealthy father, a volatile parent who at least acquiesced in his son's having to work near the Storrs campus to pay for his own higher education.

If all of this complex background were about a couple still living a suburban lifestyle in Newtown, Connecticut, it would be most inappropriate to bother looking into these matters. Just more nosiness in New England, a region first molded by the Puritan belief in knowing more about your neighbor than is perhaps healthy. I point this out here to underscore Richard Crafts's situation, as events in the mid-eighties went sour for him, and he began to contemplate ending his marriage to Helle by murdering her. If a murderer was able to dispose of his victim's remains, he must have reasoned, then the authorities could not ever lay a glove on him. No corpse, no crime. This would be particularly so if his wife were an internationally born individual who loved to travel and worked full-time in the airline industry.

Richard and Helle Crafts would eventually have three children, two boys and a girl. They were Andrew, ten, Thomas, eight, and Kristina, five, as of late 1986. Back in 1976 the couple had bought an L-shaped, ranch house with gray, wooden shingles and white trim for $73,000, set on 2.6 acres at 5 Newfield Lane in Newtown, in western Connecticut, about an hour's drive to the New York airports. Many of the families in Newtown saw at least one adult, usually the man of the house, commute daily by train or car to Manhattan. The Crafts' new home was about a mile from the town's shopping district. Once settled in, the Crafts had set out to live a suburban life on their quiet street, an existence as generic as the name of their new community. Newtown, itself, had been founded centuries earlier, in 1705, as a farming community. In 1986, twenty thousand people lived in its tranquil, hilly streets, mostly middle-class and upper-income professional families, almost exclusively white, some retired. There were younger couples with children in the community's respected school system, and there was more than a smattering of airline employees. Also like the Crafts, many households had both parents work full-time to stay ahead of the economic pressures which were looming ahead for American parents.

In the ten years Richard and Helle Crafts lived together as man and wife in Newtown, the couple had struggled, somewhat successfully, to make a good home for their growing family. However, Crafts's behaviors, which had taxed Helle's gift for patience when they were dating, became an increasing problem for their relationship. Promoted by Eastern several times, Crafts made $82,000 a year from his primary employer, a solid amount of money for the mid-eighties and a sum which today would have the purchasing power of well over $100,000. This was almost three times Helle's salary of $32,000, gross income which included much overtime. Yet, Crafts decreed that Helle and he would keep separate bank accounts and that her pay would, almost exclusively, go toward paying the household bills, including payments toward whatever was left of their original $50,000 mortgage. With his own money, Crafts went out and bought a wide variety of expensive landscaping equipment, a backhoe, a panel truck, and, most significantly, a large collection of guns. Crafts was a husband and father who would regularly drink a six-pack of beer or two in a day. This habit could make him even quieter and moodier than normal. In the early eighties, Helle and Richard would jointly buy another 3.6 undeveloped acres of residentially zoned land atop a nearby street, Currituck Road, for $37,000, putting down $13,000. Crafts liked to busy himself cutting wood on this property and on or near his home on Newfield Lane, using a log splitter. He was in the habit of giving cords of this firewood to selected friends, or his brother-in-law, David Rodgers, who lived about forty minutes away in Westport, an upper-income suburb on Long Island Sound. Crafts also paid the monthly rent on a New York apartment he kept, saying he needed it as a crash pad when coming back to New York late at night after a lengthy flight. At Crafts's insistence, the couple's home phone number was unlisted.

The gun collection gave Helle particular problems. She was afraid that one of her two sons might find his way into one or both of the two safes her husband had purchased for his collection's storage. Or perhaps, they might find a weapon simply lying around in their basement, as Helle had on occasion. That could result in either Andrew or Tom shooting the other, or himself, or their younger sister, let alone some other child. Helle had made it a practice not to criticize the temperamental Crafts, if at all possible, yet she was forced to speak up about this arsenal, which consisted of more than fifty weapons, mostly pistols, shot guns, and semiautomatic rifles. Furthermore, the fact that all of this armament cost a substantial amount of money, many thousands of dollars, further galled her.

Helle had other problems with Crafts, some of which particularly impacted the one aspect of her life she treasured the most: her three children. An introverted person, Richard Crafts seemed indifferent to his two sons and his daughter. At times, he was capable of breaking his silence with white-hot bursts of anger. At one meal, observers saw him calmly tell one of his boys to behave himself, and, when the child persisted, without changing his facial expression, Crafts shot his arm across the table and lifted the boy up by his hair, pulling away with a fistful of it. Helle would become extremely uncomfortable at times like this, discreetly intervening to protect the child, explaining her husband's actions later to her friends as infrequent and just one of his ways. But, mostly, Crafts seemed just to go through the motions of parenting. He was frequently absent from home or otherwise unavailable for attending parent-teacher conferences, birthday parties, and other traditional times when a father should participate. In 1981 Crafts was off somewhere when Helle went into labor with Kristina and, deciding not to bother anyone, or perhaps out of embarrassment, Helle calmly drove herself to the hospital for delivery of her youngest child.

During their earlier years in Newtown, Helle and Richard would appear at local stores together, but these sightings became less and less frequent as the years passed. Helle attended religious services at a local Episcopalian church, but Richard Crafts was remembered there only once, for his son Andrew's first communion. The Crafts' neighbors also did not see much of Mr. Crafts, though Helle was easily accessible and became particularly close to several. For planning purposes, Helle always posted her schedule on a calendar, though her husband seemed to come and go on a random basis. He would disappear for days on end, friends would note, and Helle would sometimes explain that Richard was at a gun show in a neighboring state.

In 1982, Richard Crafts, in spite of his flying so many hours and being away from home so much, decided to become a volunteer policeman with the Newtown force. He did not inform Eastern Airlines, a company requirement for paid outside work. This was unpaid and probably indicated Crafts's missing his service time in the Marine Corps and with Air America. He was not allowed to make arrests in this job, but he did carry a gun. His duties would include directing traffic and otherwise showing a police presence, such as at parades and other public functions. Full-timers on the force remarked how seriously Crafts took this role. When he was directing traffic outside a church one Sunday morning, Crafts got into an argument with a motorist and, at one point, placed his hand on his gun to make his point. This brought a reprimand from a police superior and raised some eyebrows. As gung-ho as Crafts was, he relished police training sessions and he even paid his own way out to Long Beach, California, to participate in a five-day seminar given by the Lethal Force Institute. Crafts also attended weekly training sessions held by the Newtown department, on Thursday nights. At this time, Walter Flanagan was the state's chief prosecutor for the Danbury judicial district, working out of offices in the superior court building there. He would occasionally conduct one of these Thursday night training lectures. A seasoned veteran, Flanagan had several big and successful prosecutions behind him as he stood before Crafts and the other Newtown police earlier in 1986. Flanagan would not specifically remember Crafts from this appearance, yet he would later become the most important player in Crafts's life and in this case.

Ironically, in 1984 Helle and Richard Crafts were confronted with a health crisis which brought the couple together as never before. Richard Crafts, who was diagnosed with cancer of the colon, had a foot and a half of his colon removed. Some lymph nodes and even a section of his liver were also taken out. On leave from Eastern, he began chemotherapy. In 1985, he was able to regain his pilot's license and eagerly went back to work, flying a normal schedule. Helle would recall to friends later that she had never felt closer to her husband than during this crisis and as she helped nurse him back to full health.

When her husband had been diagnosed with cancer, Helle took a long look at her income and decided she needed to take on other jobs, work she could fit around her flight attendant's schedule. Besides regular tag sales at their home, Helle sold Shaklee Products, which would have probably meant an extra $100 a month. She also sold other things, such as dolls and toys, and eventually opened a lace curtain business with a neighbor and fellow Pan Am flight attendant who had become her close friend, Anna Batelli.* Helle's productive business work and the neat way she kept the inside of her home contrasted with another of her husband's strange behaviors: Richard Crafts would start an ambitious outdoor project which he would abandon before its completion, giving the property a messy, even junkyard, look.

Along with several other intimate friends, such as Alyce Bennett (Arthur and Alyce were married in 1977), Anna Batelli began to see clear signs that Helle's marriage had reached the crisis stage. Besides his moodiness and potential for violence toward her and her children, his indifference as a parent, and his other selfish habits, Helle had soured on her husband due to a series of affairs she was all but certain he was having with other women, some of them flight attendants she knew. Before they were married, Richard Crafts's appeal to other women had seemed to heighten Helle's interest in him, or so it seemed to her friends. In 1986, with three pre-teenage children to raise, Helle Crafts was very actively thinking about putting an end to the pain her husband was inflicting upon her and her children.

In early 1986, Richard Crafts, now forty-nine, left his part-time

volunteer work in Newtown to take a police constable's job, at seven
dollars per hour, in neighboring Southbury. As before, he did not
notify his employer of this part-time work, as required. Soon afterward, he again paid his own way to a training seminar in New Hampshire, covering topics like Knife Counter/Knife and Lethal Management for Police. The Southbury police had heard about Crafts's reputation as wanting to become a "super cop." This bothered some of the
full-timers and, like their friends in Newtown, the earnest way Crafts
handled his new duties caused some doubts on the force.

Besides his health, his increasingly tense situation at home, and
his sense of the other police professionals' reaction to him, Crafts had
another major concern. Eastern Airlines was beginning to show
serious signs of strain. The airline was acquired by Texas Air in 1985,
which worried its employees. The entire United States air industry was
beginning to hit a profit wall, caused by government regulations, skyrocketing fuel and labor costs, and an increasingly cut-throat pricing
competition between the carriers themselves. Most pilots had tradi-
tionally preferred simply to "fly the planes" and leave the worrying
about their companies and industry to others, the higher-ups in the
three-piece suits. Now Eastern's pilots banded together and made a
valiant attempt to assure their company's future by raising enough
capital to buy the airline themselves. This effort failed. Crafts now had
to worry about his job and the security of a $300,000 company pen-
sion fund he had built up, as well as all of those other things in his life
which seemed to be going wrong, matters which directly threatened
his future, his family, and him.

All of the above brings us to the latter half of 1986. The Crafts'
neighbors on Newfield Lane had become very familiar with Richard:
how he would start an ambitious project in front of his house, use his
backhoe to dig a large trench, buy mounds of stone or fill, lay a foundation, and then never complete the task. Vehicles parked out front,
every which way, included an ancient and rusting Audi, which had no
plates. Only one of these cars seemed to be Crafts's pride and joy, a
1985 blue Ford Crown Victoria, the kind driven by the state police.

Crafts would amass huge piles of cut firewood in his back lot. This contrasted sharply with the interior of the Crafts' neat and well-kept home, in which Helle took great pride.

Helle had grown weary and apprehensive about her marriage. She began to take steps which would lead her to finally take the big step and file for a divorce from her husband. Indeed, she had stumbled onto fresh evidence that her spouse was spending nights with one particular lover, a woman she had once met and whom he had known for years, who lived in nearby New Jersey.

So, in the late summer of 1986, Helle, now thirty-nine, reluctantly retained Dianne Andersen, an experienced divorce attorney with offices in Danbury and a professional who had made something of a specialty out of matrimonial disputes relating to airlines employees. At first Helle was ambivalent about initiating this action. She had seemed to hope, she had confided to friends, that she could persevere in the marriage for the sake of her children, who would need a father, even one as moody and problematic as Richard Crafts. Andersen suggested to Helle that infidelity would be a solid basis for the cause of her suit, and the lawyer suggested that Helle retain a private detective whom she knew, Keith Mayo. Relying on a credit card slip from one of her husband's accounts, Helle Crafts had a specific name and phone number for the suspected other woman. Marie Evans,* an attractive blonde in her thirties, was an Eastern Airlines flight attendant who had an apartment in Middletown in central New Jersey. With other evidence of Richard's philandering, such as phone bills and unaccounted-for stays away from home when he was not scheduled to fly, Helle Crafts had now truly decided to forge ahead.

For all practical purposes, Helle's decision to retain Mayo ended her marital relationship with Crafts. In early September, Mayo was easily able to photograph Richard Crafts leaving Evans's apartment, even embracing his girlfriend outside her apartment's front door. This led Helle to advise her husband that she was going to divorce him and that he should start thinking about retaining his own attorney. She also told him that they would no longer sleep together. But, Helle was careful not to advise Crafts of what specific grounds she would use for the divorce action, or that she had seen photos which provided irrefutable evidence of his cheating on her. Crafts, for his part, seemed to take this news in stride and even called Andersen's office to talk to Helle's attorney, who refused to take the call. Andersen surmised, from what Crafts had said to her receptionist, that he was attempting to discover what grounds Helle was choosing to use to divorce him.

However, as in other times in his life, Richard Crafts was only playing a role by accepting Helle's announcement to end their marriage. He did not go out and consult a lawyer himself. When Helle told him, in October, that matters had moved forward to the point of her attorney drawing up a specific complaint and that he would be getting served, Crafts again appeared outwardly calm and cooperative. In November, when it came time to accept a call from a deputy sheriff with a subpoena, Crafts once claimed that the serving officer had failed to show (in reality, Crafts had not called the deputy back to confirm a time and place), and then had slipped out of his house to dodge a second attempt to serve him. In reality, Crafts had been sounding out his brother-in-law, David Rodgers in Westport, about the particulars in a divorce proceeding Rodgers had once gone through, though never specifically alluding to what Helle was doing. Rodgers told Crafts about the crippling effect of combined alimony and child support payments. These expensive hits would go along with the potential impact of a settlement which would undoubtedly mean an equal division of their two properties, the house and the tract on Currituck Road. Finally, as a melodramatic ploy, Crafts had announced to Helle that fall that his oncologist had told him that his cancer had returned and his remission was a thing of the past. He went on to say that he'd decided to forego fighting the disease any longer, meaning he would not take his medications and that he simply preferred to die. A quick call by Helle to the physician in question exposed this ruse, infuriating her and only hardening her resolve. Yet Helle still seemed to have some very mixed feelings about the finality of the steps she was about to take. Tearfully, she told several friends that she still loved her husband and that she hoped that, somehow, Richard Crafts would change and become a good husband and father. These confidences were shared with only very close friends, though.

Earlier in the summer of 1986, the Crafts had hired a nanny, Marie Thomas, twenty, who would move into their home to look after the children when one or both of the parents were out of town flying. Thomas, who also took a job working some hours at a local McDonald's, lived in a bedroom which Crafts had fashioned above the house's garage which was jammed with all his equipment and supplies. Marie Thomas would become an invaluable witness for the prosecution in the grim drama which was unfolding in the Crafts' household. But more on that later.

During that fall of 1986, as the divorce was progressing, Helle Crafts began telling friends that she was physically afraid for herself. Visiting with Alyce Bennett at her home in a shoreline village, across from its little harbor and the Long Island Sound, Helle said, "If something happens to me, don't assume it was an accident." In that same long talk with her oldest and closest friend, Helle also expressed her anger over just discovering that her husband had earlier that fall been promoted by Eastern from flight engineer to copilot, meaning a substantial increase in pay, but had never bothered to give Helle the good news. Though quiet and intensely private, Helle had also shared with Anna Batelli and at least one other couple similar concerns about Richard's violent personality and her fear for her well-being. Yet, Helle would not accept advice from anyone about trying to move out and hide herself and the children, citing her fears that Crafts's police contacts would help him find her. Once that happened, she reasoned, Crafts would file a charge for kidnapping or use the incident, perhaps, to win custody of his children from her. Helle still went about her varied roles as a mother and Pan Am flight attendant. Her meticulous calendars showed plenty of activities as the holiday season was approaching. This year would be Helle's turn to host Karen and David Rodgers for Thanksgiving dinner. Helle loved the holidays and was happy to throw herself into these tasks. She had ordered two turkeys for the occasion, which was necessary since so many at the table favored drumsticks. Helle had also sent a check to a ski lodge in Vermont for a family vacation for all of them she had planned there in January, a lot like the one Richard and she and the children had all enjoyed the previous year.

As Helle prepared to leave for a flight to Hamburg on Saturday, November 15, she must have felt confident that Marie Thomas, the nanny, would provide for her children. The trip could actually mean a break from her daily struggles with divorce, her husband, and her fears. Anna Batelli would be celebrating her thirty-seventh birthday while they stopped over in Germany. Helle had purchased a teddy bear for her close friend's present and had made plans for an upbeat little party with Pan Am's caterers. As she left her home, Helle's neighbors would not have seen anything much out of the ordinary. Crafts's truck parked up the driveway and in front of the garage, perhaps. Certainly the usual messy array of supplies and other odds and ends in the front yard. The casual observer could never have seen the darkening storm gathering over the Crafts' home on Newfield Lane.

While Helle Crafts was balancing her roles as a caring mother, busy full-time flight attendant, and a woman who was preparing to divorce her complicated husband of ten years, Richard was beginning to take the first steps along a path that would ultimately lead to horrible tragedy. Unbeknownst to Helle, in late October Crafts had purchased a 1980 silver Volkswagen Rabbit at a dealer in Danbury. This was an oddity since the family already owned Helle's Tercel, the blue Ford Crown Victoria, and a pickup truck. By this time, Helle had put aside any hang-ups about looking through Crafts's credit card and insurance correspondence and was angered to discover a USAA (San Antonio–based insurance company used by military officers) insurance slip indicating the VW purchase.

But Helle would never find out that her husband on November 10 had been busying himself buying other things, including ordering a dump truck from a dealer, McLaughlin Ford, in New Milford. This brand-new Ford 350 would cost $15,000; and the dealership promised

Crafts delivery that following Thursday, November 13. Crafts had also asked McLaughlin Ford to install a special rear hitch, one that would allow him to haul heavy equipment. Since McLaughlin employees could not do this work themselves, the new dump truck had to be driven to Bridgeport to get this work done. However, when the installation had been completed, the new truck's fuel line sprang a leak on the return trip to New Milford and had to be towed. The salesman called Richard Crafts and told him of the delay, but promised that the truck would be delivered to him on or before the following Tuesday, November 18. During this timespan, Crafts also called a nearby tree service company, inquiring about the rental of a woodchipper. He did this on the same day that he ordered the Ford dump truck, Monday, November 10. The local outfit could not accommodate him and recommended Darien Rentals which, on Friday, November 14, reserved a large woodchipper for Crafts, available for pickup the following Tuesday, November 18. On Thursday of that week, November 13, Crafts paid $375 for a new Westinghouse Chest Freezer at Zemel's T.V. and Appliances in Danbury. He would pick up this purchase the following Monday, November 17, the day prior to Helle's return from Hamburg. The customer, the store would report later, would not give his name, calling himself "Mr. Cash," and he was very specific about the dimensions of the unit. On Thursday, November 13, the same day he ordered this freezer, Crafts also drove west across the New York border to Brewster to buy a pair of fireproof gloves and a flathead shovel, bypassing several Connecticut hardware stores which sold the same goods. Richard Crafts was now bustling about, spinning his intricate and fatal web.

Helle Crafts's flights to and from Hamburg were routine. During these flights, Helle continued to display anxiety about her divorce, though this mood did not cast a pall over the planned birthday festivities for her close friend and fellow flight attendant, Anna Batelli. Also on board was Sue Miller,* another close Pan Am friend of Helle's from nearby Southbury. On its return, the Pan Am 747 battled headwinds and was an hour late, arriving in a gray dusk. Breezing through the "employee" side of customs with her friends, Helle called home to say that she'd be late. Anna and Helle rode with Sue, whose turn it was to drive the hour's journey to Newtown. They listened to reports on the car's radio from Dr. Mel Goldstein and the Connecticut Weather Center about a very unseasonable and large snowstorm which seemed to be approaching the area. All three were relieved that they'd be safe at home before the storm really hit. Sue dropped Anna off first, then took Helle home around 7 P.M. Seeing her husband's truck in the driveway, Helle said, simply enough, "Richard's home," and got out of Sue's car and went inside her home. This was the last time her friends would ever see Helle Crafts alive. She would seem to vanish into thin air.

THE CASE'S INVESTIGATION

Police are human beings. No matter how much training a person receives, the human element is still there. The Crafts case was impacted on two levels by this fact. First, the police in Newtown knew Richard Crafts as something of an odd duck, someone who gave them concern at times during his four years as a volunteer in uniform. Most of the officers had ridden patrol with Crafts, so there were bound to have been some personal exchanges. There may have even been some respect for Crafts's war record and his service in the Marine Corps. The events that were about to play out at 5 Newfield Lane would be the kind that many an investigator would look past, not grasping immediately the macabre nature of what was to transpire. If an adult is reported by her friends as missing, the police have a standard and time-honored way to deal with this kind of situation. Waiting and watching are part of this drill. In the vast majority of cases, the missing individual will turn up, in good health and with an explanation for the disappearance. If marital problems are involved (as they often are), the police reaction is to determine if the missing person has decided to return home (in this case, Denmark), to simply reassess her life, or perhaps even to move in with a new significant other. Certainly, few, if any, police investigators would imagine what actually happened between Richard and Helle Crafts on the evening of November 18 and through the next forty-eight hours. Thus, the first inquiries by Helle Crafts's friends were greeted by a wait-and-see attitude.

As the first few days since Helle was last seen passed, those concerned about Helle's whereabouts became increasingly direct in expressing their concerns for her, and another aspect of the human equation then began to show itself. Newtown Police Chief Louis Marchese was a former high-ranking Connecticut State Trooper, attaining the rank of captain in a very successful thirty-year career. Chief Marchese had even been a candidate for the top post of police commissioner and was bitterly disappointed when he did not step up to that job. Given the jurisdictional realities of the Newtown department's initial control of the Crafts case, Marchese's personality became a critical problem to be overcome when the state's top prosecutor in Danbury, Walter Flanagan, felt it was time to make changes in who was investigating this case. In short, the seventy-two-year-old chief, who was considered an autocrat in the best of times, ordered his department to put its wagons in a tight circle and to fight off any challenges to its autonomy and his authority.[1] These are the realities which the friends of Helle Crafts confronted when they attempted to get action on her disappearance.

A few days before November 18, Richard Crafts had already encountered a couple of unforeseeable complications to his plans. The dump truck was not delivered the second time it was promised, because of the leak in its fuel line. Even the VW Rabbit had been late for him to pick up. Now the storm on the night of November 18 raged through the early morning hours of the following day. Dr. Mel Goldstein today remembers this storm as being "highly unusual" for mid-November, with its five inches of very wet and heavy snow, heavy winds, and its thunder and lightning.[2] These phenomena would cause an early morning power outage on Newfield Lane, an unforeseeable event for Crafts; yet he was about to put this surprise development to his own advantage. His bad luck, on the other hand, included the fact that he could not take delivery of his reserved woodchipper, since his smallish pickup truck could not haul this large piece of equipment. Since he could not haul the woodchipper away on that Tuesday, Crafts would insist on shelling out a $260 daily rental fee for holding the machine, a move which drew attention to him from the Darien Rental Company's management. Indeed, Crafts would not pick up the woodchipper, the Asplundh Badger Brush Bandit 100, which weighed more 4,200 pounds, for another two days. And his brand-new dump truck would not be available to him then, due to more problems at the dealership.

The electrical power at the Crafts' home went out at exactly 3:35 A.M. on Wednesday morning, November 19. Marie Thomas had arrived back at 5 Newfield Lane from her MacDonald's job quite late, at 2 A.M. Marie did not notice or hear anything unusual except seeing that Crafts's pickup was not in the driveway, and went to bed. Crafts woke Marie around six the next morning and told her that she would be going to stay in Westport with the three children at the home of Karen and David Rodgers. When Marie asked Crafts about Helle's whereabouts, he told her vaguely that she was already down at his sister's in Westport and that they'd meet her there. Helle's blue Toyota Tercel was not outside. Earlier that morning, an hour or so after the power had first gone out, Crafts had called his brother-in-law, David, and told him of his plans to bring Marie and his three children there, because of the power outage. When Helle was not at the Rodgers' house, Marie Thomas again asked Crafts about her, and he became peevish, saying that he didn't know where she was. Marie, at this time, decided to let the matter drop. Crafts then left Marie and the children in Westport, and had finished his return drive to Newfield Lane by 9:00 A.M. The Rodgers might have wondered why Crafts voiced worry about his home freezing during a power outage, since Crafts (typically for him) owned a portable generator, which he could use to provide electricity in situations just like this. This unusual visit drew the suspicion of Karen Rodgers, who knew that her brother thrived in situations just like this. Perhaps, she had thought, he was using the storm as a cover for seeing another woman. The power was restored to the

Crafts' household at 10:44 A.M., though Crafts told Marie that electricity was still out when they talked by phone at 12:11 P.M. At about 3 p.m. that Wednesday afternoon, Crafts phoned the Rodgers to say that, even though the power had recently been restored, he would be later since he had slid in his own driveway and was stuck; this seemed to be another suspicious statement to Karen since she knew how capably her brother could drive in any kind of conditions.[3]

The storm had unexpectedly handed Richard Crafts an ideal window of time and privacy for him to dispose of the evidence which must have been left after a crime of violence. A criminal investigator, as I have said elsewhere, can deduce that steps have been taken to cover up a violent crime when there is an absolute *lack* of physical evidence at a scene, where there was once a bloodied corpse. However, in this case, the removal of his dead wife's remains would certainly, Crafts must have thought, mean that there could be no successful prosecution. Again, no body, no crime. Perhaps this accounts for Crafts's not being as thorough in cleaning up after the crime as he might have been. Instead, he used a portion of this fortuitous timespan to go the Newtown Banking Center and deposit in the couple's joint account a $300 check Helle had received for her curtain business. Crafts would later offer to give the money to Helle's friend and partner, Anna Batelli. Significantly, Crafts used some of this time to go to a Caldor's store in Brookfield, where, using his Visa Card at 1:27 P.M., he purchased two blue down comforters and two pillows, for a total of $257.

As preoccupied as Crafts must have been about removing various kinds of evidence and obtaining a vehicle large enough to haul his rented woodchipper, it is ironic to me that Crafts was not formulating a story to tell Helle's friends about her whereabouts. And these close friends would surely be calling for her very soon. Crafts finally picked up Marie Thomas and his children from Westport at nine in the evening, and the four returned to the darkened and empty house in Newtown.

Anna Batelli and her husband, Glen,* were not as lucky as the residents on Newfield Lane during the storm. Their power was still out well into the evening of Wednesday, November 19. Anna had been the first to try to call Helle, reaching no one several times during the day. Later that evening, Glen and she had gone for groceries and, driving by Newfield Lane, they noticed the lights on there. Once home, Anna called and Richard Crafts answered; he told her that Helle was away, offering the Batellis the use of a hot shower, if they wanted, an invitation which Anna declined. The next morning, Thursday, Anna called again, getting Marie Thomas, who said casually that Helle "must be flying." This did not compute for Anna since Pan Am regulations required a forty-eight-hour stand-down for all air personnel between flights. And Anna had already been wondering why Helle hadn't called her the previous day, since the two, as close friends and business partners, were in the habit of chatting on a daily basis. Anna called Marie back, and the nanny said that Helle's flight bags were missing, which would mean she must have gone back to work. Anna worried that she might just have an active imagination, and yet she was remembering Helle's fateful comment to her and others: "If something happens to me, don't think it was an accident." This prompted her to tell Marie that Helle had asked her to take action if she was missing. Marie denied that Helle's absence portended anything.

Later that Thursday afternoon, Richard Crafts called Anna Batelli back. He told Anna that Helle had been called to her sick mother's hospital bedside in Denmark on very short notice. Helle had called Richard from London on Wednesday morning, Richard said, en route home. What surprised Anna was that Helle had just talked to her mother from Germany the previous Saturday, and there had been no mention of any illness. Anna asked Crafts if he was going to contact Pan Am to arrange for emergency leave for his wife, since the airline had a policy which meant that Helle could be fired for missing three straight assignments while being "uncontactable." Crafts asked Anna if she could see to this chore. Crafts, when asked by Anna, gave her a phone number in Denmark that he purported to be Helle's mother's. Still without power and with a son who had caught a fever during the household's chilly two days, Anna was going to need to cancel a routine Pan Am training class Helle and she shared for the next day,

Friday, November 21. Early that next day Anna called Betty Caldwell,* a flight attendant supervisor, to make her own cancellation, and she also mentioned Helle's situation, as it was described by Richard Crafts. Betty Caldwell then advised Anna that only Helle herself, or her husband, could put in for emergency leave, a fact that Anna promptly passed on to Marie Thomas, who promised to tell Crafts.

On Saturday, Anna arrived at the Pan Am parking lot at JFK Airport for a 4:30 P.M. flight to Frankfurt, one that Helle had also been scheduled to make. Anna spotted Helle's blue Tercel parked in the Pan Am employee parking lot. While she was waiting for her flight, Anna filled in another Pan Am supervisor, Renee Denzel,* on where she thought her friend was, and Renee bent regulations for Anna by obtaining a forty-eight-hour leave for Helle. From Europe Anna called Helle's home several times hoping to alert Crafts to the fact that his wife faced a 5 P.M. deadline on Monday to request emergency leave, or, failing that, her job would be in jeopardy. Anna also tried calling the phone number in Denmark given to her as Helle's mother's, but could not get through to the home of Lis Nielsen, though she thought at the time that her language barrier might have been the problem. After arriving back in the states on Monday, November 24, Anna called Crafts and pressed him on the necessity of Helle being granted emergency leave by five that afternoon. Crafts demurred, saying that the Pan Am switchboard had been busy whenever he tried and that he was tied up with parent-teacher conferences for the children. Anna told Crafts that the Denmark phone number had not gotten her through to Mrs. Nielsen's home, and Crafts suggested that she call a cousin of Helle's in California, Poul Gamsgaard, to check. When pressed by Anna, Crafts allowed that he might be able to make that call himself, if he would be able to find time. Anna was, by now, becoming extremely concerned, anxieties she shared with her husband. As this case progressed, other friends and associates of Helle Crafts would come to the fore in demanding answers on her whereabouts, intervention which would prove crucial. Anna Batelli and these others would rise to the demands of this once-in-a-lifetime situation.

More revelations were beginning to draw unwanted attention to Richard Crafts and his behaviors. Marie Thomas and a neighbor would later recall two deep tire ruts in the snow and lawn in front of the Crafts' house, leading to the garage. McLaughlin Ford, the truck dealer in New Milford, had not been able to repair the fuel line of the brand-new dump truck, and Crafts had become increasingly frustrated. Besides holding the unused woodchipper at a $260 per diem clip, Crafts began to threaten to cancel the truck purchase if he did not immediately have the use of his vehicle or one like it. At midday on Thursday, November 20, Crafts had called his salesman at McLaughlin two times, emphasizing that he needed this truck that day to haul some very heavy equipment, including a woodchipper. Afraid of losing the sale, the dealership then offered to lend Crafts an alternative vehicle, a Ford 50 U-Haul truck they had found. Crafts was in no mood to quibble at this point, so he agreed and the U-Haul was delivered to him at Newfield Lane at 2:00 P.M. This vehicle had its company's trademark orange and gray paint on its sides and was far more conspicuous than what Crafts had thought he was going to be driving. Crafts then drove the U-Haul over to Darien Rentals and had the woodchipper hooked up, raising eyebrows there since driving off in a U-Haul with a two-ton woodchipper bouncing along behind it seemed a first.

Crafts was back in Newtown just after dusk and found that the scheduled Thursday night training class at the police department had been cancelled because of the inclement weather. He was supposed to work for the Southbury police at ten that evening. Marie Thomas had decided to stay home and not work as scheduled at her MacDonald's job, so she was there for the children. That evening, Joe Williams and his wife were driving near the Housatonic River in a region between Newtown and Southbury at around 7 P.M. As they approached the area's Silver Bridge, which spanned the river, Joe Williams heard a loud noise and came upon a U-Haul truck positioned on the bridge, a truck which had a woodchipper attached to its rear. Williams could not see well since the interior windows of his car had fogged up, but he saw a man crouching between the truck and the woodchipper, as though he did not want to be seen. This individual was wearing an olive green poncho and a floppy hat, called a "boony," commonly used in the military and by police. Williams, an avid fisherman, inched by, deciding not to stop to offer assistance since there was a car coming in the opposite lane of the bridge, and he also did not want to find himself lecturing someone for dumping woodchips into the river. This practice harmed the fish. Williams was able to notice, though, that the back interior of the truck contained two piles of wood chips and bags which appeared to be made of plastic or cloth. Crafts would later say that he was drinking coffee at a local diner during this timespan, an alibi which he could never confirm.

Wearing Levi's, Crafts showed up at the Southbury police department for his 10 P.M. to 2 A.M. shift. Danny Lewis, a municipal roads department employee on duty that night in Southbury, had remembered seeing a U-Haul truck pulling a woodchipper circling the municipal building's parking lot, which was full of trucks and plows, at around 9 P.M., and then, finding no place to park, moving on. Later, at 11 P.M. or so, Lewis recognized this odd tandem parked at the Rochambeau School's empty lot, which was a couple of hundred yards or so from the municipal building and police headquarters.

Crafts was known to hang around police headquarters after completing a shift, even one which ended at two in the morning. Southbury Constable Richard Wildman wasn't too surprised, then, when he saw Crafts, wearing a police parka turned inside out, with the high-visibility orange showing, in the Rochambeau School parking lot at four in the morning of Friday, November 21. However, seeing Crafts at the back of a U-Haul which had a woodchipper attached to it did strike the policeman as odd. Crafts was taking his personal equipment out of a Southbury police cruiser and placing it in the truck. Wildman had chatted with Crafts earlier that night, before starting his eight-hour assignment at 11 P.M., and the two had remarked about the heavy rains which had still been falling in the region. Now Wildman gave Crafts a ride back to the truck and woodchipper after he'd parked the cruiser.

Crafts told Wildman that he'd rented the woodchipper on the previous Wednesday since the violent storm had torn some "limbs" off of trees on his property, which caused Wildman to wonder out loud about the size of some tree limbs: "They must be awfully big." Later on, Crafts would tell police that he had gone directly home around 2:30 that morning, going a way which would not take him anywhere near Silver Bridge. Wildman would spot the U-Haul and woodchipper again, at 4:30 A.M., in a commuter parking lot. He didn't see Crafts this time, and a half hour later, when he pulled by the lot again, the unusual tandem was gone. Unlike his first encounter with Crafts, however, Wildman did not make any note of this second sighting in a report he filled out before he left the following morning. Richard Crafts's lies would soon be catching up to him.

Looking back at this pattern of subterfuge, it seems clear that Crafts was not that concerned that his specific movements during these critical hours would be closely scrutinized. He must have been exhausted. Yet his adrenalin would be pumping and this would keep him going. At 9:00 on Friday morning, his phone records showed that he phoned his mother in Florida. Then, at 10:30 or so, the U-Haul and woodchipper would show up at McLaughlin Ford in New Milford, where Crafts would press for delivery of his dump truck. Crafts later would say that the trip to McLaughlin from home took only twenty minutes. With a truck hauling a woodchipper over country roads, forty minutes was a far more likely estimate of that trip. He then made the return trip to Newtown. Crafts would later want to show a time period of at least a couple of hours when he would have used the woodchipper on his Currituck Road property, which was his cover story. These disparities, in and of themselves, would not seem very significant. Yet, these kinds of obfuscations and lies helped ignite police interest in this case as the days began to slowly slip by without any word from Helle Crafts or any information on her whereabouts.

Crafts would leave Newtown again after noon that Friday and drive the U-Haul and Brush Bandit to Darien Rentals where he would return the woodchipper, which cost him $900, plus tax. This, according to

Darien Rentals's time clock, occurred at 1:29 P.M. Crafts paid the bill with his Mastercard. Peter Groesbeck at the rental agency had to detach the woodchipper from the U-Haul and had had to raise the vehicle's rear door to do this. Inside the truck, Groesbeck would recall, he saw a couple of piles of wood chips mounded toward the truck's front, a gas tank, some rakes and shovels, and a medium-sized chainsaw, which he recognized as a Stihl since the agency had rented out this brand for years. None of this seemed that unusual to Groesbeck.

Crafts drove back to Newtown that afternoon and, after off-loading his equipment and getting rid of the piles of woodchips, parked the U-Haul in a Grand Union parking lot within walking distance of his home. At 5:30 P.M. that day, McLaughlin Ford finally delivered the new red and white dump truck to Crafts, who paid their salesman the remaining $11,408.80 with a cashier's check. Crafts then put in another four-hour shift at the Southbury Police Department. Several times in the previous week, Richard Crafts had appeared exhausted to people who knew him well. And well he should have. By the next day, Saturday, November 22, he was back in the air for Eastern Airlines, deadheading down to Miami where he would work a flight to Puerto Rico and finally back to New York. Perhaps getting back to his real job made him feel comfortable, even triumphant. But what he could not have anticipated, though, was the growing storm of concern for Helle Crafts and her whereabouts.

Crafts had chosen the wrong time of year to try to claim an unexplained absence by his wife from her children and her holiday obligations. (There is an eerie similarity to the Mathison case here since both murders occurred around the Thanksgiving holiday season.) Anna Batelli was, by the Monday and Tuesday of Thanksgiving week, extremely anxious about Helle and where she could be. This absence was totally unlike the vibrant mother and friend she knew so well. Then there was the matter of a highly reliable and punctual employee like Helle endangering her job status with Pan Am, especially on the brink of a divorce action against her husband. On a trip to Pan Am on that Monday, Anna saw Helle's Tercel still parked in the employee lot.

On Tuesday, Anna checked the post office box Helle and she shared in Newtown for their business and found nothing. Unbeknownst to Crafts, Helle and Anna also had rented a safe deposit box which Anna checked for any word from Helle. Again, nothing. By the day before Thanksgiving, Anna was beside herself, and was especially haunted by Helle's words of warning about her own physical safety. Anna called Sue Miller, who advised caution. Using a language-assistance operator, Anna then got through to the phone number in Denmark given to her by Crafts as Lis Nielsen's, and she was able to confirm that it was bogus. Anna shared her growing anxiety with her husband, Glen, and the two began to actively consider that Helle Crafts had been murdered by her husband.

Marie Thomas seemed to be trying to tell Anna and Glen about something. The nanny had been in the habit of dropping by to buy fresh eggs from the Batellis, who had a small hen coop in their back-yard. One news item was that Richard Crafts had bought himself a dump truck, ostensibly to build a house on the Currituck Road prop-erty, a move which Helle had never mentioned. Then, on Tuesday, November 25, Marie Thomas dropped a bombshell: On the previous Saturday, the 22nd, Marie had seen a dark stain on the master bedroom carpet, one "about the size of a grapefruit." Several days later Crafts had pulled up this carpeting, as well as the carpets in the children's two bedrooms, and had gotten rid of it. Marie also reported that her book of telephone numbers, one that included Helle's family and friends, had gone missing. She was convinced Crafts was responsible for its disappearance.

The Batellis, husband and wife, were becoming afraid for them-selves. Glen reasoned that, if Crafts were indeed a ruthless and cun-ning killer, he might snap and direct his wrath at Anna, who had become relentless in her attempts to locate Helle. Undaunted, Anna called Crafts on Wednesday, the day before Thanksgiving. No, he told Anna, he had not heard from Helle and, no, he had not had the time to call her cousin in California, Poul Gamsgaard, to recheck Lis Nielsen's phone number in Denmark. Crafts told Anna he was too

busy with chores for his children, such as keeping dental appoint-
ments. Crafts added, "It looks like I'll be cooking turkeys" for the next
day's celebration, and Karen and David Rodgers and their children
were expected. Karen would later express her surprise at Helle's
absence the next day, since her sister-in-law had invited them. In
another of the ironic coincidences that this case provided, Anna's own
son had a dental appointment that Wednesday afternoon, and she
seemed to startle Richard Crafts when the two encountered one
another at the dentist's office. Crafts went so far as to look into the
dental cubicle where the boy was being treated, to seem to make sure
that his wife's close friend wasn't simply stalking him. Crafts left
without saying good-bye to Anna.

Anna and Glen went to Massachusetts to celebrate Thanksgiving.
During the return drive, Glen suggested that he confide his concerns
about Helle to a Newtown policeman he knew. Anna objected to that
plan since she was concerned that anyone on the force might tip off
Crafts to the Batellis' concerns. Yet, the drive home late that holiday
was a watershed for Anna. Helle Crafts would simply not miss
Thanksgiving with her three children. And especially without any
word. Anna was now steeling herself to the horrible idea that the very
worst had already happened: Helle Crafts had been murdered by her
husband, and Anna would never again see her dear friend, at least in
this lifetime.

The very next day Anna had coffee at a JFK airport cafeteria with
Sue Miller and another Pan Am flight attendant, Patricia Von Berg,*
whom she had once met at a party at the Crafts' home. Anna said she
had again seen Helle's Tercel in the parking lot, and she shocked the
other two with Marie Thomas's report of the dark stain on carpeting
which Crafts had pulled up from the master bedroom. The trio of
women became ashen-faced. Patricia then blurted out Helle's same
awful warning about her personal safety that she had also told Anna.
This was the first that Anna knew that Helle had tried to warn others
about her fears for her own life. Anna and Sue then left for a flight to
Zurich, Switzerland, one they had been scheduled to work with Helle.

The two heard Helle's name unsuccessfully paged to report for the flight. Before departing, Anna told the others that she had found the name of Helle's divorce lawyer while looking through their joint post office box, and Patricia agreed to call Diane Andersen as soon as she got home, in spite of the fact that the attorney had probably taken that Friday off, which is what Andersen had done.

Patricia's husband, Fred Von Berg,* was a financial planner who had once worked for Pan Am. Upon hearing the alarming facts, Von Berg called the airline and had someone he knew there scour the airline's passenger manifestos on flights to Denmark since November 19, and there was no record of Helle being on one. Patricia called Crafts and said that she'd heard Helle's name paged and that the Zurich flight was the second job assignment she had not made. Crafts's reply was to muse about his wife's perfect record for dependability over seventeen years, and he repeated the story that his wife was in Denmark. Patricia, who was to remember that Richard Crafts had not had "two words to say to me" since they had met, said she planned to follow up and phone Helle the following Sunday, a date Crafts set for Helle's return. "You do that," Crafts rejoindered.

The circle of concern for Helle Crafts was now expanding very rapidly. Patricia Von Berg quickly called Vicki Carson,* another of Helle's flight attendant friends, who said she had not seen Helle but that Richard Crafts had told her, in a call she'd made earlier that week, that he'd heard from Helle from Copenhagen. Crafts had told Vicki the same story as he had Helle's other friends. Vicki now agreed to immediately phone Crafts back, which she did, and was told by Crafts that Helle's mother was having a hard time and that Lis Nielsen had become "soft in the head." Crafts also agreed to try to phone a cousin of Helle's in Denmark early the next afternoon to get a working phone number for the Nielsen household, though, it later developed, Crafts would be flying at that time on Saturday. Meanwhile, Patricia Von Berg, who was Swedish, could speak and understand Danish well enough to call information that Saturday. She obtained Lis Nielsen's correct phone number, which had another area code and was one digit off of the number which Crafts was distributing. Patricia now found herself talking directly to Helle's mother. She chose her words very carefully, so as not to unnecessarily alarm the old lady. Mrs. Nielsen sounded perfectly succinct and sound to Patricia, and she said she was not ill. Helle's mother inquired about her three grandchildren and, when asked, Lis said she was not planning to see Helle again until the following April, when her daughter would take a vacation with the children to visit her in Denmark.

This call by Patricia to Mrs. Nielsen shattered Crafts's cover story and would represent another bombshell for Helle's friends. Vicki Carson now sprang into action and phoned to directly confront Crafts with a confirmed set of facts which were profoundly different from what he had been saying about his wife's whereabouts. Crafts was at first silent and then lamely claimed that Mrs. Nielsen must have been lying. She had lied before, when Helle's father had become very ill. When further pressed, Crafts told Vicki that perhaps Helle had decided to visit a friend of hers in Paris, a woman named "Vivi." None of Helle's friends had ever heard her speak of such a person. Crafts also speculated that Mrs. Nielsen had garbled the facts due to a language barrier. Vicki reminded Crafts that Swedes and Danes are able to communicate well. Vicki was becoming even more alarmed and suspicious. She also reminded Crafts that Helle's job had been protected through the following Monday, but that he had better take immediate action, or the family was in danger of losing that income, a fact which Vicki tied to the recent Eastern Airlines pay cuts. To Vicki, Crafts seemed unfazed, even casual about all of this. Then she directly asked Crafts if the two had been having more matrimonial discord. Yes, but not so bad lately, Crafts said, and maybe, he replied to Vicki's next direct question, Helle had gone off somewhere to think things over.

Both Vicki and Patricia now called Alyce Bennett, who immediately became alarmed over the sequence of events and Crafts's stories. Helle would never just disappear for nine days and would not ever, in a hundred years, desert her three children without some kind of explanation during a holiday like Thanksgiving. Also, since Alyce and Helle had worked and flown together since 1969, it was also out of the question that she would blow off assigned flights and risk her job at Pan Am. Alyce quickly called Mrs. Nielsen and verified that Helle's mother had not seen her. Then, after calling the Crafts' home three times and just getting Marie Thomas, Alyce finally reached Crafts later that Saturday. Crafts had known Alyce as long as he had known Helle and seemed more talkative now. He told Alyce that he'd taken his three children to his sister's in Westport early the morning of the storm, November 19, and that he'd expected Helle to join them there. Like her other friends, Alyce knew that Helle did not like driving through snowstorms. Also puzzling to Alyce was Crafts's adding that Helle had taken a fur coat she owned, a red fox which Alyce knew Helle had stored in a cleaners in Newtown. Crafts also volunteered that he didn't know where the Pan Am employee parking lot was at JFK, another oddity that bordered on the perverse for Alyce since the Eastern employee lot which Crafts regularly used was directly across the street. Alyce put down the phone convinced that Crafts was lying, but she needed more hard facts to prove it.

By now Helle's closest friends were moving to discover what had really happened to Helle Crafts. Vicki Carson heard the latest inconsistencies from Richard Crafts from Alyce on Saturday night, and Vicki followed this up that evening with a call to Helle's cousin in California, Poul Gamsgaard. Gamsgaard would comment negatively about Crafts, and he shared the anxiety over Helle ever abandoning her children and family this way. He also knew about the marital problems the couple had been going through. Gamsgaard agreed to call Denmark, which he did the next morning. Nobody there knew where Helle was, he later told Vicki. Alyce Bennett again called Crafts that Sunday, urging him to go to the police himself or to call the FBI. Crafts scoffed at Alyce and told her that she'd been watching "too much *Miami Vice*," the popular police show of that time. Crafts added that his wife would be mortified if she later found that her absence had caused so much of a stir that she'd been reported missing. Anna Batelli had returned from her Zurich flight, and on Sunday she, too, called

Crafts to closely question him on an earlier inconsistency in his story about where Helle had gone. Crafts had told Betty Cooper,* a neighbor and friend of his wife, that Helle had gone to Denmark, while he was telling Anna he didn't know where she had gone and, only the next day, he had come up with the story about Helle going to Denmark. Crafts again changed course. This time he flabbergasted Anna by saying that perhaps Helle had gone off on a surprise vacation of her own, to a Club Med in the Canary Islands, a supposition based on some recent but unaccounted-for information he'd been able to pick up. Crafts then named several of Helle's girlfriends who might have been with her. Anna went through the motions of checking out Ellen O'Brien,* a former neighbor now living in Florida, who said she had not heard from Helle in some time. Helle Crafts's friends were now deeply alarmed and were not about to lighten up until they began finding some answers. This cordon of loyal friends was about to find a new ally, one whom they did not always enjoy, but someone who would do a great deal in getting the criminal justice system involved in the disappearance of Helle Crafts while there was still time to do something about it.

On the first morning of December 1986, Keith Mayo had no idea that anything had happened. He went to his New Milford office on that Monday, the first time he'd been there since the Wednesday of the previous week. He thought he'd be in for a quiet start to the new month, a time when he could catch up on his paperwork and pay his bills. Sue Schneider, his assistant, was there. Then, Keith Mayo's phone would ring, he would talk to Dianne Andersen, Helle's divorce lawyer, and he would embark on a three-week mission, one destined to extend to the Connecticut State Police's Major Crimes Unit. Andersen briefly told Mayo that over the weekend she had received urgent calls from three of Helle Crafts's close friends: Anna Batelli, Alyce Bennett, and Fred Von Berg, the husband of Patricia Von Berg. Andersen filled Mayo in on the alarming facts surrounding Helle's disappearance. Mayo now dashed out to consult a lawyer, Roland Moots, who had a neighboring office and who advised the private eye that he'd be much safer if a missing persons report on Helle Crafts was filed with the Newtown police. The attorney was concerned that Mayo could be about to dash into a legal trap and come out with a defamation of character suit around his neck. The necessity for a missing persons report made sense to Mayo and also to Dianne Andersen, whom he quickly phoned back. The two agreed to meet in Danbury within an hour. Mayo must have been wondering if somehow the damaging evidence his photographs represented had led directly to a tragedy.

An ex-policeman, Mayo had started with the nearby New Fairfield police force and then had moved on to join the New Milford police, since New Fairfield was smaller and a constabulary, meaning their officers were under the jurisdiction of a resident state police trooper. Mayo had also studied criminal justice for two years at the University of New Haven, where I have taught for many years. Mayo's headstrong ways had gotten him into hot water at New Milford since he had publicly accused a member of the town's police commission of leaking answers for promotion exams to preferred candidates. Mayo then took the sergeants' exam, did not place well, and decided to leave the force to start his own private detective agency. His practice was grounded in the kind of marital work he had performed for Helle Crafts.[4]

Perhaps because Mayo had met Helle Crafts, or because he had gotten a sense of Richard Crafts during his marital surveillance, or maybe because he was excitable, Mayo quickly began pressing for answers. Dianne Andersen had told him that all three of her callers had expressed concern for the Crafts' nanny, Marie Thomas, who was now the only other adult living at 5 Newfield Lane. Something could happen to the young woman if Crafts felt she was becoming a real problem for him. Mayo made a quick call for advice to an old friend on the New Milford force and then quickly found himself on the phone with the Newtown police chief, Lou Marchese.

Marchese now responded to Mayo and his pressing for urgent action, such as police protection for Marie Thomas, by letting one and all know that the chief was in charge, and he would not let anyone, especially a private detective, push into the boundary lines surrounding his authority. No, Mayo could not see anyone who would look into the case until 4:30 P.M. that day. After all, missing persons cases came up once or twice a week, and almost always the matter was settled in a few days when someone returned home. Whether or not Chief Marchese's attitude was formally passed on to his detectives and the rest of his force, this outlook began to permeate the Newtown department's reaction to Helle Crafts's disappearance.[5]

Mayo got to Danbury by 10:30 that morning and met Dianne Andersen at the court house. Andersen then took Mayo to meet Assistant State Prosecutor Robert Brunetti, who had once practiced law with a New Milford firm which had retained Mayo. Brunetti, who was nearly forty, had taken his post recently and had quickly gained a favorable reputation within the legal community as being a good lawyer and easy to access. Perhaps because Dianne Andersen was a party to the report on Helle Crafts, Brunetti decided to go down the hall to seek out Walter Flanagan, the district's chief state prosecutor. Brunetti had heard enough to let him know that Mayo could be correct about Marie Thomas being in some kind of jeopardy. And, obviously, if the prosecutor's office were too nonchalant about these reports, Brunetti could be held responsible.

Walter Flanagan quickly zeroed in on what he was hearing from his deputy. Flanagan, then forty-nine, had already proven himself to be one of the top prosecutors in the state. Old-fashioned, courtly, and tall, Flanagan was a 1960 graduate of Holy Cross College. Flanagan had been awarded his law degree at the University of Connecticut in 1963, and he practiced law with William Lavery (who would later become a judge and who would later sign a search warrant for Crafts's property) in his native Bridgeport, before moving to the prosecutor's office in 1971. Flanagan was also very aware of Lou Marchese and his iron grip on the Newtown department. Thus, he quickly recognized that the disappearance of Helle Crafts might be a situation which the local police would tend to downplay. This was particularly so since Richard Crafts had once worked there.

Brunetti left his meeting with Flanagan to make a call and then told Andersen and Mayo that he had had an inspector contact

Marchese and that the chief would not budge on the later-day meeting with Mayo. He also advised the pair to encourage Helle Crafts's friends to voice their concerns with the Newtown police and suggested to Mayo that he contact Marie Thomas and see to her safety.

Marie Thomas was late that midday for a second part-time job she had, working behind the counter of a small consignment shop in Newtown. After getting a hassle from the store's owner, Mayo was able to get a Newtown officer to call Brunetti, who okayed the girl's going to the Newtown police headquarters with Mayo. Marie, who had bleached blonde hair and looked her age of twenty, had started to sniffle when told that she would be asked about Helle's disappearance. During the half hour that Thomas talked to Mayo at the police station, Marie sketched in the details of what had happened on the morning of Wednesday, November 19. She emphasized how exhausted Crafts had appeared that day and that he had even fallen asleep at the wheel on the return drive. This interview was interrupted by a Newtown officer who escorted Marie to another room, but enough was said to further alarm Mayo about what might have taken place. There were many questions, such as: Why would Helle leave in her Tercel before dawn in a heavy snowstorm and still be expected at the Rodgers' home in Westport? Mayo also ran directly into a wall of police skepticism and felt lucky to just get a statement from Marie onto the record.

Sue Schneider, Mayo's assistant, called Anna Batelli, who promptly came to Mayo's New Milford office. After just a little of what Anna had to say, Schneider decided to take her to the Newtown police station. There Anna gave a statement to a patrolman in an interview which lasted an hour and a half. Meanwhile, Mayo and Schneider took Marie back to the consignment shop's parking lot, where she retrieved the VW Crafts had recently purchased. Mayo and Schneider followed Marie back to 5 Newfield Lane. Crafts wasn't home, and the pair felt comfortable about leaving Marie there. What had earlier been the cause of great anxiety by Mayo, was now being left to chance. This up-and-down and excitable behavior by Mayo would become a big issue in the weeks ahead.

The next several days brought a marked increase in the tension surrounding Helle Crafts's disappearance. On the morning of Tuesday, December 2, the Newtown police invited Crafts in for a talk. One of the key investigators there attested to Crafts's character as sound. At this meeting with a detective, Crafts explained that his wife had run off with her lover, an Oriental, and that he'd been covering up this fact with Marie Thomas and Helle's friends since he did not want to "air his dirty linen in public." When he was asked when he was going to file a missing persons report on Helle, Crafts explained that his wife had disappeared for a week or two before. Crafts's interrogator asked him why he hadn't stepped forward on his own, in light of the accusations which were now circulating about him. Crafts replied that he had been planning to come in and make a statement that afternoon, but his questioner did not believe him. Crafts would then sign a statement which spelled out his version of the facts. However, the Newtown police did not raise the question of the Crafts' impending divorce action. The police did zero in on a statement Crafts had made to them that Helle had a large bank account in Denmark, a red herring Crafts planted that day. Keith Mayo did not get wind of this questioning until the next day, when assistant prosecutor Brunetti told him. Brunetti made three calls to the Newtown police that Wednesday morning, the third a request for a typed report of Crafts's interview, which he would never receive. Brunetti had another important news item for the animated Mayo: Richard Crafts had agreed to take a polygraph test.

At about this time, the *Danbury News-Times* began to get wind that something was up over the disappearance of Helle Crafts. At twenty-eight, Patrick O'Neil (no relation to my coauthor) was a bright and highly energetic reporter who had already won an award. O'Neil, who covered the police beat, had seen Mayo at the Newtown headquarters with two attractive women (Anna Batelli and Sue Schneider) whom he was told were airline flight attendants. Also, Mayo had called an editor at the paper and had told him, after insisting that the newsman keep his source's names between the two of them, what had been reported by Marie and Anna. Now O'Neil began to take a close interest in this case, and his responsible coverage would help drive the investigation. This would be a positive contrast to some of the tabloid sensationalism which would appear in the weeks and months to come.

A thunderbolt of sorts now hit Mayo and the circle of Helle's friends who were pursuing Richard Crafts as the possible murderer of his wife. Crafts easily passed the lie detector test which he took on Thursday, December 4, at the state police headquarters in Meriden. Before he had been driven up from the Newtown police headquarters to take this test that morning, Crafts had signed another statement given to him by the Newtown detectives. This acknowledged that "serious accusations" had been made against him over the disappearance of his wife; that he was taking a polygraph test on that date to show his "cooperation"; and that he had not "had the opportunity" to consult a lawyer "concerning the wisdom of this undertaking."

After he arrived in Meriden, Crafts told the examiners that he had recently taken a polygraph prior to his being hired by the Southbury police. One of the two examiners used by Southbury, when contacted, told the state police that he had never observed a lie detector subject who was less responsive than Crafts had been. In total, the examiners in Meriden that morning asked Crafts nine questions, alternating between innocent queries designed to establish a truthful response pattern and very direct questions on whether he knew Helle's whereabouts and if he had murdered her. Crafts passed this test with flying colors. So much so, that one of his examiners felt his responses were a little too perfect.

There are many ways for an experienced individual to lie his way through a polygraph exam and, without going into too much detail, Crafts's experience with the CIA could have given him the knowledge to beat this test. One way some have devised to do this would be to place a tack inside a shoe and to dig a foot into this sharp object, but only when truthfully answering the set-up questions. This pain would set off a traceable reaction, similar to the recorded responses when the subject was lying, since he would not inflict this pain upon himself when responding to the incriminating questions. All of this underscores the wisdom in the courts' not allowing polygraph results in evidence, though this deeply frustrates the prosecution at times. These tests can be very effective tools for investigative purposes. But, legally the polygraph still remains inadmissible in most courts of law. Ironically, the Crafts case is just another example of why.

Mayo was shaken by the results of the polygraph. He consulted with an expert in that field and came away with the notion that someone with Crafts's background could have cheated his way through the exam. On Friday, December 5, Mayo contacted Dianne Andersen, and the two decided to call a meeting of Helle Crafts's closest friends to discuss mutual concerns and what should be done next. The following Monday, December 8, a core group met with Mayo and Andersen at the attorney's office in Danbury. The grim enclave lasted two hours and included Anna Batelli, Alyce Bennett, and Vicki Carson. The group quickly struck a consensus on the fact that Helle would never simply desert her three children during the holidays. They reviewed Helle's ominous warnings and Crafts's lies about her whereabouts. Most were meeting Mayo for the first time, and they considered him informed and committed. Andersen and Mayo left the room, and Helle's friends made plans to retain Mayo, though confidentially, since they each feared the vindictive nature of Richard Crafts and possible lawsuits. Mayo emphasized that the Newtown police considered them all as pests and would not pursue the case energetically, especially after Crafts had passed the lie detector exam. They made plans on how to raise a fund to pay Mayo. The group focused on Helle's Tercel sitting in the Pan Am parking lot as one tangible piece of evidence that should immediately be pursued. The next day, Pan Am's Betty Caldwell advised Mayo that gaining access to the Tercel was out of the question, barring a police order. Caldwell did, however, let Mayo know that Helle had made no unusual withdrawals from her account at the Pan Am credit union, except for $1,000 which Mayo knew was probably to pay for his own fee.

On Wednesday, December 10, reporter Patrick O'Neil called Crafts at his home and asked him about the investigation over his wife's disappearance. Crafts very casually replied, in effect, what disappearance? and politely got off of the phone. O'Neil had also heard about the lie detector test and could sense that Chief Marchese wasn't pushing his people on this case.[6]

The participants in the Monday meeting had asked Mayo to video-tape another interview with Marie Thomas. He did this on Wednesday and was able to ferret out more from the nanny, who had answered an ad in the *Idaho Statesman* from the Crafts the previous June, standard procedure for households in the East to recruit their help. Marie used the interview to report that two of Helle's uniform shirts were missing, as well as her toiletries, and she confirmed that a set of Pan Am flight luggage was gone, too, a fact she'd had to correct from what she'd told Anna and Glen Batelli, since she'd just found a new set which Helle had recently received in a closet. A few days after Helle had disap-peared, Crafts had told Marie that he didn't care about his wife any-more and that she was out of his life. Marie also said that she did not know of any other man in Helle's life, Oriental or not, and that the only time Helle seemed to want privacy on the telephone was when she was talking to Dianne Andersen. Then, most significantly for Mayo, Marie informed him that she'd observed a circular stain on the master bedroom rug that Helle had loved. Crafts had told her that he'd spilled some kerosene on it, an aroma Marie had noticed. This was the first time that Keith Mayo had heard of any dark stain on a carpet. Marie told Mayo that Crafts had removed the carpet and disposed of it. This fact would send Mayo on a fruitless quest to find the carpet, one that would play a huge role in unlocking the facts of this case.

After interviewing Marie Thomas, Mayo animatedly suggested an immediate meeting of the group that had met at Dianne Andersen's two days earlier, minus Andersen. Mayo also advised Bob Brunetti of these developments, and Brunetti immediately informed Walter Flanagan, who had kept very on top of what was going on in the Crafts case. Mayo arrived at Vicki Carson's home at about eight. To his amazement, Mayo heard several members express concerns that, if Crafts had mur-dered his wife, his being convicted of the crime would effectively make orphans out of the three children. Alyce Bennett put a stop to this discussion by saying she wanted "that son of a bitch, Richard" to pay for his crime, if he, indeed, had murdered her dear friend. Mayo's enthusiasm at this meeting rubbed several in the group the wrong way. The detective did not seem to appreciate the feelings of Helle's friends who were still in the mourning process, even as they tried to cope with the possibilities of what had really happened. Anna Batelli, for one, said she did not want to deal with Mayo anymore, and Alyce Bennett was chosen to be the group's spokesperson in dealing with him.

By the next morning, Mayo had turned his focus almost exclusively onto his finding the missing and stained carpet from the Crafts' master bedroom. Starting on that Thursday, the eleventh, Mayo would galvanize a team of friends and volunteers on a search which would take them ninety miles northwest over back roads to the tiny hamlet of Canterbury, where Southbury's trash was taken by a private hauler to a landfill. Mayo pursued the Southbury trail since he'd misunderstood a tip from Bob Brunetti that Crafts had been seen at the Southbury dumpster, acting in an odd manner.

On Saturday, December 13, Mayo drove to Canterbury and planned out his search, with the help of the landfill's owner. He used contributions for his search fund to hire some temporary workers and was able to round up volunteers. Starting at dawn on Monday morning, digging and searching for the next two days, Mayo's team was able to uncover a deep blue carpet which had a dark stain on it and seemed to match a swatch of rug Mayo had been able to obtain, through Marie Thomas, that had been inadvertently left behind at the Crafts' house.

During this timespan, Mayo was also able to reach out to turn up the pressure for a real investigation into the Crafts case. He notified Patrick O'Neil of his digging, and, though the reporter did not travel to Canterbury as invited, O'Neil followed the developments closely. Mayo was working through an old friend, Orlando Mo, who had worked with him on the New Milford force and had now become a state trooper. Through this relationship, Mayo was also able to begin bringing this situation to the attention of the state police's Western District Major Crimes Squad, based in Waterbury, which covered Newtown. Mo, who was the trooper-in-residence in Salisbury, another of the small towns which dot the Connecticut landscape, was now able to see that the Crafts' situation would get wider scrutiny. On the morning of Wednesday, December 17, Mayo would meet with Lieutenant James Hiltz, head of operations in Waterbury. And soon, because of the carpet Mayo's team had found, I would begin to hear in detail about Helle Crafts's disappearance and would be placed in a position to investigate.

Mayo's prompting Patrick O'Neil was also beginning to pay dividends. After worrying about whether word of the Canterbury landfill search would find its way to competing news media, the paper decided it was time to run its first story on Helle Crafts's disappearance. Later on Tuesday, O'Neil called Crafts again, this time for comment on a story he was about to run. Crafts's major preoccupation seemed to be about O'Neil spelling Helle's name correctly. As usual, Crafts ended the call with a polite and correct, "Good evening." The story ran the next morning, under the headline, "Police Seek Missing Newtown Woman." In this story, Newtown's Chief Marchese said that his department was treating the situation as a missing person case, but added that the Newtown force was "investigating all the possibilities."

Indifferent at the beginning of December, the Newtown detective force was bearing down on the case by the middle of the month. By Monday, December 8, Newtown detectives began some digging of their own. Anna Batelli accompanied one to the Newtown Banking Center, where the officer was not admitted inside to directly look at the contents of the strong box Anna had shared with Helle. Helle's jewelry was still in there, Anna emerged to tell the detective, adding that, "If you don't think Helle's dead, you're a fool." Others began checking activity on Richard Crafts's credit cards, using numbers Anna had provided them. One found a Caldor's November 19 purchase for $257.96, but there was no discovering that this was for new bedding for another two weeks. The Newtown police contacted the Danish consulate in New York and, through them, asked the Danish police to try and locate Helle there. But, despite Chief Marchese's words, the Newtown chief refused to pay the expenses for a search of

Helle's Tercel which was still sitting in the Pan Am parking lot at JFK.[7] The Newtown police were now also talking to the Southbury department about Crafts, specifically about his work schedules.

On the evening of Thursday, December 11, just as Mayo was preparing to go to Canterbury, Newtown detectives decided to phone Southbury and told them to transport Crafts, who had reported for duty, over for another interrogation. By this time, more doubts about Crafts had crept into the minds of these detectives. In their interview, Crafts was advised that Helle had hired an investigator who had documented the fact he was having an affair with Marie Evans in New Jersey. Crafts, dressed in his police uniform, looked at the photos. He denied that Evans knew about Helle's disappearance, but admitted that Helle and he had fought over his using his Visa card to make some purchases near Evans's home. They also bore down on Crafts's having rugs replaced in his house. Again, Crafts claimed he had spilled some kerosene on the master bedroom carpet. He said he had dumped the rug in the Newtown landfill a week earlier. The detectives in Newtown also closely questioned Crafts about a later-November lie he had been caught telling a Southbury police supervisor, after being caught with his three children in his police cruiser, which is against police procedures. (Crafts received a letter of reprimand for this infraction.)

In fact, as they wrapped up this interrogation, the Newtown detectives had the distinct impression that Crafts had been lying to them on several fronts. Yet, the department, dominated by Chief Marchese, was still treating Helle Crafts as a missing person. Helle's friends seemed to be on the phone at the Newtown police headquarters all the time. One officer added to the appearance of police indifference by commenting to a friend of Helle's, that she and her "friends must have been watching too much television." Considering Crafts's own reference to Alyce Bennett's watching too much of the *Miami Vice* network hit, this comment seems to reflect the suspect's mindset. In and out of uniform, Newtown officers were running into more and more questions on this case. Several sensed that Walter Flanagan was running out of patience with their chief and that the Crafts case could be taken away from their jurisdiction.[8]

The blue carpet which Keith Mayo and his troops had discovered was delivered to the state police forensic laboratory in Meriden on Wednesday, December 17. I was in Washington to give a lecture and did not return to my office until Friday, the 19th, when I first formally heard of the Crafts case in a call from Walter Flanagan. I knew Walter quite well and respected him very much. In our conversation that day, the two of us seemed to sense that we would be working closely on this matter for many days, weekends, and holidays.

In 1986, the state police forensic laboratory was located in Building #5 in the Meriden complex. This complex was formerly a reform school for delinquent youths. Today, the forensic laboratory has been moved to a new $10 million state-of-the-art facility. Building #5 was a converted, three-story, old dormitory. Although this building contained several examination rooms with lab benches for criminalists to use for examining physical evidence, not one of these spaces was large enough for the nine-by-twelve-foot piece of carpet. I made a decision that, since the carpet dug up from the dump was already con- taminated, there would be no harm in conducting my examination out- side, in the baseball field on the grounds of the state police complex. With the help of my right-hand assistant, Elaine Pagliaro, and Sergeant Martin Ohradan of the Connecticut State Police's Western District Major Crime Unit, we examined the carpet, inch by inch, looking for clues. We performed chemical tests on each of the sus- pected stains. After four hours of back-breaking work carried out on the carpet, none of the stains tested positive for blood.

I then phoned Jim Hiltz in Waterbury to tell him that the stain on the carpet was not human blood. I would conduct a more thorough investigation on Monday of the following week, with Keith Mayo, Sgt. Marty Ohradan, and Lt. Jim Hiltz in attendance. After the weekend, we spread the carpet out on the baseball field in back of my office and showed how this carpet had never been fastened to a floor. The Crafts' master bedroom carpeting was wall-to-wall, and had to have marks on its reverse side from being fastened down. I knew that I was disappointing Mayo, in particular, but he should have felt a lot better about all of his frenzied work, since he had been the catalyst for our getting into the case.

As America was preparing to celebrate Christmas of 1986, many of Helle's friends were suffering from a mixture of feelings: sadness, anger at Richard Crafts, anxiety for Helle's three young children, and dread over the fact that their friend's husband might be getting away with murder. Alyce Bennett attended a Christmas party at a neighbor's on that Saturday evening. At the party, Alyce stood in front of the large, blazing hearth and quietly told her hosts and other friends about her fears for Helle Crafts. She also expressed anger at how the police had seemed to trivialize something very awful. Her only feeling of hope was that the press and others, such as the state police, were now becoming active. Perhaps, she thought, there is still a chance that Richard Crafts would pay for what she was sure he had done.

Walter Flanagan was also preparing for the holidays. In mid-December, when his interest in the Crafts case had become white hot, the prosecutor had met with Karen and Donald Rodgers to talk things over. Crafts's sister, in particular, had been like steel, looking straight through Walter and standing up for her brother. Donald Rodgers, at that time, was still a buddy of Richard Crafts and expressed disbelief that Crafts had done anything out of the ordinary. Then, shortly before the holidays, Flanagan and his wife went to the Pequot Library in Westport to watch one of their children perform in a show. Sitting there, Flanagan looked up and saw an attractive woman, whom he could not place, standing above him, smiling, and extending her hand to him. There was an awkward second or two as Flanagan stood up and returned the lady's greeting. After this woman had departed, Ann Flanagan inquired about the visitor's identity. Then it hit Flanagan. Karen Rodgers had changed her mind, and her warm greeting could mean only one thing: Richard Crafts's sister now believed that her brother had murdered Helle.[9]

Back at his office, Flanagan was getting reports that the Newtown police were not cooperating with the office of James Hiltz. His assistant, Bob Brunetti, for instance, complained that he had not received a copy of Crafts's interrogation from December 11. On Saturday, the 20th, one of Lieutenant Hiltz's key investigators, Sergeant Ohradan, spent what he considered four fruitless hours at the Newtown station and had had to leave without Helle Crafts's dental records, which he knew were available. Finally, on Tuesday, December 23, Flanagan ran out of patience. He had already ruled that the investigation, as of December 18, would be joint, with Jim Hiltz's Major Crimes Squad in Waterbury handling all of the forensic work and the Newtown police dealing with the rest.[10]

This combined effort had a very short lifespan. Turf problems have always existed among police agencies in the United States. The FBI, state police, and local police oftentimes argue about jurisdictional and statutory authority over an investigation. The Crafts case was no exception. This type of turf problem often hinders the progress of an investigation. I have lectured around the world to the law enforcement community to stress the importance of teamwork. In theory, police investigators should work together, disregarding which agency is in charge. In my recent book, *Henry Lee's Handbook on Crime Scene Investigation*, I specifically emphasize this "team concept" needed in criminal investigation. Once in a while, a tough decision has to be made to transfer a case from one agency to another. This type of decision might hurt the egos and feelings of some people, but, in the long run, this call will prove a positive factor in solving cases. After all, our job is to maintain the confidence and trust of our citizens, to solve all cases, and to prevent crime.

Now, Walter Flanagan decreed, the investigation would be exclusively run by the state police, with the Newtown force providing assistance, if and when they were asked. Newtown was to expedite the transfer of all files. This would be a very tough step for Flanagan to take. It was especially hard on those members of the Newtown force who had truly thrown themselves into this case. Yet, facts such as Helle Crafts's Tercel still sitting in the Pan Am parking lot at a New York airport and key interviews which had not yet been typed cried out for investigation. Ironically, on the Monday before Christmas, Newtown detectives, investigating Crafts's credit cards, had discovered his earlier rental of a woodchipper. This fact hit them like a thunderbolt. But Walter Flanagan did what he knew he had to do. On that Tuesday, two days before Christmas, Flanagan also instructed Hiltz to draw up papers for a search warrant of Crafts's home at 5 Newfield Lane.[11]

More and more was beginning to come to light about what was inside the Crafts' house. On Saturday, the 20th, Karen Rodgers, had gone to the house to pick up Marie Thomas and the three children. By now deeply suspicious of her brother, as Flanagan had seen, Karen still seemed reluctant to take any direct action. While she was there, Marie showed Karen suspicious brown stains on the mattress in the master bedroom and on a towel, neatly folded and cleaned, in the laundry room. Karen instructed Marie, who had by now given notice that she would be returning to Idaho, to call Betty Cooper, Helle's friend and neighbor. James Cooper, Betty's husband and an active member of the core group of Helle's friends, went to the house in his wife's place. Betty had already been assured by Ohradan, who was reached at the Newtown police station, that Marie's invitation to enter the house would make James's entry alright. Marie showed him the mattress, which was sitting directly on the floor without any frame or box spring. Mattresses from the children's rooms were also in the master bedroom, sitting on foundations. Crafts and his children had all been sleeping in that one room for a month, Marie said. She had actually heard Crafts tell the children on one occasion, "We do fine without Mommy, don't we? See? We don't need her." As Cooper looked about, he saw what appeared to be a smear on the side of the mattress, as though something had been wiped off, plus spots the size of a quarter on one side of the mattress, and smaller spots. All of these were the brownish color of dried blood. To anyone entering the once-neat home it was quickly apparent that, in overall appearance, Richard Crafts was creating a mess inside his house similar to the one he'd sustained outside for years.

On Christmas Eve, Hiltz went to Judge Frank MacDonald, a former prosecutor himself (and later appointed the state's chief justice by Governor John Rowland), to ask that the judge sign a search warrant for Crafts's house and the Currituck Road property. All of the evidence for this warrant was circumstantial. The lies which Crafts had told, it could be argued, were merely his attempts to cover up a messy domestic dispute. And Helle's warnings about her own safety might have just been her giving way to unnecessary fears. What if they were wrong? All were conscious that, should nothing ever be developed, or if Helle Crafts were to return from some remote corner of the earth, they would be vulnerable to civil suits by Crafts against them. Walter Flanagan worried that more evidence was going to be required. But, voicing his own misgivings, Judge MacDonald signed the warrant, and his action would change my life for the next few months, starting with the very next day, which was Christmas.

It is not as though the state police and Walter Flanagan were throwing caution to the wind at this point. By now any of us familiar with the essentials of Helle Crafts's disappearance knew full well that Richard Crafts was a very intelligent and resourceful individual. It's a rule that, as time goes by, more evidence can be destroyed or altered. Therefore, the basic principle of crime scene investigation is to search the primary scene as soon as possible. This scene should be secured to prevent any tampering with the evidence or with its destruction. The scene should also be detailed, recorded, and documented. Then the scene should be thoroughly searched, and the evidence should be collected and properly preserved. As each day passed and Helle did not call her children or friends or simply walk through her front door, the investigators became more certain that they were dealing with a homicide and were more determined to bring Crafts to justice. Reports of the rented woodchipper, for instance, spread among police ranks like wildfire. So, leaving our homes to work on Christmas Day was a sacrifice for us and, of course, for our families, yet we collectively put our heads down and moved forward with great determination.

We chose to work on that Christmas, first, because of the time element and, second, because we estimated that Crafts and his three children would be away for the holiday, probably with Karen and David Rodgers in Westport. In reality, Crafts had driven his family down to

Florida to have Christmas with his mother there in Boca Raton. They had left on Monday, the 22nd. Crafts had purchased some medication in New Jersey with a credit card since his son, Thomas, had been suffering with an earache. When we entered the house, we found a note pasted to a cupboard, ostensibly to Helle from Crafts. The note was dated the 23rd and referred to the recently purchased VW, which Helle, ostensibly, did not know about, and pleaded with her to join Crafts at his mother's place. He also wrote that his Ford was not running, another lie. With a bogus date, one that could be disproved very easily with the credit card evidence, this note gave us another insight into the strange and messy mindset that Crafts was using to try and outsmart his investigators. It also told us that Crafts was very smart and was expecting our search.

Arriving at 5 Newfield Lane in the early afternoon, we had hoped to gain entry through the garage door, which we had heard was unlockable. This was not the case, and Marty Ohradan took out a small window in the kitchen door so we could enter the house. Before doing any specific work, we videotaped the entire interior to document the condition of the house. We found, as we had been told, that the home was now a shambles. Mattresses were strewn about, with a concentration of beds in the master bedroom. We used 35 mm cameras to photograph each and every article and piece of furniture for their respective positions. One major reason for doing this: To create a true representation of the scene and to counter any arguments by defense lawyers that we had rearranged any evidence to help convict Richard Crafts. This is standard operating procedure for detectives in major police agencies.

Let me take a moment here to sketch in some thoughts about working on a case over a major holiday. To be sure, Christmas is the biggest holiday in the Western world. Although there were celebrations in Taiwan where I grew up and later worked as a police captain in the Taipei police headquarters, Christmas was still not a major holiday. So, working on Christmas was not a big problem for me. But, for my family, this was a different story. After we had emigrated to the United States in 1965, we gradually picked up the customs of Western culture. We started celebrating Christmas, especially after my daughter, Sherry, and son, Stanley, were born. My wife Margaret made sure that I understood that this was an important holiday and that I had to spend my time away from the laboratory and with our friends and family.

Since 1976, we have always had Christmas dinner at the residence of Judge Anthony DeMayo and his family. At the time this tradition started, he was the chief public defender for New Haven County. Judge DeMayo is an excellent jurist and a man with a great passion for justice, and his wife, Eileen, is a most intelligent and learned lady with a very kind heart. We first met through casework. At that time I still worked full-time at the University of New Haven as a professor of Forensic Science. Once in a while, my friend Tony DeMayo needs some forensic advice and I need some career counseling. We have become very close friends. Since that first year, every Christmas we have a joint celebration and grand dinner at the DeMayos'. We also usually visit my mother, Au-Fu Lee. She raised all of my thirteen brothers and sisters after my father had died when I was four years old. She now lives with one of my sisters, Dr. Sylvia Lee-Houng. Sylvia is a professor at the New York University Medical Center. Because of my sister's guidance and support, I was able to come to the United States and finish my Ph.D. in biochemistry. To make a long story short, in 1986 when I informed Margaret that I would have to work on Christmas Eve and Day and break the tradition of having dinner with the DeMayos and visiting my mother, of course, this was a great disappointment to her and the kids. I am sure, the rest of the detectives working in the Crafts' case most likely had to go through what I went through. Disappointment from their families and a big personal sacrifice of their holidays.

Prior to our search, the Major Crime Squad received a briefing from our task force. A dozen detectives from the Western Major Crime Squad and I were now ready to work. We had all been through these kinds of investigations together many times before, so we each knew how to work with the others. We hoped to be as unobtrusive as possible and dreaded attracting the attention of any members of the media. We also were conscious of its being Christmas and did not want to unnecessarily alarm any neighbors and intrude on their holiday. We found that Crafts had thoroughly rearranged his household, and I was most anxious to determine what the household had looked like, before Helle Crafts had disappeared. Reluctantly, we decided to call Anna Batelli, who was just beginning to serve her family her Christmas dinner. Anna reminded us of her holiday duties and at first refused to come over and accommodate me. However, we called Anna back since it was crucial to our work to reestablish the master bedroom as best we could. Otherwise, it would be impossible to reconstruct the scene and to investigate the case and find the essential clues. What exactly, did the home look like when Helle came in out of the snow on the evening of November, 18? Anna, a true friend to Helle, finally agreed and was there within fifteen minutes to help us. Her assistance at this time was critical to our investigation.

We were, of course, looking for specifics. One initial analysis would be to establish the family's culture, its lifestyle, and then to determine if there had been a drastic change to this environment. Evidence of something very major happening was everywhere. The house was not just a mess, the environment had turned into chaos. The dining room table was in the kitchen, and the kitchen table sat in the dining room, which was also stacked up with bunk beds, broken down and leaning against the walls. This room also contained boxes and a bureau full of toys. A chest of drawers was laid on its side in the family room. A huge mound of ashes lay in the fireplace. These ashes clearly were not from firewood. They appeared to be the burned remains of paper and a fibrous type of material. These ashes represented a silent clue for the forensic detectives. We set about collecting these ashes, layer by layer so that later we could use an infrared technique to examine the types of material and whether or not there was any writing on the burned paper. Unopened Christmas presents were found in a closet and scattered about. One was from Crafts to his wife. It contained Danish licorice which Crafts had purchased overseas. It appeared that Crafts and his children had all been sleeping in the master bedroom. Anthony Dalessio, the seasoned investigator from Walter Flanagan's office, commented, "They're like a clan, under siege."[12]

The two bedrooms used by the children (Kristina had had her own room) were now rugless and unused. Earlier in the year, Betty Cooper and Helle had painted the hallway and the master bedroom blue, to match the carpet which Crafts had pulled up. Crafts had only pulled up about two-thirds of the rubber matting under this carpet, and the remaining third was on the side of the room which led into a vanity and the bathroom. Why would Crafts decide to pull up only some of the matting? Again, another silent clue.

I was particularly troubled by the question of what had been done with the box spring which should have been under the king-size master bedroom mattress, which now lay directly on the floor. Then I saw that each of the two boys had been using a half of the box spring as his bed. In many houses, it's impossible to fit an entire wood-framed box spring around corners and into a bedroom, so bedding stores sell sets of two to fit under the larger queen- and king-sized mattresses. Crafts had decided to keep these box springs. My focus was now becoming very intense on the bedding and this room. I looked for the brownish stains and the smear, and something inside me made me say: "Something's happened." Another silent clue was discovered.

The initial search on Christmas lasted only a half day. We did not find body parts in the freezer, and there was otherwise no major evidence to indicate that a crime had been committed. Only a few silent clues had been found. We needed time to regroup. In addition, we knew the young detectives wanted to have a chance to get back to their families for a few hours. The day after Christmas, a Friday, the team went back into the Crafts' house and worked from late morning until ten that night. Meanwhile, I set up a forensic team that consisted of some senior staff from the laboratory to start the initial examination of the evidence and to map out a scientific procedure for looking for the missing Helle Crafts. The standard procedure in this kind of search is to divide the house into several search zones, which were, in turn, segmented into smaller search areas. Each subsection would be searched by teams of two investigators, and then, a second time, by another team of two.

The primary focus of our search would be to find blood traces and any other evidence which could suggest a violent act. Or, ideally, we could find her body buried in the backyard or body parts stored in the freezer. The team was also intently interested in discovering any item which could have been a murder weapon. Of course, we were looking for any evidence of someone attempting to dispose of a corpse. When the teams went into the basement, the detectives were astounded at the size and diversity of Richard Crafts's weapons collection. This included a live hand grenade, which an ordnance expert immediately disarmed, as well as several unarmed grenades. Helle Crafts was right in worrying about all of these dangerous weapons within the reach of her two boys, if they had ever been able to open either of the gun safes that Crafts used. This collection included many clips of live ammunition, a crossbow, a large and folding hunting knife, and many guns. Among the guns found were Smith & Wesson pistols, a French Nanurrn Pistole, a Walther PPK, a Colt-45, a Finnish Sako pistol, a Browning semiautomatic, a Winchester rifle, a 9 mm Berretta, a Thompson submachine gun, and a number of others. All of these guns and weapons were seized and tagged, as a matter of routine. Again, the team was looking for a murder weapon. At the end of this long day, 113 items were taken into evidence, though this total did not include the two chainsaws found in the cluttered garage. The laboratory scientists would begin their work in carrying out a scientific analysis of each of these items, all the while looking for more silent clues.

Photographs were taken of the exterior of the house and these included shots of two deep tire tracks in the frozen mud which curved around a spruce tree. The team's photographer, William Kaminski, also went to the Currituck Road property and photographed the Ford Crown Victoria, which was parked next to a backhoe there. Kaminski, using keys he'd found in the house, also raised the trunk and photographed its interior, which was missing its matting and contained, among other things, piles of woodchips.

While the team was at work on Friday, reporter Patrick O'Neil showed up at the front door and, when he asked what was going on, was told nothing, though he was allowed to stand around outside for a while. O'Neil must have been tipped off by a neighbor or a member of the Newtown force. Walter Flanagan met with Newtown's Chief Marchese that day and formally told him what he already knew, that the Crafts investigation would be conducted solely by the state police. Marchese's only response was to tell the prosecutor, "I think you're making a mistake."[13]

On Saturday the 27th when we returned to the Crafts residence, I knew that we would be putting in a long day. The investigators had done a thorough job in photographing the house as we had found it and in restoring it to what Anna Batelli remembered. On the previous day, Martin Ohradan had asked Betty Cooper to come in and reconstruct what the master bedroom looked like for us, as best she could. Betty noticed that a dust ruffle that was over the mattress was missing. Ohradan's detectives then replaced the queen-sized bed in its original position, on a foundation since there was no box spring, and theorized that Helle had slept on the side closest to the bathroom, since that's where a stack of women's magazines was found. The dark stain on the room's carpeting which Marie Thomas had observed would have been off of the foot of the bed, on Helle's side, close to where I saw the reddish-brownish stains.

I had brought along three cases of equipment, which included a supply of luminol, a mixture of three dry chemicals which would be added to distilled water and would then, with the proper visual aids, detect bloodstains which are only barely visible or are invisible to the naked eye. Luminol is also used as a presumptive test on whether a stain is blood. (I will discuss the use of luminol in more detail at the end of this chapter.) Of course, I used a magnifying glass and a portable light source as I moved about the room, examining the walls and the floor, which was mostly bare wood now, though the foam rubber carpet matting covered about a third of the floor's surface. We then pulled down the shades and closed the curtains to darken the room. We would now apply the luminol. This is a chemical which will react with the heme portion of hemoglobin in red blood cells. I then sprayed the suspected areas of the floor, walls, and mattress. Several areas reacted with a luminous chemical reaction. These reactions indicated that the stains could be blood. By then measuring the size of the spots which had been illuminated, I also determined that the smaller droplets were of medium-velocity spatter which impacted the surface at an acute angle of ten degrees. (This analysis is covered in the Mathison chapter.) From these calculations, I was able to deduce that Helle Crafts must have been kneeling down or stooping over at the foot of her bed when she was attacked, probably from behind. She had not been lying down when she was murdered. This finding also meant that the bedding had been moved to this part of the bed when this assault occurred, since these droplets would not have soaked through. It's possible Helle was changing the sheets on the bed when her husband attacked and killed her.

I had the investigators remove a section of the mattress cover a little more than six foot by six foot to take to our forensics laboratory in Meriden for further analysis. None of the spatters had been of sufficient amount or size to seep down into the interior of the mattress. I also examined the wash cloths which had been found in the bathroom, along with the laundered and folded towel. Some of these also tested positive for blood, and they also went to the lab.

Two days later I had left the Crafts' residence to respond to two other homicide investigations I was called into that Christmas Day. As I pulled away from Newfield Lane, I was struck by the paradoxes which Richard Crafts was presenting to us as we investigated his wife's disappearance and, now, her probable murder. Meticulous and very bright, Crafts had seemed to have concocted his terrible plan very carefully: Helle's Tercel at the JFK parking lot and taking advantage of the unseasonable storm to clean up the crime scene and dispose of evidence, while Marie Thomas and the children were securely located in Westport. Yet, Crafts had apparently left behind a small but highly significant amount of blood evidence for us to find. And we still had not been apprised of his renting the woodchipper. Nor of the testimony of two witnesses who saw it being used near Lake Zoar. As master criminals go, Richard Crafts seemed to have left a great deal to chance. Martin Ohradan and his team completed their investigative work later Sunday, December 28, at about 5 P.M. They left a copy of the warrant in plain view in the family's kitchen.[14] The following day, we would hear for the first time about the woodchipper, and this revelation would electrify the air around us all. For the next several weeks our team would be fighting against time and mother nature, weather that was a particularly unpredictable force in Connecticut at any time of the year, but especially so during the dead of winter.

On that following Monday, there was a bumpy changing of the guard taking place at the Newtown Police Department, as per the orders of Jim Hiltz. Martin Ohradan sent two investigators to obtain the bulk of Newtown's work. Nothing about the rental of a woodchipper had been written up and nothing was said. Ohradan, himself, had gone to the Currituck Road property and seized the Ford Victoria, which was taken on a flatbed truck to the Major Crime headquarters in Waterbury. Ohradan and others paid particularly close attention to an abandoned mine shaft there on the Currituck property, one which had filled with water and could have hidden a body. This was drained and nothing unusual was found. Ohradan saw the wood chips there, but these made no impression on him at that time.

That same Monday, I went to work examining the mattress cover from the Crafts' master bedroom. Under a microscopic examination, we found that there were a substantial number of reddish-brownish stains on it which our preliminary testing had indicated were blood. There were three different types of stains. The quarter-sized stains, a six-by-one inch smear, and many, tiny, dot-sized spatters which were produced by a medium-velocity impact force. Now we had to do more laboratory work to establish whether these stains were in fact of human origin. Next we used an antihuman hemoglobin test to determine that the blood was, indeed, from a human source. We used some of the bloodstain to determine the ABO blood type of the stain. We found that the bloodstain was Type O, which was Helle Crafts's blood type.

There are four major blood types in the human ABO system: Type A, Type B, Type O, and Type AB. Each of these types of blood possesses specific antigens and antibodies. These antigens and antibodies could be identified in the dried bloodstains. We used a modified absorption-elution method. This method was originally developed by Professor S. S. Kind in England. My very good friend, Dr. R. E. Gaensslen and I modified the original procedure by titration of the antiserum to determine the reactivity of the antigen and, thus, made the procedure more sensitive and specific. The following table shows the antibodies in each blood type:

U.S. POPULATION IN ABO BLOOD GROUP SYSTEM

Type	Antigen	Antibody	Approximate Occurrence in U.S. Population	
			White	Black
A	A	Anti-B	40	27
B	B	Anti-A	11	20
O	H	None	45	49
AB	A and B	Anti-A, Anti-B	4	4

The next test we performed was the typing of PGM (phosphoglucomutase) Isoenzymes. The separation of genetic markers identified as red cell isoenzymes is based on their electrophoretic mobility, meaning the proteins are separated by their size and changes, when receiving electrical current. The general population can be divided into three groups: type 1, type 2-1, and type 2. We found that the bloodstain on the mattress and the tissue later found on the Lake Zoar riverbank both were PGM type 1. However, we didn't have Helle Crafts's blood sample for purposes of comparison. In addition, based on our research, we'd learned that the activity of PGM is age and temperature dependent. In general, after twelve months, PGM will lose its enzymatic activity and will become inactive. Since we had detected the PGM activity in the bloodstain on the mattress, this fact indicated that these blood spatters were more recent than old.

Everyone from Jim Hiltz on down on the investigative team was becoming very uneasy. Could anyone be convicted of a murder if there was absolutely no trace of a body? Hiltz suggested that Ohradan drop by the Southbury Police Department to ask about what they had heard. There, Officer Richard Benno mentioned to Ohradan that an individual had been observed by two witnesses late one night the week of the big storm with a truck and a woodchipper in tow. One witness, a part-time constable, had identified Crafts and had even given him a ride. Ohradan, who has an agricultural degree from the University of Connecticut, was stunned. He immediately remembered a nasty incident from the previous summer in which a twenty-five-year-old man had put a German shepherd through a woodchipper and had been sentenced to a year's probation for this, as well as being ordered to undergo psychiatric treatment. The press had played the case up and letters of outrage had poured into the *Danbury News-Times*. Ohradan immediately assigned two men to interview Joey Hine, the roads worker who saw the woodchipper on Silver Bridge, off of River Road. Even though he was an experienced homicide investigator, Ohradan was shaken. The very idea that Crafts could have been influenced by the previous summer's case into doing something so macabre got to him. Ohradan also quickly realized that it would be imperative to keep these developments quiet since the news media would grab a possible story like that and run with it. This could help Crafts. At 4:30 P.M., a Newtown officer confirmed for Ohradan that Crafts had rented a woodchipper. For all involved, this new dimension came at a critical time and could, we grasped, unlock this case for us.

The state police Major Crime Squad detectives, Patrick McCafferty and T. K. Brown, caught up with Joey Hine around noon the next day, Tuesday, December 30, at the town garage. Hine remembered the incident very distinctly. How many times would a snowplow driver encounter someone working with a woodchipper in a big snowstorm at four in the morning? Hine, a big and strong man who wore tattoos on his arms with pride, proved to have a very good memory for detail, though his recollection of what night he'd made this sighting would later prove to be a problem. After telling the detectives how he'd seen the chipper on the bridge, Hine described how the man in the orange parka had actually stepped out from behind the silent machine and directed traffic on the bridge since the woodchipper was partially blocking the road.

Hine then led the detectives directly to the spot on Lake Zoar where he'd seen these strange activities, a culvert on the bank of Lake Zoar, which isn't a lake, but merely a bulge in the Housatonic River. The detectives quickly saw coverings of wood chips on both banks. They looked like they'd been spread around by a pitchfork or a shovel. Mixed in the wood chips, they saw pieces of a light blue material and scraps of paper. McCafferty and Brown climbed down the bank and peered down at what appeared to be an envelope, which had a small nick in it. The envelope's return address corner carried the words "American Cancer Society." Both men remembered that Crafts was a recovered cancer patient. Being careful not to touch this evidence, Brown, squatting on his hands and knees, looked through the cellophane addressee portion of the envelope and was able to make out a name: Miss Helle L. Crafts. McCafferty shouted, "Something's definitely wrong here." This is an expression that I've often used when investigating a questionable crime scene.

McCafferty stayed at this location to secure the area, while Brown drove Joey Hine back to the town garage, where they'd found him. He then sped to Troop A, a state police barracks closer to Newtown, where the Major Crime Squad unit had established a command center. Brown found Martin Ohradan and shouted, "I found her fucking name on a piece of paper." Hiltz, Ohradan, and others went directly to the Lake Zoar site. Squatting down, they immediately found other pieces of mail, nicked in places, bearing Helle Crafts's name and address. (One of the lies which Crafts had consistently told was that his wife had received no mail since November 18.) The full brunt of what had apparently happened now struck these investigators. Ohradan said he'd retire if Richard Crafts had actually done so horrific a thing. Hiltz wrote the comment down in his daybook and would use it later on to kid Ohradan. Ohradan, until that instant, had had his doubts, thinking that Crafts, who seemed like he had been playing chess, was using the chipper as some sort of smoke screen, just "jerking" them around.

Using information provided by the Newtown police, investigators sped over to Darien Rental where they found the woodchipper rented the previous month by Crafts. They quickly hauled it to the Westport state trooper barracks where an investigative team of detectives and laboratory scientists waited to start their work. State Police Commissioner Colonel Lester Forst and Lieutenant Colonel John Monogan had committed their fullest resources and manpower to support the Western District's Major Crime Squad as investigators moved into a wide-ranging search of the Lake Zoar culvert. Snow was threatening and, along with anxiety about any mention of this getting out to the news media, the team worried about another layer of snow and how this could further bury the evidence which lay all around them. It was freezing out, the gray daylight was waning, and Hiltz had already decided he would not station state police to guard the site. The presence of a police cruiser or even a trooper ran the risk of drawing attention to what was going on. The evidence would be buried in snow; in reality the snow would have acted as a refrigerating agent, providing protection for any potential biological evidence, such as blood, tissue, and bones.

Later on, the state police would be bitterly criticized for not securing the area by Crafts's defense lawyers, but I endorse the judgment made by Hiltz under these unique circumstances and for this type of crime scene investigation. And I refute any notion that this decision provided any kind of window through which evidence could be planted by the police or some other interested party, such as Keith Mayo.

Meanwhile, I was mobilizing the whole laboratory. In 1986, we only had a total of 28 scientists working at the state police lab. The lab provided services which included the following sections: Serology-Immunology, Chemistry, Arson, Trace Analysis, Instrumental analysis, Firearms, Fingerprinting, Documents-questioning, Photography, and Crime Scene Reconstruction. With such a small number of laboratory scientists to provide services for the whole state of Connecticut (12 state police barracks, 143 local police departments, and 170 fire departments), our laboratory was extremely busy. With the continued successes in using forensic evidence to solve crimes, and the development of new scientific techniques, the demands on the laboratory services had also increased tremendously. I have always worked at developing a team approach to handling the more complex cases, such as the Crafts case. At any time in a major case, the whole laboratory is mobilized and will work together to examine the physical evidence. Normally, a case is assigned to one or two lead examiners, which can mean a very long time lapse before any lab results can be obtained.

Now, a few words on how we do this examination and testing work. We use a large examination table. The team members all sit around the table. Each of the team members is assigned a piece of evidence to work on, under the supervision of the senior examiner. Here is a flow chart for the examination of the physical evidence.

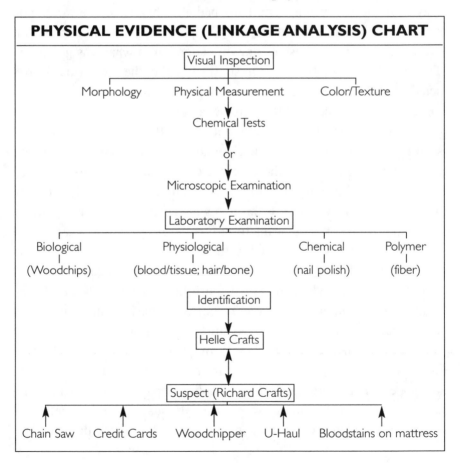

PHYSICAL EVIDENCE (LINKAGE ANALYSIS) CHART

Visual Inspection

Morphology   Physical Measurement   Color/Texture

Chemical Tests

or

Microscopic Examination

Laboratory Examination

Biological   Physiological   Chemical   Polymer
(Woodchips)   (blood/tissue; hair/bone)   (nail polish)   (fiber)

Identification

Helle Crafts

Suspect (Richard Crafts)

Chain Saw   Credit Cards   Woodchipper   U-Haul   Bloodstains on mattress

Using especially designed evidence-gathering procedures, we melted the snow inch by inch, and separated the leaves and debris from potential evidence by hand. The forensic team and detectives collected more than two dozen bags of evidence. Once a potential piece of evidence was found, it was photographed, documented, then sealed in a manila envelope. This meticulous work was done over a two-mile stretch of the Lake Zoar banks. These shreds of evidence included, gruesomely enough, strands of blond hair and tiny bone fragments, which proved to be human bone. A Shaklee vitamin label was an item collected which no one at the time recognized as that significant, since we did not yet know that Helle Crafts sold this type of product. All of this evidence was seized and taken to the Westport barracks and then was transferred to our forensic laboratory in Meriden, where a team of forensic scientists examined each piece and conducted scientific tests. Most of this critical evidence was discovered on a Tuesday, exactly six weeks after that earlier gray day in later November when Helle Crafts said, "Richard's home," as she got out of Sue Miller's car to go inside her home for the last time.

Fortunately for us all, the snowstorm which had threatened Connecticut on that last Tuesday of 1986 never showed and had moved to upper New England. After a break for the New Year (state police detectives and laboratory scientists had been working nonstop) additional evidence had been collected. This evidence was set out to dry in a room the investigators had set up in the Westport barracks. Butcher paper was spread across the floor, and saw horses supported plywood boards which formed tables. These were used to dry these particulates of wet evidence which were imbedded in the woodchips pulled from the Lake Zoar site.

Any recognizable evidence was submitted to the laboratory immediately. At the lab, the forensic team started their preliminary examinations. Dr. Bruno Froelich, a forensic anthropologist; Elaine Pagliaro, a criminalist; Sgt. Robert Mills, a trace analyst; and other team members assisted me. Each piece of evidence submitted by the police was documented, photographed, and measured. Subsequently, those pieces of evidence were further examined by using a stereo-microscope. The evidence was magnified from 5× to 40× its size. The evidence identified as human body parts was further examined by using a higher-power microscope, to magnify the evidence from 40× to 100× its normal size. Chemical and immunological tests were also conducted on this evidence.

A forensic expert consultant team was also set up to independently confirm our results. As I knew from my past experience, in this type of case we would have to prove beyond any reasonable doubt that those remains were those of Helle Crafts and that she had been murdered. Otherwise, there had been no homicide, and, thus, Richard Crafts could not be charged.

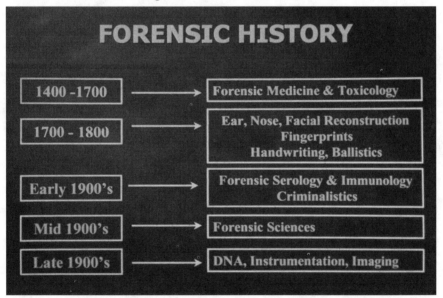

The above figure shows the development of the forensic field from medicine to human identification and criminalistics to DNA typing. Today forensic science has become so specialized that each subdiscipline has experts who have specialized in that area. Many times, it is crucial to have those specialists to examine the evidence independently, to identify the evidence, and to offer expert opinions at trial. Each of us has our limitations. The important lesson in life is to learn our limitations and to ask others to help at the initial stages of the investigation. It is also important to know that "turf" problems between agencies are a major roadblock to an investigation. A team investigative concept is the only approach for a fair and successful investigation. Realizing my own limitations, I quickly contacted a group of forensic scientists and asked for their assistance. Since the forensic laboratory and state police had no budget or funding source to pay those experts, I had to count on my friendships and "coupons," which is a common practice in our field. I would be providing lectures, services, or consultations in exchange for these other experts' services. A top-notch forensic team was quickly set up. The following is a list of experts and their areas of expertise: Dr. Albert Harper, from the University of New Haven, bone; Dr. Bruno Froelich, CSP Lab, bone; Dr. Alan Raskin, University of Connecticut Health Center Dental School, teeth; Dr. Constantine (Gus) Karazulas, state police forensic laboratory, teeth; Dr. Lowell Levine, New York State Police Forensics Center, teeth; Dr. Wayne Carver, chief medical examiner, pathology; Dr. John Reffner, University of Connecticut material science lab, fiber; Dr. Harold Deadman, FBI, hair; Dr. Bruce Hoadly, the University of Massachusetts, wood; Dr. Arkady Katsnelson, pathology; Dr. Malka Shah, medical examiner, pathology; Elaine Pagliaro, forensic laboratory, serology; Sgt. Robert Mills, forensic laboratory, trace; Deborah Messina, forensic laboratory, trace; Dr. Fred Ruzzala and Bob O'Brien, forensic laboratory, instrumentation; Dr. Robert Grensslen, University of New Haven, serology; Karen Lamy, forensic laboratory, criminalist; Herbert MacDonnell, Forensics Science Institute, blood pattern analysis; Ken Zercie, forensic laboratory, fingerprints; Robert Finkle, forensic laboratory, fingerprints. With the assistance of this forensics team we were able to find the following crucial evidence: 1. 2660 strands of human, Caucasian head hairs in eighteen bundles; 2. One dental metal crown; 3. A portion of a human tooth; 4. One piece of skull bone, identified as calvarium bone. This piece of bone was $\frac{1}{4}$ of an inch long and its edges revealed it had been cut in a traumatic way; 5. Sixty small bone fragments; 6. Three ounces of human tissue; 7. Bloodstains and blood spatter on a mattress; 8. Blue-green fibers.

By now Richard Crafts's Crown Victoria had been transported to the troop garage in Meriden. On that same Friday, a close examination of the entire vehicle was conducted. Raising the trunk, we saw the woodchips and other trace materials which had been observed on Christmas day. Inside, we found the same array of evidence as had been found at Lake Zoar: Blonde hair strands (which had also been bleached), fragments of human bone, flesh, and a faded blue fabric. These were critical pieces of evidence, but, in one of the few mistakes detectives made during this difficult investigation, these findings would not later be allowed into court. The original warrant used ten days earlier was for 5 Newfield Lane and the Currituck Road property. When the Ford was moved from where it was found on Currituck Road, the vehicle was no longer covered by this warrant. Therefore, a trial judge would later rule, the car should not have been searched when it was no longer on either of the properties covered in the warrant.

The following Monday afternoon, January 5, the state police diving team began to probe beneath the frigid surfaces off and around that culvert on Lake Zoar. The waters were in the mid-thirties so each navy-certified diver wore two insulated diving suits, one of them a thick Viking cold water suit, for this difficult task. The waters of the Housatonic were murky which meant the divers had very limited visibility. Each one, in the five to ten minutes he could withstand the cold, needed to form his own search pattern, using the sense of touch to feel as well as look for evidence. It was very demanding and difficult work. The divers initially concentrated on the areas nearest Silver Bridge. The current underneath the bridge proved strong enough to rip off the divers' face masks, so the power plant management was contacted. They adjusted the flow from an upstream dam, making the current more manageable. The first significant find in this search was made by someone on land, Sergeant Daniel Lewis, who saw a small, red, and shiny object. Pulling this particle up, Sergeant Lewis would see what appeared to be human flesh attached and recognized that it was part of a finger. The red fingernail polish would later match a bottle of nail polish we had found in Helle Crafts's bathroom.

On the fourth day, Thursday, January 8, Sergeant Scott O'Mara discovered a large green bag in the lake, one that was filled with bones. He quickly attached a flotation marker and then had to leave the water due to a nose bleed. Jim Hiltz immediately contacted me (I was in Hartford to testify in another murder case) and I tried to respond to the scene immediately, but could not get off of the stand until noon. About noon the bones were brought up and placed in a body bag provided by a Southbury auxiliary policeman who was also a mortician. Right after my testimony I drove as fast as I could and got to Lake Zoar. I could sense a great deal of excitement on everyone's part. A glance or two told me that the bag of bones was from a dead deer, probably shot out of season by a poacher who got rid of the evidence. At a moment like that, there is a sense of keen disappointment, but it is one that's mixed with humor. Unlike finding that Keith Mayo's carpet was wrong, when there was no sense of the ridiculous, the deer's carcass hit our collective funny bones and we looked at one another as we laughed together. This, of course, meant a quick return for the divers to their grim, freezing work. Many other random items came up from the bottom of Lake Zoar. Shoes, pocket books, wine bottles, and the like. It also seems that it's a repository for a library full of old school books. Maybe the kids around there have a book-tossing ritual each spring when they party at the end of the school year.

But the divers' search was about to pay a rich dividend. Sergeant Paul Krisavage would see an orange flash on the bottom in thirty feet of water. On the other end of his line from Scott O'Mara, Krisavage swam down and seized a chain saw which he brought to the surface. The serial number on the Stihl saw appeared to have been filed off, which intensified our interest. Also the chain was wrapped around the saw's housing and its bar was missing. The divers knew that would be a critical component to find. They went atop the bridge and estimated how far the bar might have traveled by throwing stones into the water. The next day, Friday, this work also paid off. Krisavage found four inches of a chainsaw bar sticking up out of the sandy bottom. By now the media had gotten a good idea of what was happening. Krisavage bootlegged his most recent find and was able to slip it into an evidence bag without any notice from a television news helicopter that was hovering overhead. The bar was immediately placed in a bucket of water, to avoid its rusting, and was immediately transported to the forensic lab. Later on, hair and fiber from this bar exhibited similar characteristics to the other hair and fiber samples we were finding.

On that Friday, the Connecticut National Guard provided us with a large tent to facilitate our search. We then launched an exhaustive search of the banks around the culvert. This was a location, most likely, that Crafts had used to try to dispose of his murder weapons and his wife's remains. For ten to twenty hours a day over the next week our investigators would be on their hands and knees in two feet of snow, digging through the freezing cold soil. Salamander heaters, powered by a portable generator, barely warmed our hands, but helped thaw the ground. We divided the ground into a series of eight-inch grid squares, and the surface of each would be scooped up and placed on a plywood table on sawhorses in our tent headquarters to be closely examined under floodlights for more evidence. All of this topsoil and other materials was put through a screen to sift out leaves and larger objects. All was then rinsed and studied. Significant items would then be analyzed on another smaller table, under a lighted, eight-inch magnifying glass. Thousands of these particles were then placed in cardboard evidence boxes for shipment to my laboratory in Meriden for detailed examination.

The search was continuing to pay off. On Saturday, January 10, Detective Joseph Quartiero found what we would ultimately determine was a human toe joint. Two days later, Detective Joseph Destanfano found an object whose surface was too smooth to be wood, and we would quickly determine that it was part of a human finger. By now I had reached out to Dr. Gus Karazulas, an excellent odontologist who had been our chief lab consultant since I'd joined the state police lab in 1978. Dr. Karazulas joined our search for ten hours on that Saturday and wasn't able to find anything. The following Wednesday, he returned and again it appeared his work would be fruitless. About midday, Gus was working on the river bank, when one of his feet slipped into the river and his boot filled instantly with freezing water. This galled him. The good doctor grabbed one last pile of debris, threw it on the table and announced that, with a frozen and wet foot, this would be it for him that day. His expression changed when he picked up a grayish object. Dr. Karazulas had found what he immediately recognized as part of a porcelain dental cap for a tooth which had a portion of jawbone attached to it.

Dr. Albert Harper and Dr. Bruno Froelich, who have been colleagues of mine at the forensic laboratory, are both anthropologists and experts in archaeology. Al, Bruno, and I were studying the bone remains we were finding at Lake Zoar. These fragments were still "greasy," meaning that they were still covered by human body fat and grease. This was not that unusual and meant that the bones were recently deposited there. What fascinated Al Harper was the condition these bones were in, the tiniest of fragments, as though they had come from a cremation, the only example Dr. Harper could remotely compare them with. Of course, we had never observed bones that had been put through a woodchipper.

The grim work at Lake Zoar continued. Using comic relief, the investigative team had named themselves the "Mud Monkeys." Occasionally the team allowed someone who had been close to the case to come down to see what we were doing. Alyce's husband, Arthur Bennett, seemed amazed at our work. Our team's efforts at Lake Zoar eventually led to the discovery of 2,660 strands of blond hair (bleached), 69 slivers of human bone, 5 droplets of human blood, 2 teeth, a truncated piece of human skull, 3 ounces of human tissue, a portion of a human finger, 1 fingernail, and 1 portion of a toe nail. This overall search would produce the final evidence needed to arrest Richard Bunel Crafts for the murder of his wife Helle Nielsen Crafts, on or about November 18, 1986.

The Crafts case was a very demanding one. All of us involved in the prosecution had to be extremely careful in building the foundation for the evidence that led to Crafts's arrest and ultimate conviction. Thus far in this chapter I have shown you, up close, just how our careful investigative and forensic work paid off. With the closure of our search of the Lake Zoar site, let us take a longer view of what would be happening in the months ahead. This would be a time that would see us go through an arrest, one aborted and prolonged attempt at jury selection, two changes of venue, and two trials.

There was still some critically important forensic work to be accomplished, but the vast majority had been completed by Tuesday, January 13, 1987, when detectives surrounded the house on Newfield Lane and finally persuaded Richard Crafts to come outside and give himself up. I want to credit Jim Hiltz and Marty Ohradan for their patience that night, since Crafts was to break several agreements on how and if he would surrender, and for Hiltz's sensitivity concerning the feelings of the three most important living victims of the murder of Helle Crafts, her trio of young children. Shortly after midnight, the Crafts children were in bed, asleep, as the arrest drama played out. Betty Cooper would then take the two boys and little girl into her custody. Characteristically, Richard Crafts would give one last mixed signal to Betty. As she entered the home, Betty passed Crafts who was being led out in handcuffs. "Thank you for taking care of the kids," he would say as he left his home for the last time.

This is as good a time as any to point out that the news media's coverage of this case was both good and bad. Patrick O'Neil of the *Danbury News-Times* had characteristically gotten wind of the arrest warrant for Crafts. He had been on top of things since the early, dark days of the Thanksgiving weekend. When asked to stay away from the residence by the state police, O'Neil complied, though he positioned himself at a distance close enough to observe the overall picture. Photographers from his paper crowding around the house could have jeopardized that evening's solemn tasks.

When news of the murder and arrest hit the regional and national media, however, the sinister side of today's journalism showed

100,000 PICK THE SCORE
Super Bowl contest - Page 43

DAILY ◎ NEWS

NEW YORK'S PICTURE NEWSPAPER®   Wednesday, January 14, 1987

CHOPPED TO PIECES

Stewardess' body parts found in Conn. lake; pilot hubby is charged

rd Crafts in police custody.

Story on page 3

The late Helle Crafts.

UOMO NAMES SPECIAL PROSECUTOR IN RACIAL PROBE – PAGE 4

through. Coverage by the *New York Daily News* epitomizes the point I want to make. "Chopped to Pieces" was the headline which the paper put on the streets, for its estimated five million readers. The *News*'s editor was a veteran tabloid journalist who had taken to appearing on PBS network shows to discuss his kinder and mellower approach to hard news. Yet, when push came to shove, the paper produced a front page which was disgraceful. This kind of ghoulish behavior led to other wrongs, such as ugly T-shirts being sold which displayed an illustration of a woodchipper under the caption, "Divorce, Connecticut Style." This wasn't funny, and the tabloid I've cited set the early and awful tone.

Walter Flanagan now came to center stage. Walter and I have enjoyed a long and productive working relationship, as well as friendship. He likes to recall that I would occasionally refer to him as the conductor of a symphony in presenting the prosecution's case. As the group's conductor, Walter moved matters toward obtaining the arrest warrant. Strengthened by what we had been finding at Lake Zoar, he had called a meeting of the principal investigators, including Jim Hiltz, his key people, my own key staff, Elaine Pagliaro and me, Dr. Karazulas, Dr. Lowell Levine, and Chief Medical Examiner Dr. H. Wayne Carver II. We were to look at the investigation from all points of view and reach a consensus on what to do, if possible. Flanagan, himself, had known that he had had enough evidence for the arrest warrant. But he did not want to lose the prosecution on any kind of technicality by jumping the gun. He was also nervous because he knew that Richard Crafts's Southbury revolver, a Magnum .357, was missing. And there were the three children. Judge MacDonald had earlier signed a second search warrant on January 9, this time without any expressed misgivings.

Walter and I spoke several times by phone that Monday, January 12, as the meeting was being set up for our offices in Meriden at 6 P.M. Going in, Walter and I felt that Dr. Carver's agreement on Crafts's arrest was most essential. After each of us summed up what we had found and what we thought, Dr. Carver sat in silence for a few moments. A big man, he then went to the room's blackboard, took a piece of chalk, and, as we all watched in rapt attention, wrote a single word: Homicide. The meeting broke up at 9 P.M. Working with lab scientists, we set about writing a point-by-point report for Walter Flanagan, who would use it as a basis for an arrest warrant which would be signed later that same night by Judge William Lavery.

Richard Crafts was initially questioned at the State Police Troop A by Hiltz the night of his arrest. He had briefly retained a local lawyer who had consented to his client's being interrogated by the state police in earlier January. Hearing this, David Rodgers, Crafts's brother-in-law and still a confidante, had lent Crafts money to retain a first-rate defense counsel, J. Daniel Sagarin, of Milford. Tall, earnest, and handsome, Sagarin had earned an excellent reputation for himself as a defense lawyer and is passionately committed to his work. Crafts would now be in excellent legal hands as he was moved to a permanent detention center in Bridgeport.

Judge Patricia Green set Crafts's bail at $750,000, at the time a record high in Connecticut. Obviously, the violent way in which the defendant was accused of disposing of his wife's body had factored into the judge's decision. To make bail, Crafts would have to come up with 10 percent of the amount in cash, which was an unattainable amount. Sagarin was on vacation and Crafts would be represented by a young associate, Tom Farver. Crafts's thirty-two-year-old lawyer moved for a reduction in bail, and a few days later there would be a hearing before a second jurist, Judge William Sullivan. Helle Crafts's close friends were terrified that Crafts would get out on bail if the sum was reduced. On the morning of the hearing, one phoned a friend whom she knew had contacts in high places, and this individual, a marketing executive for a health magazine, agreed to call the state's then–attorney general, Joseph Lieberman, who would later run as the Democratic candidate for vice president in 2000, and explained the situation. Lieberman agreed to call Judge Sullivan to express how frightened Helle's circle of friends had become. Judge Sullivan, noting that Crafts had international connections and, contrary to Farver's argument that Crafts could soon die from cancer, said the defendant appeared healthy enough to flee to anywhere in the world. Crafts's bail remained at $750,000.

By now a number of items were set aside as we cleared the decks for a battle over central issues. Helle Crafts's Tercel, when recovered by the state police from its parking spot in the Pan Am lot at JFK, yielded no evidence. David Rodgers, still loyal to Crafts, used the Tercel until it was stolen in Bridgeport when he'd brought the children to visit Crafts there. It was found wrecked a short while later. Newtown police detectives appealed to the town's police commission to investigate Walter Flanagan's taking over the case, and they directed their ire at Keith Mayo, whom they implied had planted evidence at Lake Zoar. The police commission, in a three-to-two vote turned the idea down. In early February in family court in Danbury temporary custody of the Crafts' children was given to Karen and David Rodgers. Crafts had appeared in court that day in manacles, a sight which must have disturbed his children, who were present. Up to then, Betty Cooper had taken exemplary care of the children for nearly a month. Crafts's defense team began filing motions to bar the press from proceedings, laying the groundwork for a change of venue motion later on, one that would be granted because of the wide publicity of the case.

Dr. Wayne Carver, the state's medical examiner, came up with a brilliant idea in February to rebut what would surely be a defense argument: That no substantial portion of a body could get through a woodchipper such as the Brush Bandit. The defense might argue that the two teeth, the portions of fingers, and the skull fragment had all been planted. Dr. Carver's solution? Put a cadaver through the woodchipper and see whether the bone chips would come out in the same condition. After a long and intense discussion, we decided to put the carcass of a young pig through, since the flesh from that animal was closest to human tissue. Pig skin is similar to human skin, and is also used in skin grafts and in open heart surgery. The replacement for a patient's mitral valve comes from a pig. Walter Flanagan wholeheartedly endorsed the idea. The eventual pig used in this controlled experiment weighed forty-seven pounds and was purchased from a local butcher shop. After the pig had been put through the woodchipper, most of the carcass had been reduced to a pulpy substance. What was significant for our side was that the pig's tail came through the machine intact. And all the bone fragments had similar sizes, shapes, and patterns as the bone fragments found at the river bank.

Walter Flanagan knew that Crafts's defense attorneys would try to plant doubt in the jurors' minds with another series of items which should not have been able to get through the many high-speed blades of the woodchipper: envelopes, such as the one addressed to Helle Crafts from the American Cancer Society. Eventually, Flanagan would interview the man who invented that particular envelope. The prosecutor would then combine his knowledge of the workings of the woodchipper and show that the standard, number ten-sized envelope had been sucked through the woodchipper, due to its size and relatively light weight.

In the spring of 1987, Crafts's manipulative behavior began to offend David Rodgers. The brother-in-law who had heard Crafts talk about his problems and once even heard him say, "A man's got to do what a man's got to do," was growing alienated. Up until this time, Rodgers, without Karen's knowledge, had been doing things for Crafts which could have gotten him into very big trouble with the law. One thing was to destroy, at Crafts's suggestion, sheets in the house on Newfield Lane. Another was to explore bribing a foreign-born man and woman he'd met who would swear that they had seen Helle Crafts since November 18, and on one occasion at a drug party. Rodgers, now the custodian of the Crafts' house, did nothing extra to protect it. By not installing an alarm system or even double bolts, Rodgers seemed to be inviting burglaries which could further fuel charges that evidence had been stolen and later planted elsewhere. How did things between these two veterans sour? Lucretia Crafts, Richard's mother, and his other in-laws began to infuriate Rodgers and, moreover, he did not get any expected support from Richard. Crafts, he discovered, was stabbing him in the back. Karen's brother-in-law, Malcolm Bird went into the Newfield Lane house without Rodgers's permission and took out potential evidence. Then he found that Bird had gone into Rodgers's own place without any permission.[15]

At about this time Walter Flanagan received an anonymous note from someone who seemed way ahead of the curve on the prosecution's case against Richard Crafts. This missive started with a tip that Helle's Tercel was still in the garage on the morning of November 19. The author went on to suggest that Helle's remains were in the garage that morning, in the new freezer Crafts had just purchased. The writer also said that Crafts probably had towed the Tercel to the airport that day, using a tow bar he'd later asked a relative to cart away. The author of this letter could, of course, be covering for the fact that David Rodgers, himself, had followed Crafts and the Tercel to the airport, a much more inconspicuous way to get the car into the Pan Am lot.

The note then concluded with a subject which was giving Walter Flanagan a great deal of difficulty. Joey Hine, the Southbury public works driver, had said he'd seen someone with a woodchipper and a U-Haul truck during the storm in the early morning hours of Wednesday, November 19. Crafts only took possession of the truck and the woodchipper on November 20. Hine, Flanagan would learn, had become friendly with Richard Crafts since the municipal garage was only two hundred yards from the police department. No matter how hard the prosecution tried to encourage Hine to revisit his memories of that timespan, Joey tenaciously stuck to an account that was, on its very face, inaccurate. Looking at his time cards for that time period, Hine relented enough to say that perhaps he had seen the truck and woodchipper twice, on both Wednesday morning and Friday morning. Hine's mistaking the two dates could reasonably have been caused by the fact that five weeks (from November 20 to December 30) had elapsed before detectives questioned Hine on his strange sighting. And Dan Sagarin knew all about this problem. In court, Walter Flanagan would have to go back to the essentials to meet this challenge, by introducing facts about the weather, itself, on the two dates in question.

Daniel Sagarin is an aggressive defense lawyer. When pretrial proceedings started in the Danbury Superior Court House on October 20, 1987, Sagarin objected to a ruling by Judge Howard Monaghan that attorneys for both sides would be barred from talking to members of the media. Sagarin's motion attacked this gag order as being unconstitutional. He also held that, since there had already been an enormous amount of tabloid-style coverage of the case, the damage had already been done to his client, and the defense should also have its right to make its case in the media. Sagarin would eventually win this motion and Judge Monaghan would subsequently find himself overruled by a federal judge who ruled that the defendant's Constitutional right to free speech would have been denied.

Crafts's defense team also used the enormous amount of publicity for the trial as grounds for a motion to change the venue, or location, of the trial. Almost all of the prospective jurors must have heard of this case, Sagarin would argue. Judge Monaghan initially disagreed. Then Sagarin filed motions asking the judge to suppress all of the evidence found by the prosecution in Crafts's home and on Currituck Road, because those searches were the product of search warrants that were not supported by any probable cause. These two motions, if granted, could have cut a great deal out of our case, including the human bloodstains found on the Crafts' master bedroom mattress cover, blood which was the same type as Helle Crafts's.

Judge Monaghan put aside any decision on these two critical motions and in early November pressed ahead with jury selection. By Christmas Eve, twelve jurors acceptable to both sides had been selected. Then, on January 5, 1988, after the proceedings had reconvened after the Christmas holidays, Judge Monaghan announced that he had found out that some of the jurors had not been candid on the question of their pretrial knowledge of the case. He reversed his own earlier ruling on the location of the trial, saying Richard Crafts could not receive a fair trial in Danbury. Two months later Judge Monaghan formally moved the proceedings to the New London Superior Court building and he stepped out of the trial.

THE TWO WOODCHIPPER TRIALS

Although Walter Flanagan and his fellow prosecutors could not have been happy with Judge Monaghan's decision to move the deliberations to New London, I did not view it as a loss to our side. I had heard about how tedious the jury selection process had been in the Danbury judicial district. I also knew that moving to New London would mean seeing more blue-collar workers and ex-military people in the jury pools from an area that is known as the submarine capital of the free world. But, as a forensic scientist I must ultimately leave these kinds of questions to the attorneys. The motions which genuinely worried the prosecution were the two which Sagarin had filed to try to keep the fruits of our two searches of the Crafts' properties out of the courtroom. These were still pending. All of this underscores a critical rule for the forensic professional: Strict adherence to the rules of evidence is of paramount importance; keeping in mind potential legal questions must constantly be remembered by any sound investigator.

Jury selection in New London began on March 14, 1988. This process is called *voir dire*, emphasizing the fact that individuals who swear on a Bible to tell the truth about themselves should live up to that oath. This would become a very important aspect of the first Crafts trial, since one of the twelve jurors would prove to be an erratic individual who profoundly affected the trial. In this *voir dire*, the prosecution and defense were questioning many prospective jurors who were not at all familiar with the morbid and bizarre details of this case. Things moved swiftly. All twelve jurors and three alternates were in place by March 23.

Judge Barry Schaller, on loan for the trial from the New Haven district, was assigned to the case due to his excellent reputation for being low key and polite, yet very tough when he thought he had to be. The Connecticut Bar Association polls its members on how they rate the judges in the state, and Judge Schaller consistently came out near the top in these standings. A Yale Law graduate, Judge Schaller was candid about wanting to preside, saying, "To match the interest and excitement of this trial will be hard to do."

The proceedings, which most felt would last about two months, got off to a mixed start for the prosecution's side. Judge Schaller, relying on the first search warrant's being confined to Crafts's two properties, ruled that evidence from the Ford Crown Victoria would be inadmissible, since the auto was taken from Currituck Road and searched in a state police garage. However, the judge ruled that all of the evidence directly collected on the premises set out in the warrants would be allowed in court. This was a tradeoff which the prosecution's team could live with, though the woodchips, human tissue, and fiber evidence from the Crown Victoria's trunk would have been very helpful.

I will synopsize this trial as much as possible since much of the testimony and cross examination was about the detailed forensic work I've already described. Lis Nielsen, Helle Crafts's frail, seventy-nine-year-old mother, was the first prosecution witness. Mrs. Nielsen testified in Danish, using a court-appointed interpreter, in a nervous, quiet, and dramatic way. She told how her only child had been in touch by phone or letter with her regularly, without any gaps longer than two weeks. Showing the court several of her daughter's last letters to make her point, all of this attention abruptly ended on November 18, 1986. One juror, Bart Cummings,* watched Mrs. Nielsen intently from the jury box. As Lis Nielsen answered questions, several about her being in fine health at the time of Helle's disappearance, she glanced about the courtroom. At one time her eyes met those of her son-in-law, Richard Crafts, and she nervously smiled at him. Cummings, an army veteran of the Vietnam War, saw this and immediately, he would later say, surmised that Mrs. Nielsen was hiding something. No matter what else the prosecution would do, this juror had made up his mind and had decided that Richard Crafts was innocent. This is, of course, every lawyer's worst nightmare, depending on which side this kind of "loose cannon" decides to fire on. And, of course, it is each juror's right to decide the case. But, as you will see later on, Mr. Cummings did not confine his erratic behaviors to his decision-making process.

Walter Flanagan, of course, would have no way of knowing this, nor would Brian Cotter, his top assistant prosecutor whom Walter had assigned to help him with this case. He needed a right-hand person because of the complexity of the case and the large number of expert witnesses to be called. Daniel Sagarin would vigorously challenge the dental testimony, for instance. Dr. Gus Karazulas would appear on May 11 and would testify that both the teeth found at Lake Zoar had come from Helle Crafts's mouth, comparing his own extensive x-rays (five of each tooth) with those taken by Helle's own dentist earlier in 1986. He said that his findings were being made "with reasonable scientific certainty," words which translate to "no doubt whatsoever." Dr. Lowell Levine was an oral surgeon and the dental expert who had identified the teeth of Dr. Joseph Mengele, the infamous Nazi leader who had drowned in South America in 1985, and whose services the prosecution had retained. He was not as sure as Dr. Karazulas, he said, on one of the teeth, but was firm that the second, a lower-left second bicuspid, "belonged to Helle Crafts when she was alive." Under cross-examination from Daniel Sagarin, Dr. Karazulas would say, "I have absolutely no doubt that the tooth belonged to Helle Crafts."

I would be called to the stand by Walter Flanagan in late May and would spend three days on the stand reconstructing the crime. Marie Thomas, who had been flown in by the prosecution, had already testified to seeing the dark stain, "about the size of a grapefruit" on the Crafts' master bedroom mattress cover. She related how Richard Crafts had said this was caused by some kerosene he had spilled. I showed the jury four tests I had conducted with differing fuels, one of them diesel and the other three differing types of kerosene, and how stains from all four had disappeared from sight within five minutes.

In preparing this case for the courtroom, I was very careful to back up my own observations and forensic conclusions with work from appropriate experts from around the country. We had sent the hair fibers, for instance, to Dr. Harold Deadman of the FBI's lab, and the fibers found at Lake Zoar and on the chain saw to a renowned textile expert, Dr. John Reffner. Both Drs. Deadman and Reffner testified, with Dr. Reffner explaining to the jurors how he had used infrared microspectrum photography to reach his conclusions that the fibers all

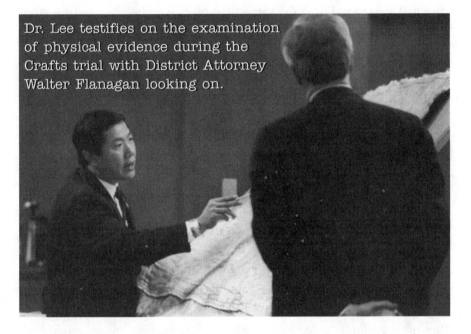

Dr. Lee testifies on the examination of physical evidence during the Crafts trial with District Attorney Walter Flanagan looking on.

came from the same source. Dr. Bruce Hoadly, a professor of wood sciences at the University of Massachusetts, showed how various machines leave distinctive cutting marks on wood chips, and how the chips found at Lake Zoar and at Currituck Road had come from the woodchipper model Richard Crafts had rented.

As the trial moved into June, Walter Flanagan finally called Joey Hine to the stand. Hine was sticking to his version of the woodchipper's time line and that he had seen it those two times in the early morning hours of Wednesday, November 19, during the heavy snowstorm. With Richard Wildman, the Southbury constable, and Joe Williams, the civilian who had seen someone who closely resembled Crafts working a woodchipper on Silver Bridge, Flanagan had already established substantial credibility with the jurors. But how would he get around Joey Hine's flat out conflict in testimony? Walter decided an end run would be needed. Dr. Mel Goldstein, whose accurate forecasts from the Connecticut Weather Center Helle and her friends had heard on their drive home, was called to the stand. Dr. Goldstein agreed that snow was falling in the dark, predawn hours of November 19. He added that cold rain had started to fall at the same time on November 20, the following night. Joey Hine then recalled that his sighting on Silver Bridge had been in rainfall, not in snow. This unstuck his testimony, and the defense was not able to shake him away from admitting to his inconsistency. After all, he hadn't been promptly questioned about events in a timespan in which, his work logs showed, he had toiled forty hours out of a total of forty-six. He had been exhausted from his plowing work, and, Flanagan was arguing, he had made a perfectly normal mistake.

The prosecution rested its case on June 7. Daniel Sagarin's defense relied on a battery of his own expert witnesses who would attempt to undermine our forensic testimony. This is often the case when analyses of blood and human tissue are brought into evidence. Sagarin and his experts did a professional job, but the collective weight of all that we had found seemed to many observers, including members of the press, to have been very formidable and difficult to impeach. Later on, there would be a good deal of discussion of how the prosecution's side had been able to spend more money in preparing its expert witnesses for their time in court, a valid point for legal scholars to ponder. Yet, with Crafts's presumption of innocence and the other advantages which our system of justice provides to defendants, those trying to balance the scales of jurisprudence should always keep in mind the total picture.

The defense team now decided to put Richard Crafts on the stand. Having a defendant waive his right to silence and take this step is a very complex decision for a defense attorney to make. In Crafts's case, Sagarin probably was working on the premise that his client would not lose his cool while he was in the witness box, one of the nightmares the defense side always has to consider. On June 16, Richard Crafts calmly told his basic version of what had happened on the morning of November 19, 1986: Helle had risen early and told him she would be driving ahead to the Rodgers' home in Westport. Crafts would go to some lengths to explain how he had spilled kerosene on his bedroom carpet. He would calmly answer any questions on whether he had harmed Helle, but would admit to her asking him to take service of the papers for the divorce proceedings she had filed against him. To observers in the courtroom, he appeared cool to the point of being cold. In his cross-examination the next day, Walter Flanagan would stand across the courtroom, so Crafts would have to look directly at him and not be able to look at the jurors as he had done the day prior. Flanagan grilled Crafts about his service with the CIA, which Crafts denied. (Seven years later in an interview in prison, Crafts would again deny he worked for the CIA, but would admit that Air America was exclusively funded by the agency.) The prosecutor also bore down on inconsistencies in Crafts's whereabouts at different times. Crafts was forced to answer, "I don't recall" dozens of times. Overall, Flanagan and Crafts fought a close duel that day, and the defense had at least survived this gamble. Many felt Crafts had come across as cold enough to have done what he was accused of doing.

The case went to the jury on June 23, following closing arguments and lengthy instructions to the jury by Judge Schaller. There were things about juror Bart Cummings, a tradesman at a large area company, which would have devastated Walter Flanagan, had he known about them. Mrs. Cummings had been in the courtroom each day of the trial and the two of them, contrary to Judge Schaller's daily instructions, had discussed the case in detail. They also went home and watched the news coverage of the proceedings, also against the jury's code of conduct as spelled out by the judge. Cummings became increasingly emotional during the deliberations. On Friday afternoon, July 1, Cummings slammed his pickup truck into a telephone pole on his way home. This meant canceling jury deliberations for the next day. The jury resumed deliberations the following Tuesday, and ten days later it was still deadlocked, with Cummings's the only vote to acquit. At 5:00 P.M. that Friday Judge Schaller read the jury the "Chip Smith" charge on how jurors should work to overcome a deadlock. Later that evening, Judge Schaller overheard juror Cummings say he would not be returning to the jury room, and during the jury's dinner Cummings could not be found. When he returned to the courthouse later that evening, Judge Schaller called a mistrial. This outcome was a bitter disappointment to Walter Flanagan and Helle Crafts's family and circle of close friends.

A frustrated Walter Flanagan would not have to wait a long time to see justice obtained. Starting in March 1989, Judge Martin Negro would preside over a second Crafts trial in Stamford, Connecticut. This proceeding would closely resemble the first, with several notable differences. Crafts's defense would now be in the hands of the public defenders' office because he had run out of funds. In this trial, he would not take the stand, though the prosecution was able to admit his testimony from the first trial. This time around, the jury took six working days to find Richard Crafts guilty of the murder of his wife, Helle. A total of twenty-three out of twenty-four jurors who heard this complicated case had decided that Richard Crafts was guilty. Crafts was sentenced to a prison term of ninety-nine years for his crime.

THE SCIENTIFIC FACTS
OF THE WOODCHIPPER CASE

The Woodchipper murder is a case in which a great many forensic disciplines came together to create a net of evidence powerful enough to gain a successful solution and justice. This was achieved, even though only fragments of the body would eventually be found. Odontology, pathology, serology, blood-spatter evidence, credit card tracing evidence, fabric and hair examination, time-line analysis, and weather evidence, were just some of the forensic fields that played a critical role in this case's successful prosecution.

I suggest that we closely analyze just one of these fields in our discussion of the forensic procedures used to solve this murder. When I walked into the Crafts' master bedroom on Christmas Day in 1986, I immediately saw some reddish-brownish stains on the queen-sized mattress that Richard and Helle Crafts used. I knew that there was a good possibility that these stains were human blood and that there could be more blood traces in that room, but ones which were not visible to the naked eye. To enhance any blood traces I could not readily see, I used two blood enhancement reagents, known as luminol and TMB (tetramethybenzidine).

Luminol is a mixture of three dry chemicals which are added to distilled water. TMB is a mixture of chemicals with ethanol and glacial acetic acid. When mixed in the proper amounts, the resulting luminol or TMB can provide a presumptive determination whether the stains in question are blood. The stains will quickly show up in a bright, luminescence with luminol and a blue color with TMB, should the source be blood. When first developed, these chemicals were used for presumptive blood-testing purposes. But, over the years, experienced investigators have been able to use luminol and TMB to bring up visually blood traces which they would otherwise miss. We apply luminol/TMB at a crime scene with a spray bottle which enables large areas to be quickly surveyed. This overview additionally permits the investigator to establish blood trails and other critical patterns. At times, these patterns can lead the investigator to see foot or handprints which would be otherwise invisible.

The application of luminol may affect some blood serological examinations, so appropriate samples should be properly collected before it is applied. Using luminol has some other requirements. First, it must be used in the dark. This can be difficult, so the room and the investigator must be prepared, including allowing the eyes to become accustomed to the pitch dark. The investigator should test the mixture on a piece of paper which has one part human blood to one hundred parts water as a positive control. Then he should apply the luminol. If he is applying it to a wall, he should be sure to spray on small amounts since large amounts will collect on the surface, causing the solution to run. This can quickly destroy the target pattern. Also, luminol will not work if the temperature is at or below the freezing level (thirty-two degrees, Fahrenheit).

The other major problem which luminol presents is the difficulty in photographing the results in the total dark. As part of the preparations, the camera equipment should be set up, off to one side. The investigator will have to take his photos at a ninety-degree angle to the target surface. Therefore, he should mount the camera on a tripod. While taking pictures, he will have to estimate the intensity of the light being produced by the pattern and should bracket his camera's light meter accordingly. The results, even in optimum conditions, can vary. I have had photos develop with as little as ten seconds of exposure and others that would not develop with three minutes' exposure. As a rule, a footprint showing a lot of detail will develop with a fifteen-second exposure while a fingerprint may not develop at all. The investigator should also try to frame the photography by providing a scale. He can carefully allow a small amount of light into the room while the shutter is open to provide this scale. Another way: He should apply fluorescent paint to a ruler, which will show up in the photograph as long as the ruler has been subjected to light prior to the photo. It is vital to take lots of photos. Eight or ten per pattern is a good average.

Obviously, using luminol and TMB to bring up the blood evidence in the Crafts' master bedroom was a critical part of my forensic investigation there. These scientific means for solving crimes are reliable but must be used only with proper preparations. Also these tests and tools are considered safe. TMB has proven to be noncarcinogenic. Criminal investigations today are a combination of old-fashioned and systematic detective work, such as checking telephone bills and credit card records, and intelligently applying modern techniques, such as blood enhancement reagents.

THE SUMMARY

The Helle Crafts murder investigation is certainly one of the most complex and variegated I have ever worked on. The first thing to emphasize when looking back at this case is its role in helping to move the American justice system away from the notion that there has to be a recognizable corpse before we can prove that a murder has been committed. As noted, this paradigm stemmed from the ancient common law notion of *corpus delicti*, meaning the necessity for proof of a body being found for proof of a crime. Whatever its origins, more and more murderers today are being brought to justice without ever finding the victims' bodies.

It seems reasonable that Richard Crafts was relying on this tradition in criminal law when he murdered his wife and set out to dispose of her remains in a way which must have seemed to him foolproof. This is why studying Helle Crafts's exemplary lifestyle was so important, as important as her husband's behaviors. Crafts's lifestyle had led to Helle's retaining a divorce lawyer and signing a divorce decree which she tried to have served on her husband. Also the importance both parents were to attach to the well-being of their three children, the three foremost living victims of this crime, was also critical. All of this analysis is critical in placing Helle Crafts's abrupt disappearance in its proper context.

In his twisted way, one can see that Crafts attached great importance to his children and who would be raising them. In 1996, Crafts told the lone journalist he has talked to since his arrest that he could escape from the Cheshire maximum security prison, "Anytime I want." He was asked why he hadn't done that. His reply, "Because that would undermine everything that I have been working for."

Walter Flanagan, his staff, and the members of the forensic laboratory and the Connecticut State Police's Western Major Crimes Squad all deserve great credit for the successful resolution of this case. In the same 1996 interview, Crafts said that he had, at that time, nineteen independent cases in litigation. The interviewer asked if all of these concerned his appeal. Recently, Walter Flanagan astounded that same writer with the fact that Crafts has not filed a single appeal of his conviction. Crafts must also have counted among those suits the one he filed against his sister, Karen Rodgers, over how she disposed of Lucretia Crafts's baby clothing business. It must have been very difficult for Mrs. Rodgers to come to terms with the fact that her brother had cruelly taken the life of Helle, her sister in law, whom she loved. And Karen Rodgers, it seems readily apparent, was an ideal choice to take custody of the children.

David Rodgers died in the late nineties and so cannot ever tell us any more. Other key figures in the case have also passed away. Lis Nielsen, Helle's mother, died in the late eighties. Keith Mayo died in an auto accident in 2000. Richard Wildman, the Southbury constable, committed suicide recently. Lucretia Crafts, Richard and Karen's mother, has died, but not before she changed her will to exclude Karen from any inheritance. What happened on the night of November 18, 1986, seems to have touched many. Certainly, Helle's grieving friends deserve great credit for persevering in her name and demanding that the wheels of justice turn. Anna Batelli, Alyce Bennett, Betty Cooper, Patricia Von Berg, and Sue Miller are just some who, when confronted with the unthinkable, had the courage to think and act.

What, in my estimation, really did happen that thundering and snowy night? Richard Crafts had probably gotten into a major verbal confrontation with his wife, after she got home from her flight from Frankfurt. The two probably argued more after the children were put to bed. Then, around ten or so, Helle prepared to go to bed and must have been exhausted. She had been on her feet since seven or so that morning, western European time. This meant that it was three o'clock the next morning in her mind when she decided to strip her bed to change the sheets. Helle was at the foot of the bed, perhaps leaning over as she worked on this chore. She would have been wearing her comfortable, older white and light blue bathrobe. Crafts must have struck her in the back of the head, from behind, once, then perhaps a harder blow, killing her instantly. According to his own statements, Crafts had had experience in killing quickly and efficiently. But blood spatter is not normally produced from a single blow. Perhaps his victim's head landed on the bed frame, producing the quarter-sized stain, which mixed with the medium-velocity smaller spatters. Or perhaps a second blow was administered.

It all happened very quickly and quietly. The three children heard nothing. Crafts was now alone with the stark evidence of the terrible crime he had committed. Taking great care to move quietly, Crafts then would move Helle's body downstairs and into the garage where he would place his wife's remains in his older freezer. Then a key moment would occur. Marie Thomas would come home late, after 2 A.M. Crafts would have to wait until he was confident she was asleep, even feigning Helle's cough when he heard Marie outside his bedroom door, since she told investigators that she had thought she'd heard that noise. When Crafts was sure Marie was asleep, as quietly as possible, he would have gone into the stormy night and gone to the Currituck Road property where he'd parked his pickup truck, which would have the new freezer in its rear. Driving the small truck back to his house, he had to navigate the back-heavy vehicle around a spruce tree in the front yard and pull up close to the garage door. This was directly under Marie Thomas's bedroom window, so being quiet was essential for this maneuver.

Once the truck was in position, Crafts would have wrestled the new and larger freezer into his cluttered garage, unpacked it, and then moved Helle's partially frozen body from the older freezer to the new one. Soon, the power would go out. Crafts would have to be exhausted by this time and dawn could not be far off. He would have to wait to take Marie and the children to the Rodgers' house in Westport. He would call David Rodgers at 4:40 and tell him of his plans to bring the family over. After all, they were without power.

Crafts woke the children and Marie and made his hasty trip to Westport. Marie would notice that Helle's Toyota Tercel was missing. With the power restored around noon, Helle's remains would have been frozen enough for him to use his chain saw to dismember her. He devoted hours that next day to lining up a truck strong enough to drag a woodchipper. On Wednesday night, Crafts would have gathered wood and taken Helle's remains from the freezer to go to the Currituck Road property where he could work in total privacy, unless some curious neighbor or cop would be alarmed by the sound of a wood-chipper in use late at night. Crafts would then put Helle's dismembered body through the woodchipper, along with cord wood, while Helle's remains were still clothed in her older, white and blue bathrobe, with her mail in her side pocket. The following evening,

Thursday, Crafts did his normal stint with the Southbury police force and then hauled the woodchipper with the U-Haul truck to the Silver Bridge section of Lake Zoar, where he was seen by two witnesses, as he finished his grim task.

There are still questions surrounding this case which will probably never be answered. How did Helle's Toyota Tercel make its way to the Pan Am employee parking lot? Did Richard Crafts actually risk being seen pulling the car behind his pickup truck, using a tow bar that had later been jettisoned? Or did some friend drive behind him when he added this macabre note to Helle's disappearance? Was that friend David Rodgers and was the anonymous note merely a way to deflect attention away from himself? After all, he could be named an accessory after the fact to a homicide if Crafts, now his bitter enemy, were to confess all.

The saddest note in this case, ironically, was articulated by Crafts, himself. Both of his defense teams picked up on this refrain. "We don't know that Helle's dead. She may come walking through that door [the Newtown police station's] at any moment." It has been sixteen years now since these tragic events unfolded. We cannot hope to ever see Helle alive. A last footnote: As I said before, I found it very strange that the Mathison case and this murder both occurred so close to the Thanksgiving holiday. There is another similarity between this case, the Mathison case, and the MacArthur case presented later in this book. Crafts worked part-time as a policeman. The murderers in the other two cases were full-time, veteran police officers.

chapter
three

THE O. J. SIMPSON CASE

If it [the glove] doesn't fit, you must acquit.
—Defense Lawyer Johnnie Cochran, in closing argument

The trial of O. J. Simpson became one of the most publicized and most complex murder trials in American history, if not world history. Perhaps because of my life's work as a forensic scientist and police officer, I resist the term "crime of the century," one that is applied every so often to a particularly notorious murder case. The 1932 Lindbergh kidnapping and the subsequent death of the couple's little boy quickly received this title. Decades earlier, Lizzie Borden was arrested for killing her parents with an ax, a case that was accorded this title. Most recently there was the Oklahoma City bombing of 1996, for which Timothy McVeigh was convicted and executed. The 1994 murders of Nicole Brown Simpson and Ron Goldman have also been called the crimes of the century, and this is a case on which I consulted. From my own perspective, each and every murder I have investigated stands out as an event so awful that, for the victims and their families, they are heinous crimes which cannot ever be matched for their abject cruelty. I find that the title "crime of the century" is more a manifestation of public and media interest in a case than anything else.

That being said, I do clearly recognize that the tragic deaths of

Nicole Simpson and Ron Goldman in the Brentwood section of Los Angeles on the night of Sunday, June 12, 1994, are landmarks in the history of American jurisprudence for a number of reasons. Just as the Lindbergh kidnapping brought out the worst in this country's media, so also did the O. J. Simpson case. Reporters covering the 1994 murders may not have climbed a ladder to force their way into a private sanctuary, as they did into the Lindbergh baby's bedchamber to steal photos for the next day's paper. Nevertheless, television cameras, the supermarket tabloids, and even some of the mainstream media all seemed to abuse their First Amendment rights at one time or another.

The media excesses did not end with the arrest of O. J. Simpson nor with the immediate weeks which followed that defendant's acquittal. During this extended aftermath, certain elements of the publishing industry also displayed a cynicism for the facts. Here is one example I find particularly galling. By the end of the proceedings, the original pool of twelve jurors and twelve alternates had been whittled down to just twelve and two. (In fact, the sequestration of these jurors for fifteen months, at a pay scale of $5 per day, raised very serious issues about our country's jury system, ones that still need to be resolved.) In 1995, about six months after the verdict was handed down, the chief executive of a major paperback publishing house appeared on the CBS network's *60 Minutes*. This publisher made a statement that each and every one of the jurors and alternates in the Simpson case had approached him for some kind of book deal. This statement seemed to cast the jury's work, at the heart of our legal system, in the same craven light as the rest of the trial's abuses. However, I know of one juror who survived the entire process with honor in tact. In point of fact, this juror had a brief telephone conversation with a reporter I know and trust who was sworn to keep secret the juror's identity. This juror had categorically refused to discuss any element of the entire fifteen-month experience with any member of the media and had *never*, repeat, *never*, approached that publisher. This juror revealed these feelings in a single, social telephone conversation, a call that was indirectly arranged by a mutual friend. Coming from a young graduate of an upscale Catholic university, the juror's actions show that we still have reason to look for the best in our fellow citizens, the ultimate jury pool. Diogenes had, indeed, found several honest women and men who had sacrificed more than a year of their lives to serve our judicial system.[1]

All of the media excesses set off by the murders of these two young victims were primarily fueled by ratings and profit. Or so it seems to me. I know that not all of the transgressions were the direct result of the corrupting influence money can have. Many witnesses, including myself, were approached by media representatives who offered to pay large sums of money in return for an exclusive interview or crime scene photographs. One prime example of cash directly poisoning the legal process can be found in the thousands of dollars which were paid early in the investigation by a tabloid television show to a prospective witness. Once this payment was established, her testimony was completely discounted by the prosecution, though her words could later have proven very powerful. However, most of these abuses seemed driven by the competitive urge for higher ratings and wider readership. Money, therefore, was indirectly behind many of these wrongs since higher ratings mean higher net revenues and higher monetary returns. And the skyrocketing public interest in this drama, as it played itself out over the course of the case's critical fifteen months, only seemed to drive the media to intensify its misbehaviors.

The O. J. Simpson case did present the American public with a wide array of issues which seemed to make the proceedings spellbinding. Race, of course, was foremost among these. An African American man is accused of murdering his ex-wife and her "gentleman caller," both of whom are Caucasian. The crimes took place in the Los Angeles area, a huge, multicultural metropolitan area where, three years before, four members of the Los Angeles Police Department (LAPD) were videotaped savagely beating an African American man, Rodney King. These policemen were acquitted by an all-white jury in a Simi, California, courtroom, and this verdict subsequently set off riots which claimed the lives of more than two dozen people and injured close to one thousand.

There were also the issues of wealth, fame, and celebrity. O. J. Simpson was one of the greatest running backs to ever play football in this country. Baseball may still be called America's pastime, but college and professional football seem to have emerged as the country's favorite spectator sport. Television viewer ratings bear this out, particularly during the Super Bowl. When asked, a surprising number of people, both men and women, can tell you what they were doing when the National Football Leagues's O. J. Simpson passed the two thousand-yards gained-in-a-single-season mark. He did this, I've been told, with a final run against the New York Jets in 1973. Still others could remember an earlier time when Simpson, then a junior in college, took the ball on the game's last play for a run of seventy-three yards, propelling his University of Southern California team to a win over their Los Angeles rivals, UCLA. This triumph meant that USC would play in that year's Rose Bowl in Pasadena. A rival on the UCLA team would win that year's Heisman Trophy, awarded to the top collegiate player. But O. J. Simpson would win the Heisman honor the following year.

O. J. Simpson's celebrity would widen after his pro football career was over. He became familiar to millions who watched television commercials which showed him racing through airports to rent his car from the Hertz Corporation and thus save his day. In this one-minute TV narrative, a little old lady in the airport calls out to her hero, "Go, O. J. Go." Already a superstar, Simpson was garrulous and his performance in front of a camera seemed effortless. Almost overnight, he developed into a knowledgeable football commentator for NBC's weekly NFL broadcasts. "The Juice," as millions came to know him, had instant entrée with both coaches and players and knew what he was talking about. Viewers respected him for that. Finally, O. J. Simpson became a movie actor, primarily known for his self-deprecating slapstick humor in the *Naked Gun* movies, which spoofed the police film genre and starred Leslie Nielsen as a deadpan, and bumbling Los Angeles detective.

To sum up, O. J. Simpson did not simply become a star athlete who smoothly transitioned himself into the broader world of sports and movie entertainment. This all meant that he would become quite wealthy, a development which seemed only normal, given his success. O. J. Simpson, who was forty-six at the time of the murders, had really come to symbolize the rags-to-riches success story, starring an individual who happened to be an African American, a hero who had totally succeeded in the broader landscape of mainstream America. And the American public liked him, a lot, for all of these accomplishments. The Horatio Alger story seemed to be alive and well in the twentieth century.

Over the years, there were a few tragedies and problems for O. J. Simpson which did come to light. In 1979 the country was saddened to learn that his two-year-old daughter, Aaren, the third and youngest child of his first wife, Marguerite, had drowned in the family's swimming pool at his home on Rockingham Drive in Brentwood. Years later and much darker, the public heard that his second wife, Nicole, had called police to this same home, and Simpson was arrested for battering her. This abuse occurred in the predawn hours of New Year's morning in 1989. Perhaps because of his favorable image, the story of this incident was buried on an interior page in the sports section of the *Los Angeles Times*, the major newspaper in Simpson's hometown. But, overall, the O. J. Simpson who was arrested for the murders of his wife and her companion was still an American hero. Thus, the stage was set for a general public that seemed to crave, as much as anything else, a tragic drama about a special hero who had fallen from grace. And, preferably, a fall by this hero from a great height.

In the O. J. Simpson case, I found myself in the unusual position of working for the defense. I was contacted in the middle of the week after the Sunday night that the crimes had been discovered. Simpson's original attorney had already been replaced by Robert Shapiro, an accomplished lawyer and friend of mine, who took over the case.

Please allow me to reemphasize what I have said in other chapters in this book: My life's credo is to work to discover the truth. My own study of forensic evidence at any crime scene is absolutely tied to establishing the scientific facts of the events in question, no matter

where the trail of evidence takes me. While I am technically a member
of one team or another, usually the prosecution, I must *always*, repeat,
always stay with the scientific facts as I am able to discover them. This
approach, a personal mission statement, has frustrated those I work
with at times, but this is the only way I can apply my knowledge,
experience, and energies to help solve a case.

I was in a task force meeting at my office in the Connecticut State
Forensics offices midweek, when Bob Shapiro called me. It quickly
turned out that I was one of the few Americans who did not know anything about O. J. Simpson. When I emigrated from Taiwan in 1965, I
had only enough money to buy a single plane ticket, one way. After I
arrived in New York, between graduate school studies and working
three jobs to make a living, I didn't have the money nor the time to
follow sports. As a matter of fact, I didn't even own a TV set. Therefore, football and O. J. Simpson were not part of my new, American
vocabulary. Bob had to explain all of this to me. My initial response
when Bob asked me to assist him was that I was way too busy and
could not make the enormous time commitment that this case was
bound to demand. But Bob Shapiro is a very good and persuasive
attorney. I listened carefully to his reasons for seeking my help, especially when he called back later that same day. Certain of the facts that
he related to me were troublesome. I then emphasized for Bob that I
would have to go straight ahead with my scientific investigation, and,
as for the forensics, we would all have "to let the chips fall where they
may." Bob understood that this could mean that my findings could end
up helping the prosecution's case. Bob Shapiro was just then in the
process of announcing that he had reached out to Dr. Michael Baden
of New York, a world-renowned forensic pathologist and a close
friend and colleague of mine; we had met thirty-five years earlier
when we worked together at New York University. Bob could not yet,
we agreed at the outset, make any mention of my name in connection
with the case, though he did tell the media that he was trying to recruit
a top forensic scientist, in addition to signing on Dr. Baden.

I also had to spell out for Bob Shapiro the fact that I could not commit to work on the case until I had cleared this decision with my own command structure. After I joined the Connecticut State Police in 1979, my superiors in the Connecticut Department of Public Safety on up to the governor had assured me that I could participate in any cases outside our jurisdiction, as long as this was done on my own time and there was no expense to the state. Still, I felt I needed to clear this case quite specifically. I phoned Commissioner of Public Safety Nicholas Cioffi, a former superior court judge and a good friend, and he quickly gave his assent, though he asked me specifically to receive a go-ahead from then-Governor Lowell A. Weicker. I was able to quickly do this, and I phoned Bob Shapiro to tell him that I would assist him only with my scientific analysis of the crime scene and would review any forensics testimony.

I arrived in Los Angeles on Friday, June 17. After getting off the plane, I did not expect to see the hundreds of reporters and TV cameramen who were waiting at the gate to interview me. When I told them that I knew nothing about the case and that I didn't even know who O. J. Simpson was, it seemed that nobody believed me. Bob had sent a limo to pick me up, which took me directly to the Encino home of Robert Kardashian, a longtime personal friend of O. J. Simpson and one of the key players in convincing Simpson to hire Bob Shapiro. I say that our presence in Encino was ironic since a group of us had just met Simpson for the first time and were pulling ourselves together as a unit to investigate the case. After the introductions, Simpson had withdrawn to a different part of the house. We then met in the library to discuss the case and to make contact with the Los Angeles crime lab and coroner's office to arrange to view the evidence and to visit the crime scene. Then we received word that there was a warrant out for O. J. Simpson's arrest. Bob Shapiro, it developed, had been in day-long negotiations with the LAPD's top command on when and how Simpson would turn himself in to the police.

You can imagine my reaction, bordering on shock, when, in late afternoon, we saw LAPD detectives and uniformed cops arrive to arrest Simpson. Bob Shapiro and Bob Kardashian could not find him on the grounds but, instead, found a letter written by Simpson. We were then informed that Simpson and his close boyhood friend, Al Cowlings, had slipped out of Kardashian's estate and were, literally, at large. Each of us was interviewed by LAPD detectives. Some of the detectives had taken my crime scene training course and knew me. We were all then advised that we faced the possibility of arrest for aiding this fugitive. Later, a description of the white Ford Bronco owned by Cowlings, along with its license plate numbers, was broadcast over the police frequencies, and, subsequently, by the news media. The vehicle was quickly spotted and, with Cowlings at the wheel and Simpson crouched in the back with a gun to his head, the Bronco led a flotilla of police and news media vehicles, under an umbrella of a half dozen helicopters used by television outlets, on a seventy-mile trip at slow speeds along California's extensive freeway system. When the Bronco went through some districts, people actually stood along the roadway and cheered for Simpson.

Cowling's Bronco would ultimately return to Simpson's Rockingham home, and he would, after some final negotiation, surrender to the Los Angeles police on two counts of murder. We learned later that all or portions of this prolonged series of events were viewed by an estimated 95 million Americans, more than had watched the previous winter's Super Bowl. Since this odyssey started near six, California time, the spectacle preempted evening television programming in the East. At Kardashian's home, we all breathed a collective sigh of relief when our distraught client was taken into custody.

After all of that, I had to block out the enormous, worldwide reaction to the arrest and stay zeroed in on continuing the technical forensics work that I had gone there to perform. During the next two days, as I continued my preliminary investigation at the primary (Bundy Drive) and secondary (Simpson's home on North Rockingham Drive) murder scenes, I knew that my initial insights had served me well. As I indicated, I will spell out these findings in the case investigation portion of this chapter. Suffice it to say, *something was wrong*. And I would be grappling with these irregularities for the next fifteen months.

And one last introductory remark on this complex and large case. Many Americans seem obsessed with the impact which O. J. Simpson's considerable personal finances had on this case and its outcome. In reality, the defendant here was most extraordinary in that he could roughly match the resources the prosecution brought to bare in this very extensive investigation and trial. There is usually a huge imbalance between what the government can do in a trial and the resources available to the defendant. The Simpson case simply began to balance the books on this score. According to one set of figures I have seen, the prosecution spent $19 million to try this case. Meanwhile, the defense costs were $10 million, excluding thousands of billable hours put toward investigation. From a personal standpoint, I received $150,000 for my consultation. From that amount, I donated $80,000 to the forensic science program at the University of New Haven, where I have taught for many years, as scholarship money for law enforcement and forensics majors. I contributed the remaining money toward the purchase of badly needed equipment and training at the State Police Forensics Laboratory in Meriden. I became a member of the defense team because I quickly sensed that a number of intractable and critical errors had been made by some of the investigators handling this case and that the alleged findings did not bare the stamp of truth. I have never regretted this decision for an instant.

THE CASE'S FACTS

Orenthal James Simpson was born on July 7, 1947, to James and Eunice Simpson in a poor section of San Francisco. He was the third of four children and would not see his father on a regular basis. The elder Simpson died of AIDS in 1985. Mrs. Simpson worked hard to support her four children and herself, primarily as an orderly and technician in the psychiatric ward of San Francisco General Hospital. Known as "O. J." from his earliest years, since he disliked the name he was given at birth, Simpson spent his formative years in the same way countless numbers of other inner-city children do. He was bigger and certainly faster than most of his contemporaries, so he was able to hold his own in the inevitable street fights he found himself in, or he was able to outrun his foes.

In high school Simpson did not excel in any way, except on the football field. At one point, when he was a sophomore and had gotten into some minor trouble, word got to Willie Mays, an African American star outfielder for the San Francisco Giants baseball team, who took the trouble to pay a surprise visit to the teenaged Simpson at the family's apartment. The budding athletic star found Mays very relaxed, without any mission statement on his mind, which made a strong and positive impression on Simpson. Later on, in his own book, *I Want to Tell You*, Simpson noted how especially impressed he was with the fine lifestyle that Mays's athletic stardom had afforded him.

After his high school years, Simpson attended City College of San Francisco, a community college where he quickly became a star on the football team and ran track. Averaging ten yards-per-carry as a running back meant Simpson was quickly noticed by big-time college football scouts. At that time, college football was beginning to command enormous attention from college administrators, the ascending television networks, and the American public. There would be no problem with the fact that O. J. Simpson had few academic skills. Since the San Francisco–area universities with teams in the big-time Pacific Coast Conference, Stanford and the University of California at Berkeley, both had excellent reputations, Simpson was more realistically recruited for football by the Los Angeles–area football powers, UCLA and USC. As many other impressionable twenty-year-olds might decide, Simpson opted for USC since he liked their colossal marching band and the school's mascot, a Trojan warrior, who would rumble around the Los Angeles Coliseum in a chariot drawn by a pair of dashing horses.

In 1968, while he was in his senior year at USC, Simpson married Marguerite Whitley, his high school sweetheart, and the two eventually became the parents of three children: a daughter, Arnelle; a son, Jason;

and Aaren, the girl who would drown at the age of two. In the spring of 1969 Simpson would become the first player selected in the overall pro football draft, going to the Buffalo Bills in the NFL's upside-down selection system. This meant that he would have to play for the team with the poorest record from the prior season. However, even before he performed in his first game, Simpson had already signed lucrative advertising contracts with ABC Sports, Chevrolet, and others.

By 1977, Simpson's football career had peaked, and all of the battering which an NFL running back is forced to absorb, even one as fast and graceful as he was, had begun to take its toll. That fall, Simpson, who was then thirty, met Nicole Brown, eighteen, a waitress at Daisy, a trendy nightclub in glamorous Beverly Hills that Simpson frequented. By now, his marriage to Marguerite was effectively over and Nicole and O. J. Simpson began to date. Marguerite and Simpson would formally divorce in 1979.

Nicole Brown went to Dana Point High School in Orange County, a wealthy California coastline suburban area about seventy miles south of Los Angeles. Nicole was born in Frankfurt, Germany, to a German-born mother who had married an American serviceman. She had grown up in America to blossom into a prototypical California beauty. Tall, blonde, and slender, she could have been the model for the girl that the Beach Boys sang about. She was the second-born of four daughters, children of a father who had returned home to make a substantial amount of money in real estate and other investments. None of the Brown girls would attain a college degree. In fact, in papers Nicole would file for her 1992 divorce proceeding, she would list a two-week sales job in a local boutique she had while she was in high school and her waitress job at the Beverly Hills night club as her entire employment background. During their marriage, Nicole and Simpson would bring two children into the world, a daughter, Sydney, born in 1985, and a son, Justin, born in 1988.

Soon after Nicole Brown had fallen in love with Simpson, she had moved into his large and expensive home at 360 North Rockingham Drive, north of Sunset Boulevard and in one of the wealthiest sections of wealthy Brentwood. The couple would marry in 1985. Simpson purchased this large, Spanish-designed property at the corner of Rockingham and Ashford Avenue for $650,000 in 1975. The house contained six thousand square feet within its stone and stucco walls and had spacious grounds whose plentiful trees surrounded tennis courts and a large swimming pool. The main house's front and sides were bordered by a six-foot-high brick wall which gave way to an iron gate in front of the spacious driveway that sat before the Rockingham entrance. There was a smaller gated entrance on the Ashford side of the property. Farther back, the grounds had three guest cottages which backed up to an eight-foot cyclone fence with heavy vines meshed together, at the property's edge. In today's real estate market, this property's value would be in the millions. Nicole Brown and O. J. Simpson had signed a prenuptial agreement when they married, one clearly establishing that Simpson retained sole ownership of the Rockingham property.

Nicole and O. J. experienced some stormy times during their seventeen-year relationship. There was the arrest of Simpson for battering his wife in 1989. Perhaps due to his celebrity status, this case was not handled in an orthodox manner. This was in spite of the fact that both Nicole and O. J. Simpson both declared that predawn morning that the police had previously been called to their home eight times. On that 1989 occasion, the investigating officer did not handcuff Simpson, who was then able to slip away and drive off in his Bentley. He would subsequently turn himself in. Even after this strange series of events, the arresting officer was unsure on whether to pursue this incident with the routines and protocols used by the LAPD for domestic violence cases.

Simpson's domestic abuse case was then assigned to a more experienced officer who was told by the city attorney's office that he should attempt to determine whether this early morning incident was isolated or was part of a pattern. Queries were made throughout the Brentwood station house. Only one of the police officers there answered that he'd also been to the Rockingham address on a domestic violence case. In a memo, Officer Mark Fuhrman wrote that in late 1985 he had been called to a scene very similar to the 1989 altercation. In that instance, the windshield of a Mercedes Benz had been shattered, and Nicole, who did not want to pursue the matter, had said that her husband had broken the glass "with a baseball bat."

On May 24, 1989, O. J. Simpson was able to enter a plea of no contest in this case and would receive a suspended sentence, two years of probation, and fines of $470. He was also ordered to receive counseling two times a week and to perform 120 hours of community service through the Voluntary Action Bureau, which specialized in criminal dispositions. With his attorney's prodding, the prosecution agreed to let Simpson avoid the group counseling sessions customarily required in cases involving domestic abuse and rage management. He would instead be permitted to undergo his counseling from a private practitioner, some of which he would later conduct by phone. And, rather than performing his 120 hours of community service in the typical fashion, such as cutting away roadside weeds and cleaning the floors and toilets in public restrooms, Simpson would be allowed to put together a fundraising dinner for his community service work, one which featured celebrity guests and elaborate corporate sponsorship. This event would raise money which would be donated to Camp Ronald McDonald, a children's cancer charity. Finally, Simpson would pay an additional $500 to the Sojourn Counseling Center, a Santa Monica battered women's shelter.

During their good times, Nicole and O. J. Simpson loved to travel together, especially when he was covering football games, and to make shopping trips to New York City. In 1985, when Simpson was inducted into the NFL's Hall of Fame, located in Canton, Ohio, the couple had walked hand in hand to his place of honor. During his acceptance address, which Simpson delivered with characteristic emotion, the honoree emphasized the critical and positive role that Nicole was playing in his life. Simpson's magnanimity toward Nicole was not just confined to her well-being. He also paid college tuition for Denise Brown, Nicole's older sister, and was able to set up Nicole's father, Lou Brown, in a lucrative Hertz distributorship in Orange County.

However, the bad times seemed to dominate this relationship, and in 1992 the couple decided to file for a divorce. They avoided a trial and signed their divorce papers on October 15 of that year. Under this agreement, Simpson would pay Nicole $10,000 per month in child support, and Nicole would keep title to a rent-producing condominium in San Francisco which he had given her. Simpson, who was then making more than $650,000 per year, also paid Nicole a lump sum of a little more than $430,000, money which, the settlement declared, would primarily be put toward Nicole's purchase of a residence for herself and her two children. Simpson, of course, would retain exclusive ownership in his Rockingham estate, as per the prenuptial agreement the couple had signed seven years earlier. For the time being, Nicole had found herself a $5,000-a-month rental at 325 Gretna Green Way in a pleasant section of Brentwood, though one that was not as wealthy as the nearby Rockingham estate. Nicole's new home also had a swimming pool and a guest house. On paper, this break-up seemed far more amicable than many divorce proceedings.

Still, there were more stormy times ahead for Nicole Brown Simpson and her famous ex-husband. Yet, both sincerely seemed to want to reconcile their differences. Several attempts were made, but none succeeded. The continuing tension between Nicole and her ex-husband erupted on the night of October 25, 1993, when she made two 911 phone calls. Nicole's voice shook with terror as she tried to get help ("he's fucking going to kill me"), all the while attempting to identify her ex-husband to the dispatcher. On this occasion, Nicole did not have any physical evidence of a beating and no charges were filed.

The guest house at Nicole's new home became the source for some of this continuing friction. While she was on a ski vacation in Aspen, Colorado, Nicole had met Brian Kaelin, a blonde, boyish-looking product of southern California, who was in his late twenties. The two struck it off as chums, and Kaelin eventually moved into the Gretna Green guest house, paying $500 per month to live there. Nicknamed Kato, after the comic book helpmate of superhero the Green Hornet ("Hurry, Kato"), Kaelin also earned some of his rent money by doing chores on the property and babysitting the two small children. In fact, Sydney and Justin took such a liking to Kaelin that they soon named the family dog, a white Akita, Kato, after their boarder. Kaelin was ostensibly pursuing an acting career in Hollywood, but seemed more typical of the directionless individuals which that area seems to attract.

Nicole was ready to buy her own property by late 1993. She had sold the San Francisco condo and knew she would have to pay a capital gains tax on that property if she did not reinvest in a new residence within eighteen months. She liked a three-story condominium in a 1991-built, two-unit building she'd found at 875 South Bundy Drive and paid $625,000 for it. The new residence would be only six blocks from Gretna Green. Bundy is the major north-south artery in Brentwood, crossing the wealthy community's major east-west street, the famed Sunset Boulevard, about a mile or so away. Nicole would be near an elementary school and a playground for the children and would be two miles or so from her ex-husband's estate on Rockingham. Her new home, which had languished on the market for months, featured a Jacuzzi, lots of marble-top in the kitchen, and a two-story living room. Nicole also planned to move Kaelin into quarters between the condo's kitchen and living room. O. J. Simpson had gone along with his ex-wife's tenant living in a guest house at the Gretna Green property, but he now intervened when he heard about Nicole's new plans for Kato's living under the same roof with herself and the children. Simpson then offered Kaelin rent-free living quarters in one of the three guest houses on his Rockingham property, an offer which Kato gobbled up.

At about this time, Simpson discovered that Nicole had been able to avoid paying federal taxes on the San Francisco condo sale by claiming Rockingham was still her primary residence and Bundy was being used for rental purposes. By now, the couple had reached the conclusion that their differences were irreconcilable. Nicole's diary would indicate an early June call from Simpson, one in which he threatened legal action with the Internal Revenue Service. On June 6, 1994, just six months or so after she had moved her children into their new home on Bundy, Simpson sent a lawyer's letter to Nicole announcing his intentions to pursue the matter with the IRS. To Nicole this meant that she would have to move out of the Bundy property so she could make it a rental. At about this time, Nicole also called the Sojourn Shelter for Battered Women in Santa Monica and said that her ex-husband was stalking her. On June 9, Nicole put the Bundy property up for a monthly rental of $4,000.

The rental sign would never go up in front of the Bundy property. Nicole Brown Simpson had already started looking for a new place for herself and her two children. She put those plans aside for the end-of-school weekend, though, since she was anticipating a reunion with her parents, sisters, and children. The centerpiece for this occasion would be her daughter Sydney's dance recital at the Paul Revere Elementary School in Brentwood, where the nine-year-old was completing the third grade. The Brown family then planned to go out to dinner at a Brentwood restaurant, the Mezzaluna. O. J. Simpson, reflecting the couple's estranged status, would not be invited to come along to the dinner by Nicole. However, he did attend his daughter's recital, sitting by himself toward the rear of the school's theater.

Simpson would later go out to dinner with Kato Kaelin, after his permanent houseguest broke a $100 bill for him. Simpson said he would need the smaller bills to tip a limo driver and a skycap at the Los Angeles airport, since he would be flying to Chicago later that night for a Hertz convention. Kaelin had been delighted by Simpson's appearance at his door and suggested that the two go out to get something to eat together. The pair would grab a fast-food supper at a local McDonald's. There is a popular misconception that this was the only time Kaelin and Simpson would go out to eat a meal together. This had happened on other occasions, though not frequently.

The Brown family reunion and dinner at Mezzaluna's proceeded smoothly and pleasantly for Nicole. The party was finished eating about nine that evening, and Nicole wanted to get her two children home to put them to bed. At about 9:40, Nicole's mother, Juditha Brown, called her daughter to say that she had dropped her glasses on the sidewalk outside of the restaurant, which were subsequently found next to the curb there. She asked if Nicole would contact the restaurant and have them returned.

Nicole had become friendly with a twenty-five-year-old, dark-haired, handsome waiter at the restaurant, Ronald Lyle Goldman, so she specifically asked for him when she made her call to Mezzaluna. Defense investigators would later establish that Goldman had already made plans for that Sunday evening, a date to go clubbing with another member of the restaurant waitstaff, an athletic, large, and attractive young woman from Oregon whom he had already been seeing. After Nicole Simpson's call, Goldman quickly decided to punch out for the night and asked the bartender on duty to please explain to the waitress that a college friend had called him, one who was in some sort of trouble and needed Goldman's immediate assistance. The bartender knew about Nicole Brown Simpson's phone call and then told the waitress where Goldman was really headed. This upset Goldman's original date and she, too, abruptly checked out and left the restaurant, letting others finish up several tables for her. This would later cause speculation about her activities later that night. Goldman, meanwhile, using a car he'd quickly borrowed from a friend, first drove to his nearby apartment and then went on to 875 South Bundy Drive.

Her mother's call was not the final time that Nicole would be on the phone that last evening of her life. She received a call from her close friend, Faye Resnick. Resnick had been Nicole's intimate friend for some time, and there would later be a great deal of controversy about what role, if any, this thirty-six-year-old unemployed woman played in the events which followed. Resnick, a narcotics addict, had stayed at Nicole's home from June 3 to June 8, when she had an overdose that afternoon and left to go into a drug rehabilitation center. Later on, there was substantial speculation about Resnick's ability to support her expensive cocaine habit since she had no discernible assets or income other than declining alimony payments from her ex-husband. Resnick had been jobless for a long time. She kept a diary, and the pages covering the five days she stayed with Nicole at Bundy were missing later on, because, she would say, of theft. Like so many of the individuals who surfaced in this case, Faye Resnick's role caused much more smoke than anything else, other than establishing that Nicole Brown Simpson was alive and on the phone with Resnick as the evening approached ten o'clock.

There is still a good deal of controversy about the timing of the next sequence of events in this case. Suffice it to say that sometime between 10:15 and 10:30 that Sunday evening several of Nicole Brown Simpson's neighbors heard or saw Nicole's Akita barking. One said the dog was making more of a wailing sound. Most of these neighbors were sitting at home doing what much of America does on Sunday nights; they were watching a favorite television show.

Pablo Fenjves lived about sixty yards north and behind Nicole Simpson's condo, and his property backed up to the same alley as did hers. With his wife, Jai, Fenjves had watched the opening few minutes of a local TV newscast. At about 10:15 that night, he heard a large dog making a wailing sound. Fenjves, forty-one at the time, was a moderately successful screenwriter. His parents were Holocaust survivors from Hungary, and he had been born in Venezuela. For a short time, after emigrating to this country, he had been employed in Florida by the *National Enquirer*. A few moments after he had heard the dog's "plaintive wail," Fenjves went downstairs to work on a script he was rewriting. He returned to his master bedroom at 11 P.M. and found his wife still watching television. The nearby dog continued to make the same troubled sounds.

Steven Schwab was also an aspiring screenwriter, though not as successful as Fenjves, who lived in a second-floor apartment on Montana Avenue three blocks away. Schwab was a creature of habit and liked to take a brisk walk with his own small dog each night after watching a rerun of *The Dick Van Dyke Show*. Schwab used a regular route for these walks, and this meant that at 10:55 he was in the alley behind Nicole's home. There Schwab saw the family's Akita, barking at a house. Schwab wondered if the dog was lost, so he approached the animal, which was friendly, and found an expensive collar, but no tags. He also noticed that there was a red substance which resembled blood on all four of its paws. The Akita followed Schwab home and patiently waited on the Schwab apartment's outside landing, while Steven told his wife, Linda, about his find.

The Schwabs were debating what to do about this well-bred dog when they were joined by their neighbor and friend, Sukru Boztepe, a freelance laser printer repairman. The Turkish-born Boztepe and his wife, Betina Rasmussen, agreed to take the dog with them, planning to let it sleep at their apartment for the night. However, when the couple got home, the Akita became too nervous, scratching at the door, and the couple decided not to keep it with them. They put the Akita on a leash to walk it, and the dog pulled Boztepe toward south Bundy Drive, where it stopped at a gate in front of Nicole Brown Simpson's condominium. Boztepe then let the dog pull him up the walkway, which was very dark and narrow, with shrubbery crowding in on both sides. The troubled Akita seemed to be beckoning to Boztepe to look farther down the walkway. Then, Boztepe would later relate: "I saw a lady lying down full of blood."

I mentioned earlier in the case that these accounts would become the sources of lasting debate. These individuals came to be known as "the dog witnesses." Their later testimony would become critical in attempts to establish a time of death for Nicole Simpson and Ron Goldman. Allow me to clarify the role of the forensic pathologist. This individual is not only responsible for the determination of the manner and cause of death, but is also extremely important in efforts to determine the time of death. Generally speaking, the forensic pathologist will base the time-of-death findings on the victim's body conditions, such as body temperature, lividity, rigidity, the degree of decomposition, stomach contents, and, finally, witness statements on the last time the decedent was seen alive. Unfortunately, even with all of our advanced forensics, it is still impossible to establish a time of death which can be considered scientifically exact. Experts can provide excellent estimates, but mostly these are still only estimates. (This issue of medical-legal, time-of-death analysis will be detailed at the end of the Sherman chapter.) Establishing this time line is critical in many cases, such as the Simpson and Goldman murders, since this data can confirm or refute a suspect's alibi. We can only hope that our continued research will provide new ways someday to determine exactly, to the very minute, a victim's time of death.

THE CASE'S INVESTIGATION

Sukru Boztepe made his grizzly discovery shortly before midnight. At 12:09 A.M. on Monday morning, June 13, officer Robert Riske was patrolling West Los Angeles in his squad car when he received a report of a crime at 874 South Bundy in Brentwood. Arriving at the address at 12:13, Riske found an elderly woman, Elsie Tistaert, who had called the police. Sukru Boztepe and his wife had excitedly banged on her front door, and the older lady had become frightened, thinking that she was about to become a crime victim herself. She had called 911. As Riske arrived, he and his partner, a female trainee, quickly found Boztepe and Rasmussen, along with the Akita, and straightened out the situation. The patrolman then walked across the street, to 875 South Bundy.

With his large service flashlight guiding him along the entrance's narrow walkway, Riske found the bloodied corpse of Nicole Brown Simpson, lying face down, at the base of four stairs which led to the entrance to her home. The pool of blood around her was large, covering more ground than her body, and was over all of the condo's tile entranceway. A restaurant menu lay near her. Riske then looked to his right where he illuminated a second corpse, that of a well-built young man whose shirt was pulled up over his head, propped against the iron fence which bordered the property. This was the body of Ronald Goldman. On the ground near Goldman's body, Riske saw a black knit ski cap, a white envelope, a pager, a torn piece of paper, and a left-hand leather glove. What Riske did not see were any bloodied shoeprints going back up the entranceway toward Bundy.

An exterior view of the Bundy crime scene.

Riske carefully moved through the left hedge bordering the walkway, past the woman's body, and made his way up to the landing. From that vantage point, the officer illuminated a walkway of 120 feet which ran along the entire northern wall of the property and which led to the alley in back. Along this route, he saw a single set of bloody shoeprints. Looking more closely, Riske also observed a trail of blood spatter next to the left footprints.

The patrolman now tried the front door to the residence, found it open, and entered. He saw no signs of any struggle or burglary there. Instead he saw lighted candles in the living room. Moving upstairs, there were more candles alight in the master bedroom, along with some in the adjacent bathroom, which had a tub filled with water. Moving quietly, Riske looked into the condo's two other bedrooms and found a sleeping child in each, a girl and a boy.

Though only a four-year veteran of the force, Riske displayed a more experienced officer's poise in this preliminary investigation. He realized that he had found a major crime scene, one that would particularly impact an upscale area like Brentwood. He knew his next move would be to radio for assistance. Just as he was about to do this on his walkie-talkie, Riske noticed an envelope on a table in the front foyer. He saw that the sender was O. J. Simpson. He had also noticed a poster of Simpson on one wall and saw photos of him at other places in the home where family pictures were on display. Recognizing the face of a celebrity at this kind of crime scene would add another dimension to the investigation. This was a fact of life for the LAPD. This development caused Riske to make his call by telephone since, as he would say later, he did not want to let any word of these homicides, possibly linked as they were to the name of O. J. Simpson, get to the Los Angeles media, who regularly monitored police radio frequencies. As Riske would later recall, he was afraid that reporters and photographers would be swarming over the crime scene before he got any backup.

Riske's initial call went to his immediate superior, Sergeant David Rossi, who was watch commander for that shift at the West Los Angeles station. That completed, he would then start taking steps to preserve the crime scene. When he had gotten the patrolman's report, Rossi quickly made a half dozen calls to the LAPD's top command. These quickly produced a steady stream of investigators and supervisors at 875 South Bundy. The first supervisor to arrive there was Sergeant Marty Coon. Soon, other uniformed officers arrived to keep any bystanders behind the yellow crime scene tape that had been put in place. Two officers arrived to take Sydney and Justin, who had been awakened but not told why, down to the West LAPD station house. More officers arrived, and they began using their flashlights to search the back alley for any additional potential evidence. Others went door to door, waking the startled residents and asking if anyone had heard or seen anything. Sergeant Rossi arrived at 1:30 A.M. to find things under control. His superior, Captain Constance Dial, joined him there. Patrolman Riske then took Rossi and Dial on a quick tour of what he had found.

Ron Phillips was a twenty-eight-year LAPD veteran and was the one in charge of the West LA detective/homicide unit which would have primary responsibility for investigating the two murders. Rossi had called Phillips shortly before he left for the crime scene. Phillips would now visit the crime scene, interview the patrolmen who had been working the case, and then call on one of four detectives who reported to him to take charge. Mark Fuhrman would take Phillips's call at his home, and he soon met Phillips at the West LA station house at 2:00 A.M. Phillips and Fuhrman did not bother waiting for Fuhrman's junior partner who had also been called. Instead, the two arrived at the crime scene ten minutes later. Patrolman Riske met them at the front gate and took the two on the same tour of what he had found. Instead of gingerly avoiding the masses of blood evidence and using the front stairs to go into the condo, the trio had decided to walk around the entire block to the alley in the rear. There they met Rossi, who now showed them what appeared to be blood smears on a rear gate. The three entered the residence through a rear garage entrance. They moved around two vehicles parked in the garage, one a Jeep.

To get into the residence, Phillips, Fuhrman, and Riske had to climb a short set of stairs. On the banister next to the stairs, they found a partially eaten and melting container of Ben & Jerry's ice cream. This piece of evidence could have provided an excellent lead to the possible sequence of events at the time of the killings. Unfortunately, there were no photographs taken at that time or other records kept to show the amount and condition of the ice cream. Also, there was no attempt made to determine who bought the ice cream or who had eaten it. The three officers then went through the interior of the crime scene. Standing and looking down from the front entrance, they could clearly see the two bodies with all the blood, whereas the wool cap, envelope, and glove evidence were partially obscured by shrubbery. They then left by a side entrance which opened onto the 120-foot walkway where they studied the shoeprints and blood spatters. Going through the rear gate, Riske showed his two superiors blood traces on its handle.

Ron Phillips and Mark Fuhrman now split up. Phillips took a call on his cellular phone from Keith Bushey, who was one of the top commanders in the LAPD. Bushey's responsibilities extended to fully one-fourth of the whole city and included the Hollywood, Wilshire, and Pacific divisions, as well as West LA. Bushey emphasized to Phillips the importance their department placed on the personal notification of victims' family members. The LAPD had been burnt in the past because the media had gone public with victims' identities prior to this personal notification. A short while later, Phillips also received word from his own chief of detectives that the case would be investigated by the robbery/homicide division, a command unit more suited to handle high profile cases. The West LA unit was now officially off the case.

Thus, Detective Mark Fuhrman's role as lead detective was over after less than an hour. Before and after being notified of this fact, Fuhrman had sat down on a couch in the condominium's living room where he wrote some initial notes on what he had observed. This is sound police practice. Whatever a person first sees and absorbs at a crime scene, such as room temperature, odors, and other transient and patterned evidence, should be correctly recorded. These essentials also include the date, time, and names of all those involved. The initial recorded condition of the evidence at the crime scene may prove as thorough as any the investigator will ever find in a case. Writing down the most minute details can both provide investigative leads and refresh the memory later on. It's also important to start exploring the investigative avenues which the observed facts present. In Fuhrman's case, he made a notation of "possible GSW," meaning that the victims might have suffered gunshot wounds. Fuhrman should not have sat on the couch in the condo. Also, he omitted some very important facts. He did not mention anything about the ice cream, the shoeprints, and the body conditions. After being relieved of the case's primary responsibility, Fuhrman and Phillips mostly waited for the robbery/homicide detectives to arrive, and Phillips had to put aside any direct plans for notifying the victims' families. Fuhrman busied himself directing the police photographers, who had arrived at the crime scene.

An hour and a half later, shortly after four in the morning, Detective Phillip Vannatter arrived at Bundy. He was a twenty-five-year LAPD veteran, with fifteen of those years as a detective, and he was a senior member in the robbery/homicide unit. Taking over, Vannatter quickly met with Phillips and Fuhrman for a briefing. Told by Phillips of Bushey's desire to have O. J. Simpson and the other family members notified in person as soon as possible, Vannatter decided to wait, preferring to keep studying the crime scene. A half hour later Tom Lange, another LAPD veteran and Vannatter's partner, arrived. Phillips and Fuhrman were meeting these two detectives for the first time. Permit me, at this point, to inject a word or two on these individuals. During the course of my forty-five-year career, I had lectured to thousands of detectives on forensics and criminal investigation and had become very acquainted with some of them. I knew that the detective is a special breed of professional. All were bright, devoted, and took pride in how they did their work. They would not have been at that crime scene at that hour of the morning, and they would not work days, nights, and weekends on their cases if things were otherwise.

By now Phillips was becoming increasingly nervous about not acting on Bushey's order to personally notify the families and, in particular, O. J. Simpson, of the murders. Vannatter now decided that all four would go to Simpson's residence, wherever that might be. Fuhrman then recalled the 1985 domestic dispute he had found at the couple's home on Rockingham when he'd been a uniformed officer. Also, patrolman Riske had already run a trace on license plates found on the Jeep in the garage and had given Fuhrman the 360 North Rockingham address. This solidified Fuhrman's recollection.

The four detectives used two cars to drive to Rockingham, and they soon found themselves in an extremely upscale neighborhood. Earlier in his career, Vannatter had spent four years assigned to West Los Angeles, and he had never had cause to be on North Rockingham. In the darkness, the police strained to find the Simpson address. They immediately noted that the residents there did not need to park on the streets. But one vehicle stood out for Vannatter, a recent vintage, white Ford Bronco. The Bronco was additionally conspicuous since it seemed to be parked at an angle. However, this fact was never confirmed in any police photos. In fact, police photos show the Bronco was parked in a perfectly straight and normal fashion. The detectives soon saw it had been left directly in front of the Simpson house's address numbers, 360, which were painted on the curb.

Looking from the curbside, the four saw that there were lights on upstairs in the large house, behind the imposing, six-foot brick wall which guarded the property. Vannatter approached the iron gate and pressed the buzzer there. There was no answer. A couple of lights dimly gleamed from inside the house. Two expensive cars sat in the driveway in front. The detectives now took turns ringing the buzzer and still received no response. A plaque proclaimed that the property was protected by Westec, and, by chance, a vehicle marked Westec happened by and the police flagged it down. The driver gave the police O. J. Simpson's phone number. It was about 5:30 now, shortly before the California dawn, and Vannatter called into the house on his cellular phone, only to hear Simpson's voice on the answering machine.

Fuhrman let his three seniors continue their vain attempts to raise someone in the residence. He wandered over to the Bronco and shined his pocket flashlight inside. He saw some papers in the back seat, which were addressed to Simpson. A short while later, Fuhrman called to Vannatter, "I think I've found something on the Bronco." Vannatter came over and Fuhrman showed him a small red stain slightly above the exterior handle on the driver's door and four small red stains at the door's bottom, on the door sill, which looked like smears. Vannatter quickly determined that the stains resembled blood. He then had Fuhrman run the Bronco's license plates, and the owner's name came back as the Hertz Corporation. All four were familiar with O. J. Simpson's employment history with that corporation. Vannatter now stepped aside with Tom Lange, his partner, and the two discussed the situation. They agreed that a criminalist would be needed to start testing the blood-like substances which were visible on the Bronco. However, it could be a substantial period of time before one arrived, even an hour or two. They had left a violent crime scene back at Bundy, and there was no telling what the situation inside the Rockingham estate might be and whether any immediate help was needed there. Vannatter would later testify that he was concerned that someone inside could be in immediate need of assistance. The two returned to Phillips and Fuhrman and said that they would not wait for a search warrant before entering the Rockingham property. This decision would prove to be one of the real bombshells in the O. J. Simpson case. Much like a decision made in the heat of a battlefield, it is impossible for the average observer to appreciate the kinds of pressures of a moment in time like this one. And, even though the evidence later found at the Rockingham residence would be admitted, notwithstanding this decision, the criticism levelled at the LAPD for this move set a tone which would never leave any of the future developments or judicial proceedings.

Mark Fuhrman volunteered to scale the brick wall, which he did, and then opened the gate manually, letting the other three into the grounds. For a few moments, they vainly tried to awaken someone inside by ringing the bell at the front door. Getting no answer, the four walked around to the side of the house, where they saw the estate's three guest cottages. Phillips peered into the window of the first and said he saw someone inside. He then knocked on the door and quickly got a response. A very drowsy Kato Kaelin opened the door and answered that he did not know the whereabouts of O. J. Simpson. Kaelin, almost asleep on his feet, suggested that the police ask the resident in the guest house next door to his, Simpson's daughter, Arnelle.

Leaving Fuhrman with Kaelin, the other three awakened Arnelle Simpson, who said she also did not know where her father was but suggested that they go to the main house to find out. Arnelle asked if Simpson's car was parked outside the Ashford gate, and Vannatter gestured toward the Rockingham entrance where they'd found the Bronco. Using her key, Arnelle then let the detectives into the residence and, after a few moments of indecision, she dialed Cathy Randa, who had been Simpson's personal secretary for many years. O. J. Simpson had taken a late-night flight to Chicago, Randa told Vannatter, after Arnelle had awakened her at her home. He was staying at the Chicago O'Hare Plaza. Simpson was there to appear at a Hertz convention, a visit which was supposed to include playing a round of golf later that day.

At 6:05 A.M., Phillips called the hotel and was put through to

Simpson's room. Introducing himself and choosing his words very carefully, he informed Simpson, "Your ex-wife, Nicole Simpson, has been killed." At this point, Simpson became very distraught, saying, "Oh, my God, Nicole is killed? Oh, my God, she is dead?" Phillips then attempted to calm Simpson and informed him that his two children had been taken to the West Los Angeles police station, a move which Simpson immediately challenged. This drew the explanation that the police did not know where else to take them. Simpson then told Phillips that he would be returning to Los Angeles on the first available flight, ending the conversation. Phillips handed the phone back to Arnelle who suggested to her father that his friend, Al Cowlings, be called to pick up the children at police headquarters. O. J. Simpson's dialogue, itself, would later prove very controversial since he did not ask Phillips how his wife had died and how that might have impacted his children and their being taken to police headquarters. At this time, for the police record, Simpson did not yet know of the two murders.

While this drama was first being played out in the main house, Detective Fuhrman continued to question Kaelin. Looking into his blurry eyes, Fuhrman wondered about his mental condition. To resolve any doubts, Fuhrman took a pen and passed it under Kaelin's eyes, a time-honored police test for determining sobriety. Kato passed and Fuhrman asked the houseguest if anything unusual had occurred on the prior evening. Yes, was Kaelin's answer. About 10:50 or so Sunday evening, he had been chatting on the phone when he'd heard several loud thumps on his bedroom wall behind him, the wall nearest the street. They had come with enough force to shake a painting hanging next to the room's air conditioner, and Kaelin had actually wondered if there would be an earthquake.

Fuhrman quickly finished up with Kaelin and took him to the house, to wait with the other three detectives. Aided by his pocket flashlight, he returned to the cottage and went around to its rear to see what might have caused the banging Kaelin had experienced. Moving slowly in the predawn gray light, Fuhrman found that the dwelling's rear and a tall chain-link Cyclone fence formed a narrow pathway behind the cottages, covered with leaves and twigs. He said he was trying to determine just where Kaelin's bedroom wall would be and had moved about twenty feet down the pathway when he spotted a dark object lying on the ground. Upon closer examination, Fuhrman would later testify, he saw that it was a right-hand leather glove, similar to the glove he had observed on the ground at the Bundy murder scene. Shining his light directly onto this glove, Fuhrman also observed that the glove had no leaves or twigs on it and was covered with a dark substance which seemed sticky, since parts of the glove were adhering to one another. Fuhrman then continued down the pathway, encountering as he moved a short distance farther and for the first time, cobwebbing. He followed along the fencing until he reached the property line, retraced his steps, and joined the others in the main house, where he reported his findings.

Fuhrman's report to Vannatter about seeing a leather glove along the pathway, one which was for the right hand and which appeared to be covered with blood, set the police investigation into overdrive. Normally, when a spouse or an ex-spouse is found murdered, the police automatically suspect the surviving party to the marriage. This is especially true if the victim is female, and particularly if there has been some history of spousal abuse or some other discernible motive. Vannatter now assigned his partner, Detective Tom Lange, to inform Nicole Brown Simpson's next of kin. The veteran Lange knew that the family lived seventy miles away in Orange County. This meant he would be taking the chance that the press would discover her identity and that the family might find out about their tragedy through the media during the hour or so it would take him to drive south to notify them in person. At 6:21 A.M. Lange decided to forgo the LAPD's in-person notification policy, and he phoned the family's home. Nicole's father, Lou Brown, answered Lange's call. He took the news quite calmly. However, Nicole's older sister, Denise, had picked up an upstairs extension and, upon hearing the horrible report, began screaming, "He did it. He finally did it." Lange asked Denise whom she was talking about and she, without hesitation, replied, "O. J." Though inadmissable as hearsay and pure opinion in any court of law, Denise's hysterical response only served to fuel the detectives' suspicions about Simpson.

Still at Rockingham, Vannatter declared that location a secondary crime scene. He then sent the other three detectives back to Bundy and was particularly interested in their making a comparison of the glove at Rockingham which Fuhrman had showed them and the one lying near the two murder victims. He would await the arrival of the criminalist he had requested. The Rockingham house and grounds were now bathed in the southern California early sunlight, and Vannatter used this visibility to make his own investigation. Walking out of the house, he found several drops of what appeared to be blood on the driveway near the two cars parked there. These droplets appeared to be in a line from the Rockingham gate to the house's front entrance. Moving out through the gate, Vannatter went to the Bronco, where he saw what appeared to be blood on the console between the vehicle's two front seats. Peering in from the passenger's side, he also saw more traces on the inside of the driver's door. Vannatter retraced his steps to the house's front door and, entering, he saw three droplets which appeared to be blood in the foyer.

The criminalist, Dennis Fung, arrived at Rockingham at 7:10 A.M. He quickly performed a presumptive test on the red substance found on the Bronco's driver's side door. This test, while not conclusive, showed that the evidence likely was blood. A few minutes later, Fuhrman returned from Bundy to tell Vannatter that the glove at the murder scene was for the left hand and appeared to be a match for the right-hand glove along the Rockingham pathway. Vannatter now decided to formally ask for a search warrant for the Rockingham location. He left Fuhrman and went to the West LA station to write out his request.

Many experienced police detectives develop good working relationships with individual prosecuting attorneys. Vannatter had networked with one prosecutor who had particularly impressed him in work they had done together on a murder case which relied heavily on blood trace evidence. Before he started to write his search warrant affadavit, he decided to call Marcia Clark for her advice on this case.

Vannatter called Clark at home that morning and asked her if she thought he had enough evidence to have the warrant approved. Clark shot back that she thought that he had enough to make an arrest. Clark had only one major question for Vannatter: Who is O. J. Simpson? Thus, Marcia Clark was in on the case and, with her characteristic enthusiasm and work ethic, would find herself in the role of lead prosecutor. Vannatter completed work on his affadavit by late morning. In it he indicated that O. J. Simpson had made an "unexpected" flight to Chicago late the previous evening, an allegation which flatly contradicted what Cathy Randa had told him that dawn. This misstatement would prove a powerful weapon in the defense team's future effort to have all of the evidence found at Rockingham excluded. Toward noon, a magistrate signed Vannatter's search warrant, and he drove back to the Rockingham location to continue his investigation.

Coincidentally, O. J. Simpson's hurried return flight from Chicago was landing at the Los Angeles airport at about noon that day. During this flight his celebrity status meant that other passengers recognized him and one, a friend named Howard Bingham, had chatted with him. Later, Bingham would say he did not notice anything at all unusual about Simpson's demeanor. Simpson's departure for the airport the night before, late Sunday evening, June 12, would prove an important legal battleground in the coming months. And from the prosecution's standpoint, a key witness would emerge who would, with his credibility, play a large role in creating a time window just wide enough for Simpson to have committed both murders and still be back to Rockingham in time to catch his flight to Chicago. However, this time window is extremely narrow. Maybe possible. But just barely.

Allen Park was new to his job as a limousine driver for the Town and Country service. He had been assigned to pick up O. J. Simpson at his home on Rockingham at 10:45 that Sunday night and to drive him to the airport for his 11:45 P.M. flight. Since Simpson would be his first celebrity passenger on his new limo job and he wanted to get it right, Park had decided to get there twenty minutes early. When he pulled up on Rockingham, he saw a largely darkened house, and he eased his vehicle around the corner onto Ashford. He did not, he would later testify, see the white Ford Bronco parked on the street. At about 10:40, Park rang the bell in front of Simpson's Ashford gate and got no response. Next he tried the Rockingham gate's bell and still did not get any response. Park was now worried. Each minute after the quarter hour meant that much less time to get his passenger over the freeways and to the departure areas in time for his flight. Park now used his car's cellular phone and called his boss. He made other calls, one to his mother to chat with her about the problem. Later on, cellular phone records would corroborate his statements. Park kept ringing the bell for the house. Nothing.

Park's nervous boss called him back. The driver could not report any development. A few minutes after that call, Park saw a man emerge briefly from in back of the house and disappear again. This would be Kato Kaelin. Then, in front of the house, an African American man, who was approximately six-feet tall, well built, and who looked to weigh about two hundred pounds walked into the Rockingham front door and disappeared into the house. Lights began to go on inside the house, first downstairs and then upstairs. Park hit the front bell again, and this time O. J. Simpson answered. The gate was then opened. Upon entering the house, Simpson told Park that he had overslept, had just gotten out of the shower, and would be down in a few minutes. Kaelin now reemerged, according to Park, and the three loaded Simpson's bags into the limousine's trunk, although Simpson insisted on handling a small, black duffel bag himself. Park and his passenger left just after eleven, and Park needed to make a right-hand turn. Something on the curb obstructed his view at that time, maybe a vehicle which had not been there when he had pulled up forty-five minutes earlier. But Park was never able to say that this obstruction of his view was a white Ford Bronco. Also, in his initial statement, Park did not mention this obstruction. Only after continual interviewing by police detectives did Park agree that a vehicle had arrived that blocked his view.

On Monday, Simpson arrived at Rockingham just before 1 P.M. The streets in front of his residence were teeming with newspaper

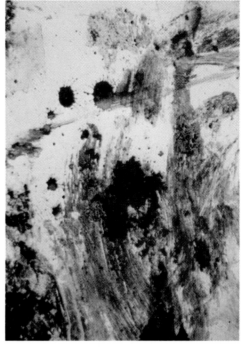

Medium-velocity impact blood spatter and blood smears were found on the spare tire in the Mathison van.

Blood drops were found under soil smears in the Mathison van.

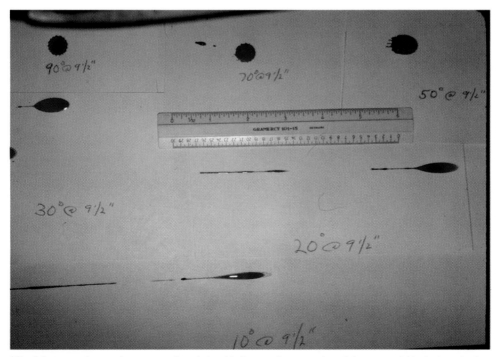

Blood drop experiments demonstrate the relationship between impact angle and shape essential in the investigation of the Mathison case.

Handprints in the Mathison case were found after using blood enhancement reagents.

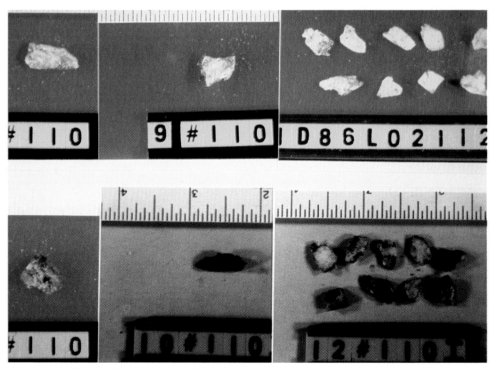

Sixty-nine small bone chips were recovered from the Lake Zoar riverbank in the Woodchipper case.

One of the bone fragments from the Woodchipper case was identified as human calvarium (inner skull) bone.

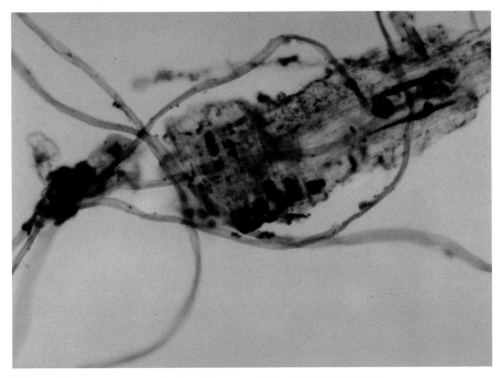

Fibers and tissues were discovered on the chainsaw used in the Woodchipper murder.

A close-up view of the Bundy Drive crime scene in the O. J. Simpson case. Large amounts of bloodstains were seen on the walkway.

The glove found by Mark Fuhrman at the Rockingham Drive crime scene in the O. J. Simpson case.

A pair of torn underpants found on the floor next to the bed in the Shermans' bedroom, with scallop pattern in elastic band visible

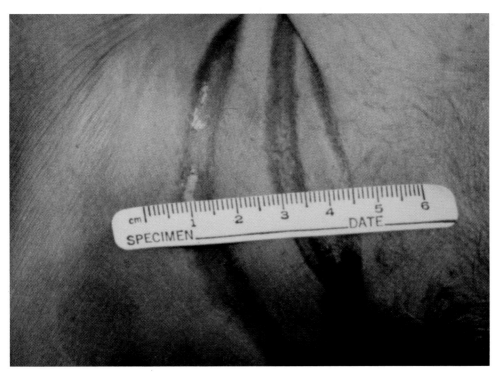

Ellen Sherman died of ligature and manual strangulation. Three parallel strangulation marks were found at autopsy.

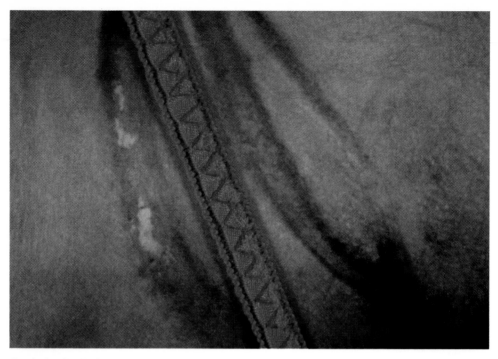

Overlaying the elastic underpants with the ligature marks on Ellen Sherman's neck shows the same pattern and measured features.

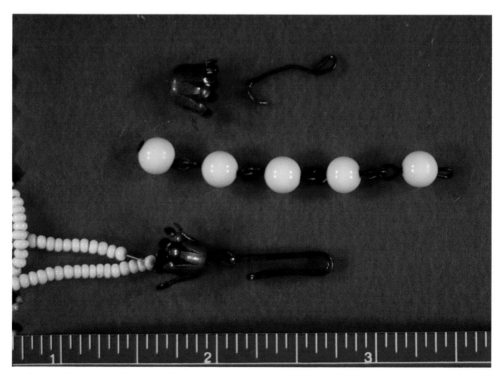

Broken beads from a necklace were found in the bedroom from the Sherman murder scene.

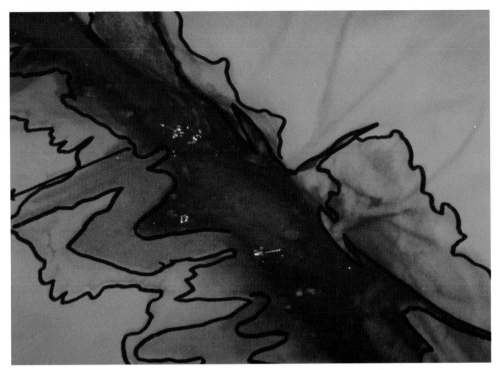

A close-up view of the bloodstain on the MacArthurs' bedsheet.

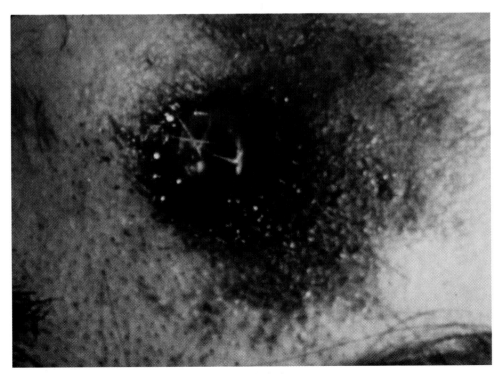

A close-up view of the bullet entrance wound in Pilar MacArthur.

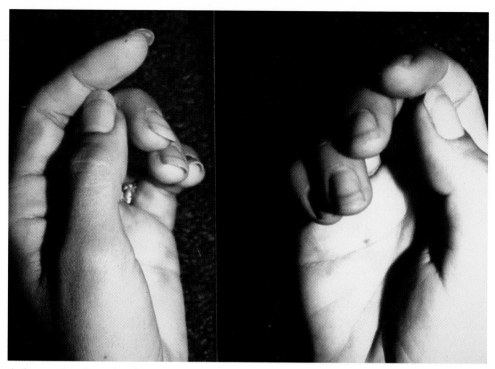

A close-up view shows that Pilar MacArthur's hands have no blood-spatter deposits.

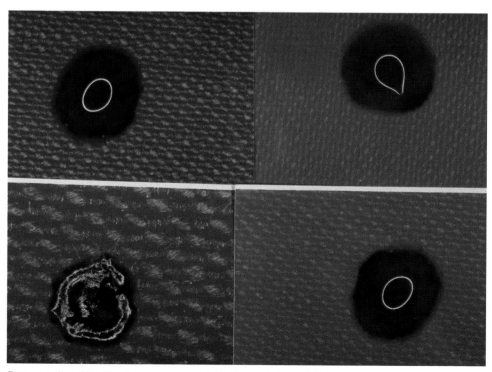

Reconstruction of the MacArthur crime through blood coagulation and drying experiments.

reporters, photographers, and TV news crews. Vannatter was inside the house but had already instructed one uniformed officer, Donald Thompson, to detain Simpson, even to "hook him up," police jargon for handcuffing him. The lead detective made it very clear he did not want anyone else entering the house since his team was in the process of carrying out its search warrant. Later, Vannatter testified under oath that he did not remember being that specific about handcuffs with Thompson, saying he had simply directed the officer to bring Simpson directly to him. The only African American police officer to play any kind of a role in all of this case, the younger Thompson, a nine-year LAPD veteran would, like Patrolman Riske, display a good deal of public relations know-how in the way he carried out what he thought Vannatter had ordered when Simpson arrived home.

Before his return flight, Simpson had phoned ahead from his Chicago hotel room to Howard Weitzman, the criminal defense lawyer who had helped Simpson navigate his way through his 1989 arrest for spousal abuse, and had asked the attorney to meet him at his Rockingham home on his arrival. Joining Weitzman at Rockingham that midday were Cathy Randa, Simpson's secretary; his business lawyer, Skip Taft; and Robert Kardashian, Simpson's long-standing close personal friend and golfing buddy. Walking toward his main gate, Simpson had to wend his way past the media. Simpson left his bags with Kardashian and moved through the gate; police would not allow any of the others to go in. Brad Roberts, Mark Fuhrman's partner, was the first police detective Simpson would talk to, and, when told about a blood trail being found which led to his front door, Simpson, according to Roberts, began to hyperventilate and muttered, "Oh, man. Oh, man. Oh, man."

As Simpson got to his front door, Patrolman Thompson placed his hand on him to detain him. However, instead of putting cuffs on Simpson in full view of the media, Thompson led him to a less-exposed part of the yard, near an elaborate playset put there for the children. Away from the media's eyes, Thompson handcuffed Simpson, placing his hands behind his back. However, one particularly tall and creative TV cameraman, Ron Edwards of KCOP, was able to place his camera on top of the exterior wall and record Thompson's actions. This dramatic footage was broadcast to millions of Americans. O. J. Simpson had not yet been charged with anything and his being handcuffed so preemptorily was seen by many African Americans as unfair, an act of racial profiling.

Weitzman was quickly allowed to enter the Rockingham grounds and joined Vannatter and his client in the side play yard. Weitzman asked the detective to remove the cuffs, which Vannatter promptly did. In the process of uncuffing Simpson, Vannatter noticed a bandage on the middle finger of Simpson's left hand, riveting his attention because of the blood-drop evidence to the left of the footprints at the Bundy crime scene. Once freed, Simpson quickly assented to immediate questioning by the police at the robbery/homicide unit's offices at the LAPD's central headquarters in downtown Los Angeles. Once there, after the twenty-minute trip, Weitzman asked to talk privately with his client. When Simpson and Weitzman emerged, the lawyer told Vannatter and Lange that Simpson preferred to talk to them without his attorney being present. Weitzman had only one request: That the questions and answers be completely recorded, which was agreeable to the police, who quickly provided a tape recorder.

The thirty-two-minute question-and-answer session of Simpson by the two detectives would prove doubly controversial. First, O. J. Simpson's friends and even some acquaintances of his rose as one to protest the fact that Howard Weitzman had ever agreed to allow his client to enter a police interview room under the circumstances of his wife's murder without the benefit of his lawyer being present. No matter that Simpson, himself, had insisted that this be the case. Vannatter had started the questioning by reading Simpson his Miranda rights, which advised him that he could remain silent if he so chose, that whatever he did say could be used against him in a court of law, and that he had the right to have a lawyer present. The sum total of all of this criticism, broadcast over the media, soon led to Weitzman's being dropped and being replaced as defense counsel by Robert Shapiro.

Weitzman's being discharged as Simpson's defense counsel over this police interview, the only time investigators would ever question Simpson, can be considered paradoxical. That's because a glimpse at the session's transcript shows that the questions posed by the two detectives proved ineffective. During that thirty-two minutes, O. J. Simpson gave contrasting accounts of how he had sustained the cut on the finger of his left hand, mumbling at one point that he had cut it when he had hurled a hotel water glass against his bathroom's wall after being notified of his ex-wife's death. (Subsequently, police found a broken glass in the bathroom sink of Simpson's Chicago hotel room. Whether any tests for blood were taken there and what those results may have been has never become known.) Next he said that the cut had been sustained at an earlier time and, finally, he said he could not remember exactly how the cut had occurred. Simpson was also allowed to gloss over his 1989 spousal abuse arrest and the couple's angry and extensive history of marital discord. Simpson said, at one point, "I was never really arrested," a statement which went unchallenged. Simpson's account of what he was doing during the later evening hours when the murders actually occurred was equally vague. He mentioned that earlier that evening he was at his daughter's dance recital, had somehow left to get flowers for Sydney, and that he had declined an invitation from the Brown family to join them all for dinner at the Mezzaluna. When told by Vannatter that the police had found blood inside the Bronco, Simpson volunteered to have his blood tested, as well as be photographed and fingerprinted. At a final point, the two detectives pointed out to Simpson that they were questioning him because he was Nicole's ex-husband. He responded by saying, "I know that I'm the number one target."

When the interview was completed, Simpson and his two lawyers left and returned to his home on Rockingham, where dozens of police were still conducting their search and where, outside the gates, the media presence was taking on a circus atmosphere. The case, it was soon obvious, was exploding into international proportions. Word of the police interview, without the advice of counsel, soon spread, and the major networks had already begun bringing in cadres of their own legal analysts to review matters on the air. Without exception, these experts criticized the decision to let Simpson be questioned without his lawyer at his side. The cast of characters who would take center stage in this drama, some of extreme importance, was lengthening. Some were getting into the action through a different role than the one they would eventually play. One of the first of the legal analysts to go on television and criticize the decision to let Simpson go into his questioning alone was a brilliant and charismatic African American attorney who had become prominent in southern California for his work defending minorities and their civil rights. He is a man whom I would work with and would get to know well and one whom I admire greatly, Johnnie Cochran.

On the prosecution side of the equation, Marcia Clark's entry into the case, through Vannatter's chance early morning phone call, would prove equally portentous. Clark, who lived in nearby Glendale, was an up-and-coming prosecutor in the vast Los Angeles District Attorney's office. Known as a workaholic who had made a hobby out of studying criminal cases, Clark had proven herself a scrappy, quick-witted, and resourceful litigator. The daughter of parents who were born in what is now Israel, Clark, forty-one, was twice divorced and had two small children, boys aged three and five. Gordon Clark, the boys' father and a computer programmer, shared custody of the children. Marcia Clark, given the head start Vannatter's call had provided her, worked hard to expand her role in the case, an assignment which seemed tailored for her list of strengths. Clark would naturally be working under Bill Hodgman, also forty-one, who was director of operations in the Los Angeles District Attorney's office. Hodgman, as boss of the criminal division, was an excellent lawyer who had compassion and a solid grasp of human nature. He would seem the ideal balance for Clark's impassioned style. Later, Christopher Darden, the thirty-eight-year-old African American son of a shipyard worker from Richmond in the Oakland area, would also become a key player on the prosecution team.

By now Hodgman and Clark were acting as the prosecution's

cocounsel. Clark was a key player in the decision, reached by prosecutor concensus on the evening of Thursday, June 16, to move ahead and arrest O. J. Simpson the next day. Since the initial call from Vannatter, Clark and the rest of the team had worked tirelessly to assess the case's evidence, particularly the blood evidence. LAPD Criminalist Collin Yamauchi was working with a blood sample provided by Simpson, which had been drawn shortly after his Monday afternoon questioning. The LAPD's nurse then gave the blood vial to Vannatter, who placed the sample in his back pants pocket and then finally drove the twenty miles to the Bundy scene, where he then walked around the crime venue, until he gave this crucial evidence to Fung. Fung would then put the blood in the back of his van for the remainder of the day and eventually pass it on to Yamauchi, hours later, when it was at last properly stored.

Vannatter could have simply walked to the serology section of the LAPD's crime lab at the central police complex, and, after it had been properly identified, should have had Simpson's blood placed in a properly secured refrigerator for storage. This was a very serious mistake, one which led directly to an even bigger mistake. Any physical evidence used in court should meet both legal and scientific requirements. When Vannatter took the defendant's blood back to the crime scene, he may not only have caused deterioration and compromised a blood sample, but he could also have set off a devastating legal problem with the chain-of-custody issues pertaining to evidence handling.

Yamauchi's preliminary tests of this blood sample were conducted that Tuesday and Wednesday. Because of the importance of this case, Yamauchi's superiors decided to forgo the ABO blood-typing tests (see the Woodchipper chapter for a full discussion of this technique) and directed him to perform tests using DQA, a simplified form of DNA (deoxyribonucleic acid) testing. (DNA testing will be discussed at the end of this chapter.) This meant the breakdown of the samples into a possible twenty-one types, instead of the four types of blood groups which result from the ABO testing. Yamauchi found that the blood from the Bundy pathway matched Simpson's, meaning that only about 7 percent of the population could have left those blood traces. Also, his tests of the blood on the right-hand glove found behind Kato Kaelin's guest house matched a combination of O. J. Simpson's, Ron Goldman's, and Nicole Simpson's. These findings were reported to the prosecutor's office, which led to the Friday warrant for Simpson's arrest. It would, of course, be weeks later that the defense team would discover that these critical blood identification tests had been performed on a blood sample taken from Simpson which could have been tainted.

As I examined the Bundy crime scene, I would become aware that Vannatter's lapse with the Simpson blood sample was not the only police miscue. The entire Bundy location seemed to have been subjected to unprofessional evidence treatment. To permit access to the bodies, the technicians and police there had used bath towels to mop up large quantities of the blood which covered the entranceway. They had also deposited gloves, towels, and other materials on Ron Goldman's body. These were huge mistakes. Even though photographs would show the extent and configurations of this blood evidence, the forensics team should not have been in so great a rush to eradicate this crucial blood evidence. Crime scene investigators have to be certain that all relevant samples of this blood evidence have been collected, properly documented, and stored in a refrigerator. Later, a videotape broadcast by a local TV station showed police detectives and forensic technicians walking through and stepping on the blood evidence, some without any of the required coverings and gloves, and debris thrown on top of a victim's body. Also, while detectives searching the master bedroom in the Rockingham location came across a pair of men's socks on the carpet at the foot of the bed, there was no close-up photographic documentation taken before they collected this evidence. Six weeks later, the LAPD would claim to find Simpson's blood type on both socks and Nicole's blood on one of the socks. There is no mention in the original crime scene police notes of whether the blood was present or on the overall condition of these socks. These socks and this blood evidence would also become another critical battleground, as well as another example of the shoddy investigative work performed by some of the LAPD detectives.

Arriving in Los Angeles four days after the murders, my initial examination of the Bundy scene had to rely primarily on police crime scene photographs. What I saw in these was most revealing to me. Not in terms of what was collected and later tested, but because of what evidence they had failed to collect and test. There were many unexplained blood droplets on Nicole Brown Simpson's body. The victim had been wearing a light-textured dress that evening, with her back exposed. As she lay face down on the ground in front of the steps to her condo's entrance, several low-velocity, vertical blood droplets had deposited on her back. The origin of these blood droplets was clearly from an area directly above the victim. (See the Mathison Chapter for a discussion of analyzing the location of a blood source by determining the shape and pattern of blood drops.) These vertical blood drops were overlooked and ignored. Once the victim's body was placed in a body bag, that blood evidence would be obliterated. Subsequently, her body was washed by the medical examiner's office, and all the blood evidence was lost. What could be more revealing as to the DNA type of an assailant, one who was killing the victim with a knife, than matching the DNA type of those blood drops?

To place this critical oversight in perspective, let me reiterate how those blood droplets had gotten onto the victim's back: They had landed from the top downward. These blood droplets were later washed from Nicole Simpson's back at the Los Angeles morgue. Testing this blood could have revealed the identity of the murderer or, perhaps, someone assisting the assailant. If this blood had been identified with thorough DNA analysis as O. J. Simpson's, the case would have been closed. If the blood had not been similarly established as Simpson's, then the entire case would have had to move in a different direction. Throughout this lengthy investigation and trial, both sides put forward possible scenarios. Some of these were not, I will say kindly, grounded in logic. The prosecution later had to respond to criticism because it did not collect and test these blood droplets. Some on the prosecution team even tried to explain that the blood drops came from the Akita's wagging tail. Several LAPD officers at the scene reported that they did not see any blood on the Akita's fur.

I must add here that I do not take any pleasure in reporting this grievous oversight. Someone, more likely than not, standing directly over Nicole Simpson's body had deposited blood drops and had to be involved in the killings. It is equally sad for me to report that the prosecution claimed that Nicole Brown Simpson's killer had applied his foot to her back, as indicated by patterns resembling a footprint. But subsequently, Dr. Baden was able to point out that those patterns were actually patterns caused by lividity. (Lividity is a reddish pattern of settled red blood cells in the blood vessels.) Ron Goldman's body did not yield any similar evidence. Goldman may have walked into the crime scene as the first murder was taking place and found himself trapped by the assailant (or assailants) in the entryway, a killing ground surrounded by the white metal fence. Goldman was savagely stabbed twenty-eight times, and some of these wounds on his arms and hands were classified as defensive wounds. An able-bodied and large young man, Goldman had put up a good fight in the last few minutes of his life. The bloodstain patterns found on his blue jeans also confirm this. But the prosecution insisted that this killing was quick and would, therefore, fit into the time window they were already attempting to establish for the crimes. The leather glove and knit ski cap found in the entryway attested to that.

After some considerable negotiation, the prosecution finally agreed to allow us to examine the Bundy scene. However, we were prohibited the use of any chemicals or instruments for testing, and our examination had to be concluded within ten minutes since the police had not finished their examination. We did find evidence that I considered critical: Several shoeprints which were distinctly different in style and size from the other shoeprint evidence found on the Bundy grounds. These images, which prosecutors later claimed were a marking in the concrete surface of the walkway, were never adequately (chemically) analyzed by the prosecution's forensics team and could have been caused by a second assailant. Forensic experts at the FBI meticulously studied the shoeprints which led down the walkway. These shoeprints were identified as size twelve and made by Bruno

Magli. Similar attention should have been paid to this second type of shoeprint. Establishing the source of those second prints could also have changed the direction of the investigation into these murders.

After this one brief visit to the Bundy crime scene, we then went to the Rockingham residence to conduct our scene analysis. Naturally, we were especially interested in the area where the second leather glove had been found. In particular, we looked at the space behind Kato Kaelin's residence where he said he'd heard the loud thumps the night of the killings. We inspected the fence behind the guest house from the street side and tried to comprehend how an individual, even a gifted athlete in great shape, could have scaled the cyclone fencing there, with its additional thick covering of vegetation on top of the fence, and then vault over this fence and land behind Kaelin's residence without damaging any of the vegetation. O. J. Simpson was once a very great athlete. However, by the time he left football, his body, particularly his knees and legs, showed the effects of a very savage beating for which he'd undergone several operations. When Simpson simply walks down the street, he visibly allows for the chronic pain in his knees and legs. Even in his prime, however,

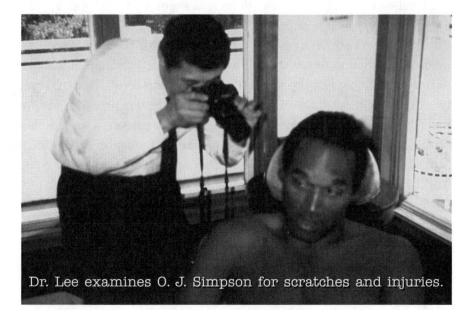

Dr. Lee examines O. J. Simpson for scratches and injuries.

Simpson would not have been able to vault that fence. As I said as I made my investigation, "Only a helicopter or a Kung Fu master from a movie could make that leap."

We reported our preliminary findings and observations to Robert Shapiro and the rest of the defense team. Soon, the media started to call the defense, a "dream team," a term which came out of Olympic basketball. This kind of thinking only added to the pop-culture atmosphere the Simpson case generated. Those of us in the meeting room were more bemused by this than anything. Besides Dr. Michael Baden, Shapiro had reached out to Alan Dershowitz, the renowned Harvard law professor and brilliant lawyer. F. Lee Bailey, who had successfully fought for a new trial and ultimately won the exoneration of Dr. Sam Sheppard, also came on board. Bailey, throughout the forty-plus years of his career, has established himself as peerless in the art of cross-examination. Also joining the team was Bob Blasier, a Harvard graduate, a former assistant district attorney, and a superb organizer. I have already mentioned Johnnie L. Cochran and my immense respect for him. Likewise, I found Gerald F. Uelman, the dean of the Santa Clara University Law School, a very warm-hearted individual and an extremely competent attorney, though his quiet manner belied his aggressive approach to defending his client.

Two New York attorneys also came on board, both passionate in their determination to see that all blood evidence admitted in a court of law be accurate and properly collected and preserved. One of these two, Barry Scheck, is a world-renowned DNA legal expert who was in his mid-forties at the time of the trial, but a person who has the wisdom of a much older man. A professor at the Benjamin N. Cardozo School of Law in Manhattan, Scheck also works as the head of a New York legal organization, the Innocence Project, which is dedicated to freeing innocent individuals who have been wrongly convicted. Peter Neufeld, Scheck's associate at the law school and in the Innocence Project, also lent his considerable talent and dedication to the case. Considering the importance that DNA and other forms of blood evidence would play in this case, it's not surprising that Scheck, Neufeld, and I were to work very closely together over the course of many hours and nights during the next year. There were other very talented lawyers on the defense team, such as Carl Douglas and Shawn Chapman, and we were supported by an excellent team of investigators and legal assistants.

To deal with the scientific demands of the case, the defense team also consisted of the following: Herb MacDonald, a world-renowned blood pattern expert, considered by many as the father of bloodstain analysis in the United States; Dr. Barbara Wolf, an excellent forensic pathologist, whose post is at the Albany Medical Center and whose energy and keen observations created a new dimension of excellence for the defense; Dr. Edward Black, a world-renowned forensic DNA expert, who brought with him excellent laboratory skills and theoretical experience; Chuck Morton, a renowned scientist and trace evidence expert, whose knowledge and experience in hair and fiber analysis added appreciably to the overall effort; and Larry Ragel, former lab director for Orange County Forensic Lab and excellent crime scene expert.

This defense team was not setting to work in a vacuum. We were faced with what seemed a mountain of forensic, medical, time-line, and factual data which we had to sort out and place in perspective. We also had become aware that our work would get a lot of attention. The world's populace had responded to the initial reports of the murders and the evidence which had been found. Public interest and media coverage seemed to create a firestorm of interest, one that almost seemed a national obsession. The following weekend, *Time* magazine and *Newsweek* both printed O. J. Simpson's frowning police mug shot on their covers. But *Time* took the extra step of having an artist touch up Simpson's somber face, creating a scowling effect. This caused an uproar, one that was not confined to the African American community. In addition, the television footage of Simpson being handcuffed, even by an African American officer, only fueled this outrage. Polls quickly began to show a deep division across the land in how the two dominant American races, black and white, saw this crime. The race card,

as it later became known, was playing itself and was not the manipu-
lation of some sinister force. Public relations had thus been established, early on, as a critical part of how this case would be handled.
Intitial polls showed that a majority of Americans, 60 percent, still felt
Simpson was innocent.

The prosecution had one enormous advantage, however: the fact
that the Simpson case would go to a grand jury in the Los Angeles court
building on Friday, June 17. This legal body, made up of a panel of
twenty-four private citizens, would hear the barest basics of the prosecution's case against Simpson. The accused would not be present, nor
would his lawyers, so the defense could not cross-examine any of the
witnesses. There would be no presiding judge. Led by Marcia Clark,
the prosecution would have a field day, since their side did not have to
present all of its evidence, and thus be pinned down to a specific
strategy. Whatever it took to get an indictment against Simpson for the
two murders was all Clark and her colleagues would have to put forward. This forum was by far the best route to take for the prosecution
to put the defendant on trial. The alternative would be a preliminary
hearing, a much more balanced courtroom proceeding, one where the
defense could cross-examine prosecution witnesses and better protect
O. J. Simpson, all under the watchful eye of a judge. In such a contested
hearing, the prosecution would have to commit itself to certain legal
strategies, ones it would have to live with for the duration of the trial.

The grand jury proceedings moved ahead for several days. One
day's proceedings actually saw Marcia Clark completely discredit one
of her witnesses, a young woman who claimed to have seen O. J.
Simpson driving his white Bronco erratically at about 10:30 that
Sunday night, speeding from the direction of Bundy toward Rockingham. Clark dropped her because the young woman had accepted
$7,600 for interviews on a tabloid television show and a newspaper.
However, this strange maneuver would look like a speed bump in the
prosecution's path compared to what resulted when someone in the
Los Angeles Attorney's office, on Wednesday, June 22, leaked a tape
of Nicole Brown Simpson's two, rapid-fire, hysterical 911 phone calls

in October of 1993. The sounds of panic and terror in Nicole's voice during these calls for police riveted listeners around the country. Opinion polls quickly established that the airing of these tapes had switched the 60 percent innocent rating the general public had given Simpson to 60 percent who thought him guilty.

The defense instantly saw this and counterattacked, charging that the release of these tapes had poisoned the grand jurors. Working from San Jose, Gerland Uelman collaborated with Alan Dershowitz in Israel, where he was on business, to craft a motion (the first of hundreds they would file) that the grand jury be dismissed and that the proceedings be immediately turned over to a preliminary hearing. At the least, they asked, the defense ought to be allowed to question the grand jurors on what they'd already heard on the case. Gil Garcetti, the Los Angeles district attorney, an elected official, had added to the furor by publicly opining that Simpson could confess and go for manslaughter. The presiding judge conducted his own private investigation of the grand jurors and found that several had, indeed, heard the 911 tapes. By now, even the prosecution was wavering, and they filed their own motion to disband the grand jury and go the preliminary-hearing route. The Judge agreed and the preliminary hearing would start four days later, on Tuesday, June 28. The defense had caught a break. Race and public opinion were now in the forefront of a legal proceeding which should not, by definition, be influenced by those considerations. There is an axiom in the law that most pretrial publicity works for the prosecution and to the defendant's disadvantage. This was one time when the other side's quick score would backfire.

Since this trial was taking on such huge proportions, average citizens in the Los Angeles area were constantly calling in reports to both the prosecution and defense about what they might have seen or heard during the days leading up to the murders. Occasionally, one of these leads would amount to something. The owner of a downtown Los Angeles store, Ross Cutlery, contacted the prosecution and reported that O. J. Simpson had been in his shop a few weeks before the crimes and had bought a pricey folding, Stiletto knife. Police presented the same kind of knife to Dr. Irwin Golden, the Los Angeles deputy coroner, who had performed the autopsies on Nicole Brown Simpson and Ronald Goldman. Dr. Golden indicated that there were possibly two knives used in these murders. He then rendered an opinion that this type of knife was, indeed, the murder weapon.

During the preliminary hearing, Detective Tom Lange had to admit that the coroner's office was not contacted for ten hours after the murders. The coroner's office mislabeled fluid from Nicole Simpson's body, discarded her stomach contents, and Dr. Golden changed his estimated time of death for both victims, finally testifying that 75 percent of his forensic findings placed the times of death after 11 P.M., a blow to the prosecution's 10:15 P.M. time-of-death theory. In another blow to the prosecution, Dr. Golden rendered his opinion that two different weapons could have stabbed the victims to death, based on contrasts he'd found in the knife wounds. Dr. Baden had noted that there were a total of sixteen mistakes. Once she had learned of the knife purchased by O. J. Simpson, Marcia Clark quickly moved to demand a second search warrant of Simpson's Rockingham home. The police again searched the premises and still found no knife. Of course, reports about this possible prosecution breakthrough had reached the media, and this is what dominated the news as the Thursday, June 30 opening of the preliminary hearing arrived.

Gerald Uelman was able to get this latest firestorm under control. Simpson had told Uelman exactly where in his house Uelman could find the knife he'd bought and never used. Uelman then went to the Rockingham master bedroom, looked into shelves which were behind a pair of mirrored doors, and saw the knife in its original box, exactly where O. J. Simpson had said it would be. The knife did not appear to have ever been used, as Simpson had said. This discovery, of course, had placed Uelman in a very delicate position since he was in danger of being declared as a witness, should he actually touch the knife. Dean Uelman, as I have previously noted, is a very experienced and very bright lawyer and thus he would handle this whole situation superbly. The morning the hearing was to start, Robert Shapiro and

Uelman approached the superior court judge in the Los Angeles court who handled miscellaneous matters, explained their dilemma to him, and told him where the knife was still located. This judge then decided to appoint a jurist as a legal master, a sort of impartial referee, who would take custody of the knife.

Retired superior court Judge Delbert Wong filled this role. When all these court matters were taking place, I was in Seattle attending an American Academy of Forensic Science (AAFS) annual meeting and had just given a speech there. I received an urgent phone call that informed me that I had been asked by the court to examine the knife to determine if it bore any evidence of having been used, which would be contrary to what Simpson had said. Of course, the prosecution was informed of the judge's decision to ask me to perform the tests for the court. Neither the prosecution nor the defense objected to my being named as the court-appointed expert, a fact which gratified me. The object of scientific investigation is to find the facts and the truth, no matter where this search leads. I flew to Los Angeles and began my examination of the "mystery envelope" right away. I tested the knife thoroughly and found it in pristine condition, even with the price tag still pasted on it. There was no blood, tissue, or hair found on it. I also processed the knife using the cyanoacrylate-fuming method (there is a discussion of this technique for developing fingerprints at the end of this chapter) and found fourteen latent fingerprints on it. Neither side would ever question these findings. Judge Wong then placed the knife back in a brown manila envelope, which he then sealed with evidence tape and delivered to Judge Kathleen Kennedy-Powell, who would be presiding at the preliminary hearing. This "mystery envelope" was placed on the bench in full view of the millions watching the proceedings on live television around the world. The whole thing played like a Perry Mason episode, and this "mystery envelope" would conveniently provide the climactic ending. Only real life does not work that way. Once apprised of the fact that the knife had never been used, the prosecution dropped the subject like the red herring it had all turned out to be, and both sides proceeded with the hearing. I did not mention the name of the judge who had appointed Judge Wong as the special master. His name was Judge Lance Ito, an individual who would become a critical player in the coming trial.

Let me add some footnotes to this episode. First, the contents of the "mystery envelope" were never revealed until the end of the trial. Second, the knife's being in pristine condition was never leaked to the media, a rarity for this trial. Third, the corrupting influence of money on the pool of potential witnesses was again felt when word of the knife's existence came to light. A salesman at the cutlery store had accepted $12,000 from a supermarket tabloid for his story. This would badly impeach anything he would have to say. I was contacted by numerous TV and print representatives to reveal the contents of the "mystery envelope." The tabloids initially even offered me $50,000, a sum they raised to $100,000, for a photo of the contents. Not to preach, but my own professional standards and ethics are not something that money can buy. Finally, the tone of the entire trial was set during this first hearing, particularly during argument about the "mystery envelope." The prosecution and the defense exchanged fiery statements, some very personal, and this kind of bitter dialogue would dominate the proceedings for the next fifteen months. This made for many dramatic scenes, some even about the racial origins of respective counsel, and almost all of these were caught on live network television. Indeed, the American public would view 115 days of this coverage. But this personal rancor did not, in my opinion, best serve the cause of justice. True, our entire legal system is driven by human beings who have deep feelings about their adversarial roles. In the final analysis, I feel, this courtroom acrimony made the reserved and professional manner of Alan Dershowitz, Barry Scheck, Peter Neufeld, Gerry Uelman, and some others stand out in a very positive way.

At this point I would like to describe briefly some of the forensic ground that I was covering in my analysis of this case. (Again, I remind the reader that DNA analysis will be presented at the end of this chapter.) Many of the blood samples sent out for DNA analysis came back as "inconclusive." Much of this had to do with the collection and handling of the blood evidence: Blood samples sitting in a hot van for hours, blood samples which were not properly stored. Blood drops should be collected by transferring blood onto a moistened cotton swab. These blood swabs should then be thoroughly air-dried before being packaged and sealed. Otherwise, bacteria and fungi will consume the sample. The LAPD crime scene technicians collected the blood by transferring the blood onto pieces of cotton swatches. I found impressions of bloodstains on the paper containers (called "paper bindles") in which the blood swatches were kept, proving that these samples had not been dried before being packaged. This represented foolproof evidence that the swift-drying process had not been carried out. Especially troubling was the fact that some of the bloodstains on the bindles could not match the shape of the swatch. These findings also became an issue during the trial.

At the preliminary hearing, the entire tone of the trial to come was established during argument on the prosecution's request to obtain hair samples from O. J. Simpson to compare with hair from the ski cap found at the Bundy scene. With Shapiro arguing for the defense and quoting me, he declared that three hair samples from each side would be sufficient. This amount would be more than adequate for the microscopic comparisons that Marcia Clark argued her side wanted to do. However, the defense reasoned that the prosecution had other purposes in mind. Judge Kennedy-Powell told the court she was prepared to order a total of ten hair samples. This would have been an adequate number. However, Marcia Clark pressed on, introducing her own expert, who proved, under Shapiro's cross-examination, to only have performed administrative duties for the last several years, instead of keeping current in a laboratory in the rapidly changing field of forensics. After much acrimonious debate and considerable time, the judge finally upped the number of hair samples "to at least forty but no more than one hundred."

More themes for the coming trial were set during the preliminary hearing. Detective Vannatter testified that he had asked Mark Fuhrman to leave the Bundy crime scene and accompany him to Rockingham to provide assistance. Fuhrman, however, then testified that he'd been included by Vannatter since he "didn't know the area," and that Fuhrman should "lead us up there." Even more critically, Fuhrman testified that he had found the white Ford Bronco parked "in a very haphazard manner," with its rear and front a foot out of line. Gerald Uelman would point to photos taken two hours later, after detectives had arrived at Rockingham, which showed the Bronco parked normally. Fuhrman, whose history for racist behavior would later surface and figure prominently in the coming trial, also testified that he had seen a set of stains on the door on the driver's side, consisting of "three or four lines, red-stained lines" at the doorsill window. A demonstration later showed clearly that the surface that these stains were reportedly on was not visible when the Bronco's door was closed. Seeing those stains, Fuhrman said, prompted him to look into the vehicle's interior, with the aid of his flashlight.

Much of the preliminary hearing's six days of testimony from its twenty-one prosecution witnesses and its debate orbited around these kinds of issues. One critical argument would be about probable cause and whether Vannatter and the three other detectives had a right to enter and search O. J. Simpson's property, including the Bronco, without first obtaining a search warrant. Uelman crafted a scholarly and excellent motion to dismiss the case. A ruling against this search would have meant that all of the evidence found at Rockingham that Monday morning would have been declared inadmissable. The fourth amendment of the Constitution provides this "due process" protection. Judge Kennedy-Powell would hear this debate and would decline making this critical procedural ruling, forwarding that decision to the ultimate trial judge, Lance Ito. Judge Ito would ultimately rule for the prosecution, thus admitting the evidence, holding that the police were entitled to enter those grounds because of the crimes at the Bundy scene, the blood trace evidence at Rockingham, and their stated desire to protect possible injured persons at the Rockingham scene.

The defense lost this particular showdown, and on July 8 Judge Kennedy-Powell would order O. J. Simpson arraigned on the two murder charges. On July 18, Johnnie Cochran joined the defense team, and his impact would make a profound difference. At Simpson's arraignment on July 22, Simpson would offer his plea this way: "Absolutely 100 percent not guilty." During the preliminary hearing the critical battle lines had been drawn for the overall trial to come. The defense now had to go to work and attack the prosecution's case at its point of maximum vulnerability: eyewitness statements and physical evidence. Especially the blood evidence, how it had been collected, how it had been contaminated, and whether this blood evidence had been the subject of tampering. Did the mistreatment of the blood evidence include any misconduct? Put another way, did some person or persons, in their zeal to convict O. J. Simpson, tamper with the blood evidence and plant the defendant's blood at several critical locations? Six months would roll by and the defense team would work night and day, following up all possible leads, to be prepared for the trial when the first gavel fell in January 1995.

THE SIMPSON TRIAL

Largely because O. J. Simpson did not keep to the negotiated surrender schedule on June 17, he was denied bail and would remain in a lockup in the Los Angeles Criminal Courts building. This was one major factor in the defense team's efforts to bring this case to trial as soon as possible. During the time between the preliminary hearing and the start of the trial, I had been flying cross-country on a few weekends to examine the forensic evidence. When I was home in Connecticut, I used weekends for the Simpson case since I had a number of other cases to work on to fulfill my responsibilities as director of the forensics laboratory for the Connecticut State Police. While in Los Angeles, I worked either in the LAPD crime lab or in other independent laboratories to reexamine the earlier pieces of evidence. (I want to take this opportunity to thank the many Los Angeles crime lab scientists for their courtesy and assistance.) In the earlier stages of this work, we generally met at Robert Shapiro's offices, but later we moved our meetings to Johnnie Cochran's offices. The defense team would work long into the evenings, and we would send out for meals regularly. Much has been written about how the team's members got along with one another. Or, rather, didn't get along. For my part, I liked the entire group and found the interplay of so much legal and scientific talent very fascinating. I've already discussed the contrast in styles each of these talented individuals represented. Of course, since I was specifically dealing with scientific evidence, I was able to move straight ahead with my findings. All the team members were very honest and highly respected by their peers in the legal and scientific communities.

When the trial actually started in earnest on January 24, Judge Lance Ito was selected to preside. The bespectacled and bearded Judge Ito would prove a meticulous jurist, one who always seemed to work very hard to please both sides. Early on, Judge Ito had permitted the proceedings to be televised live, and this added an enormous dimension to public interest in the trial. One network, PBS, made the decision to forgo the attempt to cover the trial day by day and to present only its highlights from time to time. They seemed to be the only ones to do this. The television cameras caused a major disturbance in the first few days of the trial when one of the three courtroom cameras inadvertently and very briefly presented the face of one of the alternate jurors. The television producers themselves brought this lapse to the judge's attention. This deeply troubled Judge Ito, and he considered banning the cameras but the next day decided to continue to permit the live telecasting. This problem did not reoccur, and I often wonder whether the cameras' presence in court were a help or a hindrance in seeking justice in this case.

Much has been said and written about the racial makeup of the jury which was sworn in to try the case. This is another area of the proceedings about which I do not want to express an opinion. Suffice it to say, reflecting the racial makeup of the population of the downtown Los Angeles area, the twelve jurors and twelve alternates were predominantly African American. The exact racial makeup of the original twelve jurors was: nine African American members, eight of whom were female; two Caucasian females; and one man of Hispanic origin. Of the twenty-four original jurors and alternates, the count was: fifteen African Americans, six whites, and three Hispanics.

Before the trial would be completed, ten alternates would move into the regular jurors' box. Five of the original twelve had reported that either they or a family member had experienced some negative involvement with law enforcement. Two of the original twelve had college degrees. Not one juror read a newspaper regularly. And nine thought that O. J. Simpson was less likely to have murdered his ex-wife and Ron Goldman because he had excelled in football. Both the prosecution and defense counsels said they were pleased with the makeup of this jury. The twenty-four jurors and alternates went into sequestration in a downtown hotel on January 11, 1995. They would now, as Judge Ito instructed them at the end of each day's court proceedings they attended, not be allowed to discuss the case in any way with anyone, including one another.

The prosecution's side suffered a real setback on the evening of January 25. Bill Hodgman and Marcia Clark were in Gil Garcetti's office discussing the trial when Hodgman felt a pain in his chest. He got up and tried to exercise this discomfort away. When this did not relieve the pain, and at Garcetti's suggestion, Hodgman was rushed by ambulance to the California Medical Center where doctors heard an irregularity in his heartbeat. Hodgman was hospitalized, but soon had recovered enough to resume working on the case from his office. His courtroom role was effectively ended with this cardiac problem. Christopher Darden stepped into his role as cocounsel to Clark. Hodgman, with his quiet and understated manner, was an ideal partner for Marcia Clark, whose fiery outbursts in court would become famous. Hodgman's leaving the courtroom was a loss for his side. (I did not mention the enormous press response to this development; that's since each and every turn in the road was greeted by intense news media coverage. This would remain the case for the next ten months.)

During the opening days of the trial, Judge Ito issued his decision to allow the admission of the Rockingham evidence. In another finding for the prosecution's side, Judge Ito also ruled that the prosecution could enter evidence on O. J. Simpson's record of spousal abuse, as long as they could show relevance. However, Judge Ito also ruled that the prosecution would not be allowed to introduce a diary Nicole had kept as events led up to her divorce settlement since it would be hearsay. Another important ruling by the judge favored the defense: Evidence of Detective Mark Fuhrman acting or speaking in a racist manner would be admissable, but, again, contingent on the defense's showing relevance. These rulings would prove critical, and doubly so when, toward the end of the trial, an individual stepped forward with the recorded tapes of statements Fuhrman had made over several years. The defense lost a motion to explore Fuhrman's military and LAPD personnel files. Finally, the prosecution decided that it would not bring O. J. Simpson to trial for the two murders under threat of the death penalty. Surveys show that jurors selected to sit in judgment for capital felony cases are, overall, more willing to return guilty verdicts in all cases.

As we prepared for the trial itself, several critically important questions were on our minds. Many of these questions revolved around the blood evidence. Following the preliminary hearing in the summer of 1994, the prosecution's DNA-testing results had come back, and they were quickly leaked to the news media. Major headlines appeared proclaiming that bloodstains found at Bundy matched O. J. Simpson's. The DNA tests showed that the odds of someone other than O. J. Simpson being the blood source were 170 million to one. This was an enormous escalation from the preliminary testing which had shown that this blood type was found in 48 percent of the general population, meaning that in the Los Angeles area alone the blood could have been produced by as many as 8 million people. Judge Ito ruled that the defense had the right to split samples and conduct its own DNA testing, though the defense would only be permitted to use 10 percent of the blood sample taken from O. J. Simpson. This amount, in many cases, would not be enough for testing.

Initially, both the prosecution and defense believed that the results of the DNA testing of the blood evidence would make or break this case. The defense would have to work tirelessly in developing a strategy to deal with the evidence. Ultimately, the trial we were approaching would generate 126 witnesses, 857 pieces of evidence, and hundreds of thousands of pages of court transcript.

At the beginning of the trial, we had formulated, at Johnnie Cochran's request, a list of critical questions to answer. These are spelled out in Cochran's book, *Journey to Justice*. Here I will paraphrase some of these questions and add other critical issues:

1. Why was Detective Fuhrman alone outside the Rockingham crime scene for eighteen minutes? Why are there no notes to reflect what he did for those eighteen minutes?

2. Why was the glove found at Rockingham still damp with blood at 6 A.M. after allegedly being dropped at 10:45 the prior evening, especially in light of the small amount of blood smeared on it?

3. What exactly is the state's theory on how the other glove got there? And why was there no blood found on the dried leaves or ground, when a bloody, wet glove had been dropped there?

4. In light of the shoeprints and the number of knife wounds, isn't it equally probable that there was more than one killer? If the prosecution is wrong about this, can't it also be wrong about the defendant committing the crimes?

5. Since the killer would have to be covered with the victims' blood, why wasn't there a large amount of blood evidence on the supposed getaway vehicle or on a path to the van?

6. There were Caucasian hairs and other fibers found on the ski cap and gloves that did not match the victims'. From whom did they originate?*

7. With the very narrow time window left to commit this double murder, how did O. J. Simpson carry out these actions by himself?*

8. Why was only one of Mrs. Brown's lenses found in the envelope? Where was the other?*

---

*Questions I added

9. Why was Nicole's blood found on the inside of the sock, but not on the carpeting and outside of the sock? How was this blood transferred?*

10. Who was the source for the blood droplets observed on the back of Nicole Brown Simpson, and why wasn't this evidence collected and analyzed?*

These were strong and compelling questions with which we would start the trial. Notice that none of these questions has anything to do with race or some of the other issues many Americans still associate with this proceeding.

The defense team also raised critical questions during its cross-examination of state witnesses:

1. Dennis Fung would contradict testimony he had given before the aborted grand jury proceeding and at the trial.

2. The prosecution's collection procedures for blood samples and the question of who collected each sample were challenged.

3. Why did the police investigators fail to collect the piece of white paper found near the body of Ron Goldman?

4. Who placed a blanket over Nicole Simpson's corpse, one that had been taken from inside the condo and could have, through fibers, cross-contaminated the evidence found on her person?

5. Were Juditha Brown's glasses and their case collected after Ron Goldman's body had been dragged over them?

6. Why had the police investigators not collected any evidence until after the coroner's office had left the scene?

7. Why were incorrect procedures used for the collection of physical evidence at the scene?

8. Why were important biological specimens not collected during the autopsy?

9. Why were no chemical-enhancement techniques used to develop or enhance the shoeprints at the Bundy crime scene?

10. Why didn't the criminalist and the other detectives notice any bloodstains on the pair of socks found at the foot of Simpson's bed?

The defense, after undermining the LAPD's crime scene procedures, now would go for much bigger issues: The blood evidence found on the rear gate at Bundy, or the blood evidence originally seen by police, included in his notes by Detective Mark Fuhrman, was not collected until July 3, three weeks after the murders. In his direct examination, Fung had simply admitted that he had somehow missed this smudge, which would have been on the inside handle precisely where a killer would have opened the gate. And this is where Barry Scheck was masterful. The prosecution had begun its case claiming "a mountain of evidence" that would convict O. J. Simpson. When the defense was finished, the blood evidence from the back gate and from the socks would seem to create a mountain of doubt.

When most attorneys, even very good ones, are conducting very technical cross-examination, the expert on the stand knows a great deal more about his field of expertise than the lawyer asking the questions. Take it from me, Barry Scheck and Peter Neufeld know the field of DNA from top to bottom. They had noticed something very strange about the DNA findings from the blood trace on the gate, as compared with the DNA testing of the blood spots from along the Bundy pathway. The blood samples from the pathway contained DNA which had substantially degraded. This meant that a lesser quantity and quality of the blood was available for DNA testing. The PCR-testing technique (polymerase chain reaction), which is not as precise, had to be used. The blood traces from the back gate, however, had more intact DNA, and, therefore, could be subjected to a far more precise form of testing, called RFLP (restriction fragment length polymorphisms). But how could this be? The blood on the gate had sat outside, in the elements, for an extra three weeks, subject to the hot California sun and other environmental forces. Nobody was able to answer this critical question. Also, the police crime scene photos, taken the day after the murders, did not show any blood sample on the gate. Yet, in a photo taken on July 3, the blood smear on the gate handle was clearly visible. All of this was devastating. Something was wrong here. That expression spread through the defense team like a rallying cry.

Where would someone obtain a sample of O. J. Simpson's blood to smear it on the rear gate at Bundy? The defense team had also noticed something peculiar about the way the LAPD nurse had drawn blood from Simpson on June 13. The nurse, a man named Thano Peratis, had testified at the preliminary hearing that he'd drawn a standard amount, eight milliliters. Then the defense experts reviewed how much of this blood sample had been used up in each step of the testing, a very extraordinary step. Working backwards, and utilizing testimony Peratis had taped, it was established that all of the testing, at most, must have consumed only 6.5 milliliters. Where had the remaining 1.5 milliliters gone? Again, something was very wrong here. In still another breakthrough, the defense presented an expert witness, Dr. Fred Rieder, a world-renowned toxicologist, who had found EDTA (ethylenediaminetetracetic acid), a blood preservative, in the blood samples from the Bundy gate, the pair of socks, and other areas. EDTA is present only in a test tube as an anticoagulant, to preserve a blood clot. How would that have ever gotten there?

Barry Scheck also postulated that Ron Goldman's blood found in the Bronco had been planted by Fuhrman (the only person Scheck actually named), an act which F. Lee Bailey had already suggested when he cross-examined Fuhrman earlier in the trial. Scheck also suggested that Nicole Brown Simpson's blood had been planted on the pair of socks found at the foot of O. J. Simpson's bed. The defense team studied the LAPD's original notes and saw that there was no mention that blood was found on these socks. Then, a few weeks later, somehow blood was discovered on them. The prosecution presented its own DNA witnesses to present the findings of this testing. With more DNA matching numbers running into the billions, all of this should have been the crown jewel in the prosecution's case. The defense also was assisted here by Herb MacDonald, a world-renowned blood-spatter expert, who testified that he had found the location and the condition of the bloodstains on the socks to be extremely questionable. Those bloodstains carried DNA which matched that of Nicole Brown Simpson. However, all of this testimony and hard work about this blood evidence by the defense created a large cloud of doubt, one that seemed to have rolled in and settled over the courtroom. It's been written that there was more DNA evidence presented in this case than in any other in American history, but in the end, the jury did not pay much attention to the DNA results.

There were more developments in the prosecution's case, but only a few that are important enough to warrant further discussion. Nicole Brown Simpson had kept a safety deposit box in her bank which police investigators opened and found photos of Nicole that showed she had been battered. When the prosecution's attorney, Christopher Darden, was presenting evidence of spousal abuse by Simpson in his direct examination of Denise Brown, Nicole's older sister, he displayed one of these photos on a screen for the jury to see. Robert Shapiro instantly objected, and Judge Ito called both sides to one of the trial's many sidebar conferences. Darden could not establish any foundation for the photo, such as where or when it had been taken as well as by whom. The judge admonished Darden verbally for presenting this image to the court, ruled the photo inadmissible since it lacked any foundation, and directed the jury to ignore it.

Another ruling by Judge Ito involved physical evidence. Police investigators, with some help from the FBI, had established that Nicole Brown Simpson had purchased two pairs of Aris leather gloves, size extra large, on December 18, 1990, at Bloomingdale's, the upscale department store in New York City. These gloves, especially in that size, were quite rare, according to testimony from an expert in the field. In a court session in late June, just before the prosecution rested its case, the gloves were entered into evidence. Even though Bill Hodgman and Marcia Clark had decided not to let O. J. Simpson demonstrate whether these gloves actually fit, Christopher Darden, who was handling this testimony for the prosecution, agreed to let such a demonstration go forward. Trying on the glove in full view of the jury and the vast television audience, Simpson hopped from one foot to another, attempting to pull the glove over his large hand. There is an old and honored saying in the legal profession: Never ask a question, unless you know the answer. Johnnie Cochran would take full advantage of this mistake in his closing statement.

On this note, the prosecution rested its case on July 6, 1995. I would be testifying under direct examination as a defense expert in late July. The following are some of the issues which were raised. A second type of shoeprint, with a parallel-line-design sole pattern, was discovered at the Bundy crime scene. These were bloody shoeprints. Was there another assailant? Later, the prosecution would argue that a second murderer would have had to leave more footprints and other kinds of evidence. However, there were many pattern imprints on the Bundy walkway. Those imprints were not chemically enhanced. Therefore, whether or not there were additional shoeprints present there was a fact which could never be established. Moreover, various blood-spatter patterns were found at the Bundy scene. I demonstrated how blood-spatter formations occur, showing how blood moves out of and away from its exit wounds. Attorney Scheck focused on what I thought, in my professional opinion, about the way the blood evidence had been handled during the course of this investigation. One of the most important findings, I testified, was that the bloodstain patterns were discovered on the "paper bindles," which indicated that the swatch which had picked up the blood had not been properly dried out. However, the laboratory findings showed that those swatches were dried overnight. At the end of my testimony, I summed things up by saying, "Something is wrong."

Having presented the highlights of the Simpson trial, I've decided to wait to this point in the narrative to discuss one last bombshell that rocked these proceedings. During the prosecution's case, Detective Fuhrman had been closely cross-examined by defense lawyer F. Lee Bailey on his racial attitudes. Fuhrman's responses were clear and to the point. He did not use racial slurs and had not performed his duties in a racist manner. This position was challenged by a witness, Kathleen

Dr. Lee testifies in the courtroom with Johnnie Cochrane looking on.

Bell, who had said she and others had heard Fuhrman talk in a most racist manner. These conversations had occurred at a Marine Corps recruiting station where she had worked and at a local bar. Fuhrman's calm responses to the questions posed to him, by even one as expert as Bailey, had tended to offset the charges of racism. However, late in the trial, during July and August, a second witness, Laura McKinny, who had taped many hours of her conversations with Fuhrman, stepped forward. Played in the courtroom, Fuhrman is clearly heard delivering racist statements and relating events during which he said he had behaved in a most racist manner. All of this dialogue with McKinny had been recorded for her future use in writing screenplays for a proposed television series. Fuhrman would end up exercising his Fifth Amendment right to refuse to testify on the grounds that his answers could be self-incriminating. And perjury is a crime.

Both sides completed presenting their cases and on Tuesday, September 26, 1995, the summations began. This is ironic since jury selection for the trial had commenced exactly a year earlier. Johnnie Cochran had emerged as the chief defense counsel, and it was a forgone conclusion that he would deliver one of the two defense summations. Cochran's rise to this position had been obvious from the start of the trial. However, the prediction a year earlier of Barry Scheck as the lawyer who would deliver the second defense summation would have been a tremendous longshot. This is true because of the tremendous legal talent assembled on the defense team. Author Jeffrey Toobin makes this point very well in his excellent one-volume history of the case, *The Run of His Life: The People v. O. J. Simpson.*

Johnnie Cochran had built strong credibility, it seemed, with the jurors. His closing statement touched many of the critical aspects of the case. Cochran, who even seemed to surpass himself with his charisma, hammered away at police irregularities and the terrible shadow that Mark Fuhrman's racism had thrown over the investigation. The portion of Cochran's peroration which will stay with many viewers was his treatment of the leather glove's not fitting onto the large left hand of O. J. Simpson. "If it doesn't fit, you must acquit," Cochran sang out again and again. Cochran called out another powerful argument: "If you can't trust the messengers, watch out for their message." His summation seemed spellbinding. Barry Scheck, with his thoughtful and logical approach, then moved into position. Scheck seemed to devastate the prosecution's forensic evidence. He called out that the LAPD had created "a cesspool of contamination." Scheck hammered away at the prosecution for the preservative EDTA found in the blood evidence on the bedroom socks and in the blood smear found on the rear gate at Bundy. And he underscored that both of these blood traces were discovered weeks after the crime. I was more than flattered when Barry Scheck cited my findings and feelings: "Something is terribly wrong with the evidence in this case."

The case was ready to go the jury on the afternoon of Friday, September 29. Judge Ito would not allow deliberations to begin before the weekend, so the twelve jurors had to spend one last weekend cooped up in their rooms, eating hotel food. Shortly after nine the following Monday morning, the jurors began. An early poll taken by the jury showed that ten were for acquittal and two found Simpson guilty. Within three hours, the jury had arrived at its unanimous decision of not guilty. In one last delay, which had to be very frustrating for the jurors, Judge Ito ruled that the decision would be announced in open court the next morning on October 3, at 9 A.M. Pacific time. The look on Johnny Cochran's face as the acquittal was announced, together with his placing his arm around his defendant, is now a well-known image. And the concept that forensic science must always be objective and used only to establish the actual facts was upheld. The upholding of this rule of law was the trial's ultimate victory.

The jury's quick decision to acquit set off a firestorm of vividly contrasting emotions throughout America. African Americans rejoiced unabashedly. The LAPD's incompetent investigation of the two murders and its history for racial abuse, most recently displayed in the Rodney King affair, had drawn the black community together. This was especially so in the large urban areas where the decision to acquit Simpson represented a kind of validation of their fears of the police. American whites, on the other hand, were horrified, calling the acquittal a reverse form of lynching. This reaction, in turn, infuriated the black community. The trial had, indeed, exposed the deep chasm in the two, very disparate Americas. The white world, for the most part, comfortable, middle class, employed, and often suburban and rural. The black community, angry, lower income, crime-plagued, and more in the inner-city or located in poorer rural areas throughout the South. For myself, I was deeply gratified at the decision and happy that the case was finally completed. Of course, I knew, firsthand, the problems which lay beneath the surface of the prosecution's evidence.

THE CASE'S SCIENTIFIC FACTS

Over the past decade, extraordinary interest and excitement have been generated by the use of DNA (deoxyribonucleic acid) in forensic science, primarily because the molecule is highly stable in stains and is found in almost all human cells (except red blood cells). Therefore, DNA is statistically highly informative for the purpose of establishing a sample's origin. In addition, many high profile cases, such as the

William Kennedy Smith rape trial and the O. J. Simpson double murder trial, have increased the legal profession's and the general public's awareness of and interest in the genetic typing of biological evidence.

DNA, the hereditary material of living organisms, is primarily found in the cell nucleus. DNA is organized into long, threadlike structures called chromosomes. In addition to the DNA, chromosomes contain associated proteins, predominantly histones, that organize the DNA into its native conformation. In most human cells, there are forty-six chromosomes, one set from each parent. Most cell types have two sets of chromosomes and are referred to as diploid. The important exception to this rule is found in male and female sex cells (gametes), which are haploid. Sperm and egg cells contain only one strand of DNA (sperm with male DNA and egg with female DNA). The fertilized egg, the zygote, possesses forty-six chromosomes, twenty-three maternally derived and twenty-three paternally derived.

DNA is polymer (a long chain of chemical building blocks). Its individual units or building blocks are termed nucleotides. Each nucleotide consists of a five-carbon sugar (deoxyribose), a nitrogenous base, and a phosphane group. Only four types of nucleotides are found in DNA. The sole difference between them is which base is bound to the deoxyribose at carbon number one: adenine (A), guanine (G), cytosine (C), or thymine (T). The bases A and G, with two nitrogen rings, are called purines. Bases C and T have a single ring and are termed pyrimidines.

The functional DNA molecule is actually two strands of DNA intertwined, forming a double helix that is tightly packed in the cell nucleus. This structure was first proposed in 1953 by a pair of scientists, an Englishman, Dr. Francis Crick, and an American, Dr. James Watson. They conducted their research in England and were awarded the Nobel Prize for their discoveries in 1962.

The informational content of DNA comes from the linear arrangement of the four nucleotides (primary sequence); in other words, the genetic "alphabet" contains four letters (A,C,G,T) that are repeated in specific patterns (called genes). A gene, thus, is defined as the physical and functional unit of heredity—a segment of DNA that carries the information or "codes" for a functional protein. The human genome contains 3 billion base pairs (bp) of DNA, coding for an estimated 50,000–100,000 genes. Genes are situated in discrete regions, commonly referred to as genetic loci, on the forty-six chromosomes. In addition, most genes exist in multiple forms, called alleles. A single genetic locus may have many different alleles. This variation is termed genetic polymorphism. However, each individual can have no more than two different alleles for a single gene. Collectively, however, a population may have multiple alleles at any given locus, and that genetic polymorphism is the molecular basis of forensic DNA typing.

Items that can be subjected to DNA analysis are generally limited to things that are biological in nature. This listing includes blood and bloodstains, semen and seminal stains, tissues and cells, bones and organs, hairs with follicles, urine and saliva (with nucleated cells), and dental pulps. In addition, to nuclear DNA, another type of DNA— mtDNA, has been found in cytoplasma. mtDNA (mitochondrial DNA) is maternity-linked, inherited from the mother only. mtDNA has been found in hairs, bone, nails, and other biological samples. Other types of biological evidence, such as tears, perspiration, serum red blood cells, and other body fluids without cells are not amenable to DNA analysis.

Many legal challenges have also been raised in court because of this new and powerful technique. These issues and challenges can be grouped into the following categories:

Genetic issues. DNA is the genetic blueprint of the human body. Half of this blueprint is inherited from the paternal side at conception and the other half from the maternal side. Over the years, many issues have been raised and, to a large extent answered, including: Whether or not a person's DNA is unique in a population; whether DNA remains constant throughout one's life or to what degree do mutations occur; whether or not all the body cells in the human body have identical DNA patterns; and whether or not chemicals, environmental factors, or medications can alter a person's DNA patterns. Science has determined that DNA is unique for each individual, except in the case of identical twins, and a person's DNA remains constant throughout his life. There is no longer any question concerning the genetic issues of forensic DNA typing.

Technical issues. Any procedure in scientific testing is only as good as the scientist's ability to perform such a test. A standard procedure will not guarantee the reliability of the testing results. It is not unprecedented to learn that incorrect or fraudulent results were reported by forensic pathologists and forensic scientists. Thus, there have been incidents in which individuals have been wrongly arrested or even convicted through faulty analysis of the evidence or erroneous witness statements. Quality assurance and quality control have become two essential areas in forensic DNA typing. The FBI laboratory, with the American Society of Crime Laboratory Directors and its Laboratory Accreditation Board, has been actively developing standards for quality assurance and quality control. In addition, criminalist certification programs have also been offered through several national groups. It is essential that each DNA examiner possesses the qualifications required and has sufficient training in forensic DNA typing. Also, each DNA typing laboratory should ensure adherence to the highest standards.

Matching issues. The ultimate goal in the analysis of any physical evidence is to achieve sample individualization (specifically establishing the identity of a person). The common route for achieving such a goal is the comparison of the known sample with the questioned material in its physical, chemical, and biological properties. One of the simplest and most effective methods of comparison is pattern matching. If the questioned sample exhibits the identical patterns as the known control, then these two samples must share the same origin. The mechanism of DNA matching is essentially the same as that of fingerprint or ballistics-recognition matching. It is basically a matter of pattern recognition and comparison. If two DNA profile patterns are exactly the same, a match should be declared.

Statistical issues. It is meaningless to examine two patterns and proclaim a match without attributing some statistical significance to the results. It is necessary to couple an analysis of the probability of a random match between two samples with the specific loci analyzed. That is, for a given population, what is the frequency that two unrelated individuals would have the identical DNA patterns at the analyzed sites by chance alone? The conflict among population geneticists arises because it is impossible to survey the entire world's population. One means of estimating this frequency is to take a random sample of the population and determine the frequency of each allele and genotype.

Contamination issues. There are two ways to transfer physiological evidence: direct and contact deposit. For example, if during commission of a crime, the victim's blood transfers directly to a suspect's clothing, subsequent DNA typing will indicate that the questioned bloodstain found on the suspect's clothing could have originated from the victim, providing a direct link beween the victim and the suspect. Or if a suspect receives an injury during commission of a crime, a bloodstain found at the crime scene could provide a direct link between the suspect and the crime scene. This type of a DNA-testing result has significant forensic value and provides powerful information for the crime scene's reconstruction.

The second possible mechanism is through secondary transfer, such as a perpetrator fleeing the crime scene and leaving a trail of the victim's blood along a pathway. Any individual subsequently walking by may pick up the bloodstain on his or her shoes. Although DNA testing provides a direct link beween the victim's blood and the second individual's shoes, this type of link through secondary transfer is of limited value in crime scene reconstruction.

DNA analysis of a piece of physical evidence containing physiological fluid provides information only as to how such physiological fluid was transferred. The results yielded cannot be used exclusively in attempting to prove or disprove an alibi. For example, DNA extracted from a rape kit may link a male suspect to a victim, but this DNA typing does not yield information distinguishing rape from consensual sex. Therefore, any DNA-testing result should be considered only as a scientific finding of DNA analysis. Interpretation of such results should be made with extreme caution in conjunction with additional information, such as crime scene analysis, patterns, examination, and the consideration of other physical evidence.

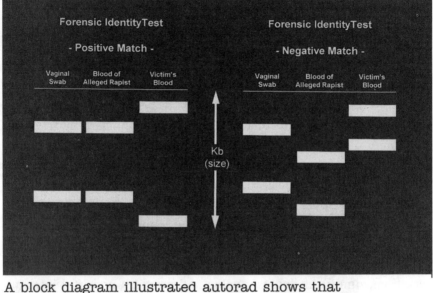

A block diagram illustrated autorad shows that
DNA found on the walkway has an identical profile
as alleged rapist's DNA.

In conclusion, successful analysis of physical evidence by DNA technologies relies on the ability to locate, collect, preserve, and isolate relatively intact DNA molecules in sufficient quantity for analysis. Although DNA is among the most stable of biomolecules, certain factors exist that can limit the ability to recover useful amounts of DNA. These factors include age of the sample, environmental conditions, contamination, and the methodologies used for isolation procedures. The methodologies developed by the forensics community have proven successful in most cases in achieving identification of sample DNA. At times testing fails to produce results, *but it has yet to produce a false positive*. Once a result is obtained, it should be interpreted cautiously, especially if mixed stains are indicated. The potential impact of DNA analysis on the criminal justice system in general and on forensic evidence in particular cannot be overstated.

Courts throughout the United States have admitted DNA evidence, and their appellate courts, including the respective supreme courts, have rendered favorable decisions after reviewing DNA profiling. When defense challenges have arisen against DNA evidence, or the courts have balked at admitting it, such reluctance is usually based on the grounds of how common or rare the reported DNA profile is in the U.S. population. In other words, the prosecution must demonstrate the significance of the DNA match, based on population genetics.

In August 1993 the Washington Supreme Court became the first state high court to endorse forced genetic testing of all persons convicted of sexual offenses or violent crimes. Such testing is destined to generate a DNA database to identify and prosecute future sex offenders or violent criminals. Washington is one of more than thirty states that has enacted similar statutes. Although opponents of such forced testing believe it is a waste of money and an unnecessary invasion of privacy with the sole purpose of investigating possible future crimes, the Washington Supreme Court found a "rational connection between the DNA-testing statute and law enforcement." In addition to establishing guilt in criminal acts, DNA profiling can serve the cause of justice by establishing innocence as well. In fact, the DNA test results actually exclude the named suspects in about one-third of the submitted cases.

Fingerprint evidence is another prime example, as I said earlier in this book, of a recently developed forensic technology which is now totally accepted by the general public, as well as the scientists, courts, and the rest of the legal community. However, even in gathering fingerprint evidence, forensic investigators are making solid progress in widening our ability to find, record, and compare fingerprints. The latent fingerprint is one which is not readily seen, even with a magnifying glass. The latent fingerprint has to be enhanced to be visible. Over the course of time, many forensic scientists have explored new and improved ways to develop and recover latent prints. Most recently, we have seen new dimensions opened up in latent-print processing techniques, ones that have revolutionized the field of fingerprint identification. More than 250 new techniques have been created for latent-print development and fingerprint identification. In addition, computer image enhancement and the automated fingerprint identification system (AFIS) also have been used in fingerprint work.

When I was asked by Judge Delbert Wong to study the knife which O. J. Simpson had purchased several weeks before the murders, I reported that I'd used a cyanoacrylate-fuming procedure to discover fourteen latent prints on the knife's surfaces. This process makes use of superglue. In 1982 U.S. Army investigators working in a military laboratory in Japan, as well as investigators at the Bureau of Alcohol, Tobacco, and Firearms in this country, found Japanese fingerprint examiners were able to develop latent fingerprints in a new way. They used alkyl-2-cyanoacrylate (superglue) to develop latent fingerprints.

Cyanoacrylate fuming has been successfully used in developing latent prints on surfaces as diverse as plastic, electrical tape, garbage bags, Styrofoam, carbon paper, aluminum foil, finished and unfinished wood, rubber, copper and other metals, cellophane, rubber bands, and smooth rocks. The equipment and materials required include cyanoacrylate and a fuming tank—a cabinet or other suitable container with an adequate ventilation system. The investigator should first place the item on which the latent prints are to be developed into the cabinet. The item should be suspended from the upper portions of the cabinet, if possible, to allow its surfaces to be totally exposed to the cyanoacrylate fumes. Then two or three drops of the cyanoacrylate should be put into a small porcelain dish, which should then be placed in the fuming cabinet. Then he should allow the items to be exposed to the fumes for at least two hours, at which time whitish-colored fingerprint patterns will appear. The developed prints in any of these processes may be further enhanced by dusting them with regular or magnetic fingerprint powder or treating them with chemicals.

It's possible to accelerate this process to between one and two hours by using a fan to circulate the fumes around the target surface, which increases the rate of contact. Applying heat to the circulation process is another way to accelerate the process by twenty to forty minutes. The investigator should place a heating apparatus under the porcelain dish containing the superglue or otherwise arrange for heat to impact the dish. The heat hastens the polymerization process of the cyanoacrylate and increases monomer volatility, resulting in faster vapor release and, thus, faster development of the latent print. Finally, a chemical acceleration procedure can hasten this process. This requires 0.5 M sodium hydroxide and cotton pads or some other absorbant medium. First, the investigator prepares 0.5 M sodium hydroxide by dissolving 2 g solid NaOH in 100 ml of distilled water. Next he puts a clean cotton pad, cotton ball, or other absorbant medium into the dish. Then he puts two or three drops of liquid cyanoacrylate onto the absorbant surface and adds two drops of 0.5 M sodium hydroxide solution to the absorbant surface. He must allow the target surface to fume from thirty minutes to an hour, until the whitish-colored print appears. For field services, the investigator can use a superglue-fuming wand. This is a portable superglue-heating wand developed by the Alaska crime laboratory. This wand can be carried by the crime scene investigator to any location for fuming cars, furniture, windows, doors, and even an entire house.

The acceptance of fingerprint evidence by the courts has always been predicated on the assumption that no two persons have identical fingerprints, not even identical twins. However, "fingerprints match" have recently been challenged in court for lacking standards on minimum number of friction ridge characters which must be present in two fingerprints in order to establish a positive match.

THE CASE'S SUMMARY

The O. J. Simpson murder trial has become a landmark in several ways. The DNA evidence took on a preeminent role in this case and became a particular source of study and legal precedent. In a court of law, any evidence which has been obtained illegally is subject to being excluded by the trial judge. Failing that, the appellate courts regularly overturn convictions due to appeals arguments which the defense can make challenging the admission of this kind of evidence. These rights are all set forth in the Fourth Amendment's due process provisions. Criminal defense lawyers call this kind of evidence, "the fruit of the forbidden tree."

At the very least, the blood evidence collected from O. J. Simpson and from the crime scene was handled in a very shoddy manner. This failure to properly collect, store, and preserve these blood samples led directly to the evidence's being contaminated and rendered unsuitable for proper DNA testing. The fact that 1.5 cc of blood was missing from the known amount of the blood sample taken from O. J. Simpson was also most disturbing. Add to that the fact that the EDTA preservative was found in the samples taken from the pair of socks found in the master bedroom at Simpson's Rockingham home and in the blood taken from the Bundy gate, and these irregularities suggest more than simple investigative incompetence.

The Simpson case also became a national landmark for other reasons. Few of these reasons are positive. The media's malfeasance, particularly their corrupting the process with money paid to witnesses, is one. Then we have the specter of a publisher likely overstating his case, accusing all of the jurors and alternates of trying to sell him a book. Another issue was the leaking of information to the media, such as lab test results, before and during the trial. Still another is the deep racial divide the case uncovered and exacerbated in the country at large. This racial antipathy went far beyond the post–Rodney King atmosphere in Los Angeles. And to some degree the nation still does not seem to have gotten over the O. J. Simpson case. Finally, the case raised new questions about the efficacy of allowing live, televised broadcasting. What if, instead of early in the proceedings and only briefly, the cameras later on had shown the faces of all of the jurors? Would a late-proceeding mistrial be worth the benefits of the live broadcasting? I seriously doubt that. Also, there is the nagging question as to whether witnesses and others directly involved in the trial played to the cameras.

These are only some of the questions and issues which the Simpson trial has exhibited for many to ponder. For myself, as a forensic investigator, the DNA questions are the most important. As previously stated, I am a person who sees the search for scientific evidence as one and the same with the search for the truth. I am most gratified that the great majority of police officers and forensic scientists around the world feel the same way and all have a very high professional and ethical set of standards. As our ability to analyze, test, and individualize blood and medical evidence keeps improving, so must our attention to the basic principles of proper handling, identifying, and preserving these unique avenues to the truth. Our entire American system of jurisprudence is grounded in the concept of equal protection and fair play for all. We can demand no less, no matter where the trail of forensic evidence takes us.

chapter four

THE SHERMAN CASE

To the world's best partner.
> —Inscription on a bracelet given by
> Edward Sherman to his wife, Ellen.

The Ellen Sherman murder case is about the importance of establishing the victim's time of death. This is a question that is within the province of the forensic pathology field but, even today, does not provide exact answers. The average person knows that a body, under normal conditions and for a certain number of hours after death, will stiffen, a process known as *rigor mortis*. Additionally, the body's red blood cells will slowly settle in the capillaries and other blood vessels in the lowest portions of the body, forming a pinkish pattern. *Livor mortis* then sets in. Some even know that this stiffening of the corpse's limbs, caused by rigidity in the muscle system, will abate another twenty-four hours or so later. But even to the medical forensics expert, there are not that many such telltale signals to establish the exact time of death.

At the time of her death, Ellen Sherman was thirty-eight and her husband, Edward Robert Sherman, had just turned forty-two. This heinous crime would provide the prosecution team with a number of formidable challenges. Mrs. Sherman, who was five-and-a-half months pregnant at the time of her death, was found strangled late one

August weekend. Friday evening of that weekend her husband had left
to go to Maine for a sailing trip with four other men. At first appearances this would seem an airtight alibi. At that time the couple's only
child, Jessica, twelve, was at summer camp in a nearby town. When
Ellen's body was found at dusk on Sunday, August 4, 1985, the man
who discovered her murder had opened the master bedroom door and
walked into a room that was extremely cold, because the window air
conditioner had been turned up to full force. This abnormally cold
temperature would serve to slow down body decomposition, compli-
cating the ability of the medical examiner to estimate the time of
death. It would later develop that the individual who went into the
Sherman home was the victim's employee and had once been her
lover. At the time of this gruesome discovery, her husband and his
shipmates were sailing and fishing in the Buzzards Bay area of Massachusetts, near the Cape Cod bridge. Sherman, who had had a long-
standing relationship with a coworker at the community college where
he taught marketing, even fathering a child in 1984 by this mistress,
had been making a series of ship-to-shore phone calls from the sailboat. He was asking friends to find his wife's whereabouts since he
said he had been unable to talk to her by phone. Edward Sherman
would be finally notified by police the following Monday morning of
his wife's death.

When the police arrived at the murder scene on Sunday evening,
they found the bedroom at a normal summer temperature since the
first witness and paramedics called in had not bothered to close the
door. This meant that there was no way to establish exactly how low
the room's temperature had been. But, there were several methods for
determining Ellen Sherman's time of death that assisted the medical
forensics investigation in this case. One of these is the scientific study
of the victim's stomach contents. Unlike some involuntary physiological and muscle systems, the digestive process stops almost instantly
upon a person's death. In this case, Mrs. Sherman's supper of linguine
and a red seafood sauce, probably clams, had stayed in her stomach for
a considerable amount of time while her body lay in the refrigerated

bedroom. When examined, these food remains had not moved down to her small intestines, a process which normally requires five hours. This would be a critically important factor in this case, especially when leftovers from this dinner were found by the detectives in the couple's refrigerator.

My own direct investigation in this case would primarily focus on reconstruction of the crime, an examination of the cause of death, what kind of weapon was used, the positioning of Ellen Sherman's body on the bed, an analysis of fluids which had come from her mouth and nose, and the discovery of forty semen stains on the couple's satin upper bedsheet. I would also work closely with the state's chief medical examiner in her investigation.

The Sherman case is also illustrative of the importance of persistent police work. Investigators had zeroed in on Edward Sherman as the prime suspect from the moment he was first questioned on the Monday after the murder. The Shermans had been going through a very stormy time in their marriage, and Ellen had openly talked to friends about divorcing her husband, who had carried on a number of affairs, including the one which resulted in his fathering a child. Edward and Ellen were business partners, yet Ellen owned majority control of this operation, a fact she mentioned when talking to friends about the divorce. Also, as the Sherman investigation painstakingly moved forward, a teenage witness would step forward to tell about a bogus, one-way phone call she had remembered overhearing Edward Sherman make on the night of his wife's death. This would buttress the prosecution's case. But, I am getting ahead of myself.

FACTS OF THE CASE

Edward and Ellen Sherman were married in 1969 in New York, near Ellen's Long Island home. Ellen Sherman was brunette, highly energetic, friendly, and attractive. Her husband was a solidly built, balding man whose heavy dark eyebrows gave his face a brooding look which matched his long periods of silence. The couple moved to Connecticut in the early seventies. Edward Sherman had been a high school teacher in the Bronx, opting for that career, perhaps, because it conferred a draft deferment status on those in the profession during the Vietnam War. Yet, his penchant for violence showed itself early in his teaching career in New York when he choked a student who had been in a fight with another student. Sherman had choked the student after he'd intervened to break up the fight. Also, earlier in the sixties, Sherman had married a woman in Chicago, but that union was short-lived and ended in an annulment. He was accused of assaulting his first wife.

After the Shermans settled in Connecticut in the early seventies, the couple bought a Cape Cod–style, two-floor house in the Black Stone section of Niantic Village in East Lyme, a comfortable shoreline community about ten miles west of New London. The Sherman home was less than a mile from the waters of Long Island Sound. Most of the houses around them were owned by summer residents who used these residences exclusively for vacationing. Sherman landed a position as a marketing instructor at Mohegan Community College, in Norwich, about ten miles from home. This teaching position provided him with summers off and a generous state benefits package. Sherman's IQ was considered very high, though it had never been recorded, and he was a member of the Mensa society. Ellen had used her excellent organizational and creative skills to run a business the couple had started, which they named Ad Graphics.

Ad Graphics was successful, so the Shermans hired artists and other employees for their offices on the Boston Post Road in Waterford, another shoreline community immediately east of Niantic. Sherman became publisher of an ambitious and profitable magazine, the *Showcase of Homes*, which presented photos, listings, and other details on many of the residences for sale in New London County. Ellen Sherman owned 51 percent of the shares in Ad Graphics, a move her husband endorsed since the business would be run by a woman, and thus be able to take advantage of certain kinds of existing federal assistance programs that encouraged minority- and women-owned enterprises. Ellen earned substantially more at the business than her husband, who explained that this arrangement let the couple take advantage of more tax deductions. Ellen, according to Ad Graphics's employees, did the vast majority of the work, however. In the early eighties a woman named Elizabeth Caulfield had participated in the business with the Shermans, but she eventually left in 1984. In 1982, Caulfield had discovered that Edward Sherman was using the business's name to conduct private banking business. Consequently, Caulfield had Sherman sign an agreement that he would not repeat this practice and, if he violated this trust, he would be responsible for paying her $50,000.

As a married couple, the Shermans led an unusual lifestyle. Edward Sherman became involved in a number of extramarital affairs, a behavior which Ellen condoned. In one instance in the mid-seventies, police were called when a former girlfriend awoke one night to find Sherman standing over her in her bedroom. No charges were filed, but this former lover said he had once struck her. He also was accused of choking another former girlfriend in 1974. Then, in 1977, Sherman became romantically involved with a married woman who also worked at Mohegan Community College. This mistress, who had a two-year-old son, divorced her husband in 1978, about the time Sherman urged his wife to abort a fetus he had fathered. A neighbor and very close friend, June Rossiter,* would relate that Ellen Sherman had said she'd aborted a second baby, at her husband's urging. In 1982, the mistress also had an abortion, which was her idea, Sherman later would say, adding that he was not sure he was the father. And Ellen Sherman was urged by her husband to have affairs of her own; she would later say that she had gone to bed with three other men. Len Fredriksen, an employee at Ad Graphics, was one of her lovers, though this sexual part of their relationship lasted for a very short time.

Sherman continued to pursue other romantic interests, in addition to his wife and mistress, something both women seemed to tolerate. Then, in early 1984, his mistress became pregnant and in November gave birth to Sherman's daughter. Ellen Sherman had dreamed of having more chil-

*Denotes pseudonyms

dren, something her husband had strongly opposed. News of the new baby in her husband's life so upset Ellen that she won a commitment from her husband to have another child, as long as Mrs. Sherman promised to do all the "logistical work" needed to raise the baby. Mrs. Sherman had her doctor remove a contraceptive device in December of 1984.

Ellen Sherman had met her husband's mistress several times, once having coffee with her at an Old Lyme restaurant, where the two talked. But now Ellen had become outspoken about the mistress's role in her husband's life. In the first few months of 1985, Ellen phoned the mistress at a time when she suspected her husband was in her home in Groton, located on the eastern side of New London from Niantic, and broke the news to her that she would be having her own baby. Ellen was particularly pleased, she told the mistress, that her due date coincided with the birth date the year earlier of her husband's out-of-wedlock child. On April 2, Jessica, the couple's daughter, ran away from home but for only a few hours. This episode could have been caused by the growing tension between her parents.

The acrimony between the two women and Edward Sherman mounted. The mistress had begun to give ultimatums to Sherman to get a divorce from Ellen or break off the relationship with her. Sherman expressed interest in helping support his mistress's daughter financially and had set up scheduled times when he could visit the child. While Ellen Sherman was overjoyed at her pregnancy, she also began to pressure Sherman to return home permanently and take on the normal role of father and husband. On June 16, Father's Day of 1985, Edward and Ellen Sherman had a family fight which lasted all day. (Holidays, as we've seen before, can often be the backdrop for escalating friction within a troubled marriage.) Sherman threw a broken television set across the room into a wall and also tossed stereo speakers, as well as pulling out a loose banister from a staircase railing. He raged at his wife over their home being in a broken-down condition. The next day, Ellen was forced to postpone an amniocentesis appointment at her doctor's office, because she was bleeding from her vagina, a result of the previous day's fighting. A close friend and neighbor, Sandra Wright,* witnessed a substantial part of this terrifying, hours-long fight. On the following Monday, Ellen's employees saw her wearing dark glasses indoors and far more makeup than usual. Her staff at the office, where she was quite popular, also saw Ellen in tears; and one worker said that her hands shook the entire hour she was there. Edward Sherman's domestic violence was not confined to his wife; his mistress would later testify that he had kicked her in the head.

After the Father's Day tirade, the relationship between Ellen and Edward Sherman began to disintegrate. In the next few days, Ellen would order her husband to leave the house. She did this when she suspected he was at his mistress's home; she and Sherman actually passed one another in Groton one weekday, as Ellen drove her car there with her husband's clothes and his bag packed. Meanwhile, the mistress had told Sherman that she expected a decision on his divorce immediately and that they would not be seeing one another until, and if, he had decided to permanently end his marriage. Sherman then asked his mistress if she would "still be there" for him once he had become single, and she replied that she would have to think things over. In the next month, the mistress would ask two real estate agents to price her Groton house for possible sale.

Sherman had become an avid sailor. Ellen and he had purchased a sailboat earlier that spring, so he went to live on the boat. After a couple of weeks, Ellen agreed to take her husband back, especially after he gave her his assurance that he had made a decision to abandon his relationship with his mistress, except for staying close to the daughter he had fathered with her. Late in June, Edward Sherman's cousin, who lived in Tolland in northern Connecticut, spent a Sunday with the couple, some of the time at their new boat, and she would later say that the two seemed very happy together, even "acting like newlyweds."

Ellen Sherman was interested in writing and had been at work for months on a novel, one which portrayed a husband who has a mistress, kills his wife, turns the air-conditioning up to full force, and leaves her corpse behind in their locked house. Ellen never actually showed this work to Sherman, but her daughter, Jessica, printed out the text from her mother's computer and gave it to Ellen's mother, Mrs. Rose Cooper, of Pembroke Pines, Florida.

In July, Ellen Sherman again began to suspect that her husband was still spending time with his mistress, a feeling which would prove accurate. She now began to confide to close friends, including Len Fredriksen at work, that she had run out of patience with her husband's behaviors and would divorce him. "I can take care of myself and our children," she effectively told her select friends. Ellen also sketched out the fact that she would be able to come away from the divorce with the business, the couple's house, and child support payments. This would, in her words, "leave him nothing." Sherman and his mistress were now house-hunting themselves, looking at a property on one of New London's oldest and most picturesque streets. With her husband, Ellen Sherman looked into selling Ad Graphics, and the couple asked a business broker to determine a price they might expect for it. Ellen asked the broker whether the payment for the business could be made out in two checks, one each to the husband and the wife, and he assured her that was possible. Edward Sherman would later say that, as far as he was concerned, he was just going through the motions. This was contradicted by an agreement the couple had signed with the broker that required them to sell, once their sale conditions had been met. Sherman would make a similar disclaimer about not seriously looking for a house to buy with his mistress and only going through the motions to please the salesperson.

In pursuing his passion for sailing, Sherman had become very friendly with a group of other sailors who would occasionally get together to sail a vessel back to the New London area for a boat owner. In July four of these sailing buddies and Sherman agreed to drive to Rockland, Maine, a five-hour trip, and navigate a thirty-two-foot sloop back, setting sail the morning of Saturday, August 3.

Toward the end of July, the Shermans' on-again, off-again marriage seemed to be back on. This was in sharp contrast to Edward Sherman's relationship with his mistress. On July 31, however, she agreed to let him drive her and their daughter home from work, since she did not feel well. He did this, prepared a dinner for the family, and then borrowed money from her to take a cab back to the college to get his own car so he could drive home. Earlier that week, the Shermans' daughter, Jessica, had left to spend ten days at a children's summer camp in nearby Chester.

Ellen did not react to her husband's late arrival home on July 31, but she was hurt that Sherman would be going off on a sailing jaunt the following Friday, August 2, since that was his forty-second birthday. That birthday Ellen worked in the morning, had a light lunch (a grilled cheese sandwich) at an East Lyme restaurant, and then joined her husband to go swimming at a YMCA pool in Westbrook, fifteen miles west of their home. The couple returned to their house midafternoon, and around four Ellen, wearing khaki shorts, was seen walking the family dog, by a neighbor. As they awoke that Friday morning, Ellen gave her husband a birthday card which featured a kiss from two very red lips on its cover and asked, "Do you know who's sending you this card?" Inside, in equally bold red lettering, the card answered itself with, "You'd better." Ellen had signed it, "Guess Who?" Late that afternoon, when she had finished her walk, Ellen Sherman gave her husband a birthday present of a milk shake maker she had purchased two days earlier, and the two shared a chocolate chip milk shake.

On his birthday, Sherman had sent a letter to Jessica at camp saying that her parents missed her and promising that Ellen would come out to visit her that Saturday. During that Friday, Edward Sherman had had two conversations which would later prove crucial. He spoke with Anita Simon,* the daughter of one of his fellow boaters, Everett Simon.* Anita, a teenager with whom Sherman had chatted about movies in the past, was working at her father's East Lyme hardware store. On this occasion, Sherman had asked Anita if she'd seen a new HBO movie, *The Blackout*, which had premiered the night before. Anita hadn't, so Sherman briefly described the film's plot, which featured a businessman named Ed, who had killed his wife and children at home one night and then had turned up the house's air-conditioning full force to delay their bodies' decomposition over the following weekend.

In the other encounter, Sherman happened to meet his neighbor, Charles Wright,* outside the Niantic post office. Wright's wife, Sandra,* was a close friend of Ellen's and someone who had witnessed the bitter Father's Day fighting. Wright told Sherman that the couple was going to New Jersey and then Manhattan for the weekend, so Sherman went back to his car and produced a roadmap of New Jersey to help them. Phone calls Edward Sherman would later make to the Wrights and others after he left and was on his sailing trip would become critical to the prosecution's case.

After the dinner hour on that Friday, Edward Sherman did some other strange things. After 7 P.M., while he waited to be picked up by Stanley Mueller,* one of his sailing buddies, he pulled out of his driveway and slowly drove up the incline of his street. After a hundred yards or so, he encountered a neighbor, Charles VonKrack of Hastings, New York, who was walking with his family. VonKrack had observed Ellen Sherman during her earlier walk with her dog. Sherman now stopped his car in a manner which seemed to block the roadway and proceeded to chat amicably with the VonKrack family. Over the past few summers, VonKrack had struck up a chatty friendship with Ellen Sherman but had never received so much as a wave or a nod from Edward Sherman. Just as this conversation was ending, Mueller's car approached and Sherman turned his car around. He then pulled his vehicle back into his driveway, sprang out, opened his trunk, pulled out his sailing bag, and hopped into Mueller's car.

Sherman was not wearing his customary tinted aviator-style sunglasses as he got into Mueller's car; he would buy a similar pair at L. L. Bean in Freeport, Maine, early the next morning. In response to Mueller's question, Sherman said his wife was too busy to come out to say good-bye. This seemed odd to Mueller, since it was not, in his estimation, like Ellen Sherman to refrain from making some kind of friendly and personal contact and to wish them well on their sailing trip. Sherman also seemed oddly dressed for the trip, wearing long pants and two long-sleeved shirts which were buttoned at the wrists. The other four crew members would all wear shorts and single summer shirts.

Edward Sherman had been pushing Mueller and his other buddies for an earlier departure all along. Initially, the group was to leave around 10 P.M., which would get them to Rockland not long before dawn, a practical time since the boat they would be sailing would not be available until eight in the morning. First, the group had adjusted their departure time forward to 8:30 and then, finally, at Sherman's urging, to 7:30, when he was picked up. Sherman then persuaded Mueller to detour over to the Niantic boataminium where he had moored his craft, so he could do some last minute checking on its padlock and battery. They now doubled back to pick up another crew member and would stop at a package store just before its mandatory 8 P.M. closing time, to pick up some beer. Then the trio would go to the Albright* home for the final two crew members, where, as it later turned out, Sherman would do something which was beyond strange.

Jamie Albright was then the eight-year-old daughter of another sailing buddy, Bill Albright of Old Lyme, who owned an auto repair shop which specialized in foreign cars. When Sherman and the others arrived at their home, Mrs. Albright was on the phone talking long distance to her mother-in-law about the condition of a relative who was ill. Sherman, shortly after his arrival, asked if he could soon use the phone since there were some important details he wanted to tell his wife. Jamie, who was in the next room, had wanted to make a call to a friend and was mindful of an Albright family tradition which held that the phone would be available to the next person who had asked for it. Thus, when Sherman got on the phone, the child was miffed. Jamie, who had the habit of eavesdropping on her mother's conversations, picked up the phone and heard Sherman carrying on a stagy, one-way conversation, with only a ringing signal on the wire.

Sherman concluded this phony call with the comments, "If you need anything, go to the neighbors. We're leaving to go now.... Goodbye, honey.... I love you, too." These final words were spoken especially as though Sherman was responding to a statement by someone at the other end. All the while, Jamie Albright heard nothing but the ringing signal. The sailors then left and drove the five hours to

Maine and boarded their sailboat the next morning, after shopping at L. L. Bean. After the boat got underway, Sherman repeatedly used the ship-to-shore radio telephone to try to reach his wife, since he said he had to provide her with the numbers for the padlock securing their boat and he wanted her to make sure that he'd turned off the vessel's battery. When the couple had purchased the boat, the seller had made the padlock's numbers as easy as possible for the Shermans to remember. They matched the boat's registration numbers, which were displayed on both sides of the bow in large block lettering. Then on Saturday evening, when the sailboat put into the harbor at Gloucester, Massachusetts, so the five could go to a seafood restaurant for dinner, Sherman again went through the motions of trying to phone his wife.

Sherman wasn't the only one having trouble getting through to the family's number that weekend. As early as 6:30 Friday evening, an hour before Sherman left the house, phone calls to Ellen were going unanswered. Her brother, Frank Goldstein, of Huntington, Long Island, had just received a letter from his sister and wanted to talk to her about what she'd written. Goldstein then called his sister's number every half hour, until a last call at 10 P.M. when he gave up. On the following Sunday, Sherman began to express misgivings about Ellen's whereabouts to his crewmates, and he began to make more ship-to-shore calls. One was to see if Ellen was at the Wrights', even though he'd been told the previous Friday that those neighbors would be out of town for the entire weekend.

In the early evening, Sherman called another neighbor, June Rossiter,* Ellen's close friend. Rossiter did not like Edward Sherman and the way she thought he pushed her close friend around, constantly putting her down. Rossiter was a blonde country singer from New Orleans who performed under the stage name, Melissa Taft.* Sherman told Rossiter that he was concerned about not reaching Ellen and asked her, according to June, to go to the house to check on his wife, a request Sherman later denied making. Instead, Rossiter called Ellen's coworker, Len Fredriksen, who also lived in East Lyme, and he agreed to drive over to the Sherman house to check around. Fredriksen was worried about his friend. The last time he had talked to Ellen Sherman was at the office on the previous Thursday, and her swollen face showed that she had been crying. He asked her what was wrong, and she said, "I have to talk to you." Those were the last words he would ever hear from her.

Len Fredriksen drove directly to Ellen Sherman's house on Park Court and was unable to get any response to the doorbell, though he saw lights on inside and outside and heard an air conditioner running. Next, he went around the structure and tried to look in a window to see if he could find Ellen at home. He saw that the living room blinds were pulled down, which was unusual. After tapping on windows to try to get a response, Fredriksen pried open a screen on the house's porch and let himself into the house through a window. He moved through a foyer and the kitchen, which had piles of dog feces on newspapers that had been laid out on the floor. Becoming increasingly anxious, Fredriksen went up the central staircase and knocked on the door to the master bedroom. He heard nothing, so he slowly opened the door and immediately felt a cold blast from the room's air conditioner which was on full cold. In the graying light he saw Ellen Sherman's nude body lying on the bed, face up. Fredriksen advanced and tried to find a pulse. Just then, the phone rang and he picked it up. The caller was Edward Sherman's mother, Mrs. Charlet Sherman, of Margate, Florida. Fredriksen said only, "Hurry up. I can't talk," and hung up. He then called 911 for the East Lyme police and paramedics. Next he called June Rossiter, broke the tragic news to her, and she replied that she would be right over. She arrived at the Sherman house within five minutes and found Frederiksen sitting on the house's front steps. His head bowed and buried in his hands, Frederiksen said, "June, we've lost her."

THE INVESTIGATION OF THE CASE

I was at home on Sunday evening, August 4, 1985, when the phone rang and I was told about the murder. I immediately dropped everything I was doing and left for the crime scene, which was a little less than an hour's drive from our house. Margaret, my wife of thirty-eight years, is very used to these kinds of sudden interruptions in our home life. I was a police captain in Taiwan when I first met Margaret and, as I've mentioned, she knows all too well that having to go out the door at any hour of the day or night, in any kind of weather, is simply a part of my professional obligations.

By the time I entered the Sherman house, a number of police officers, detectives, and paramedics had been in the master bedroom, so the room did not feel extremely cold to me, the way it had when Len Fredriksen had opened the door. Once the paramedics had gone in, the door had been left ajar, so the warmer air in the rest of the house had been moving upward and into the bedroom. I looked on the bed and saw the nude body of Ellen Sherman, pregnant and lying in a supine position. I could plainly observe two deep and very red ligature marks around her neck. I saw beads from a broken row of a necklace that she had been wearing. Off to the side of the bed, I also saw her torn, blue, bikini-style underpants, which had been stretched out of shape. I also saw a bra and, to the side of the bed, a white slip. There was a third, thinner abrasion mark on her neck, one that seemed pressed into her flesh.

The scene of the murder—
an exterior view of the Sherman residence.

I took out my big magnifying glass and laser equipment and began to closely study the entire murder scene, paying particular attention to the wounds on the neck and stains on the bedsheets. As I more closely examined the stretched-out underpants, I recognized a pattern in the elastic band which went around the wearer's waist, and I compared this to the pattern I had observed on the victim's neck. They were very similar, though the pattern on the waistband seemed a little narrower than that found on the body. There is a tendency to reach a conclusion at a time like this, one that I have always resisted. I would need to bring the underpants back to our forensic laboratory in Meriden to make a precise comparison of those two patterns, but I felt that there was a good chance the underpants had been used as a ligature in this murder. I was equally confident that the killer had also strangled his victim with his hands, accounting for the two florid abrasions. In my inspection of the victim's underpants, I found no traces of blood or semen-like materials.

While I looked closely at this crime scene for traces of transfer evi-

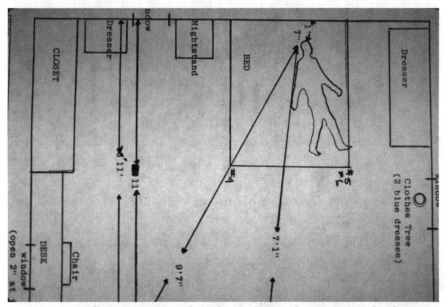

Crime scene sketches show the master bedroom.
The victim's body was found in the bed.

dence, I was also concerned about things I had not seen or had not been otherwise experiencing. If a human being has been dead for more than a few hours, the body begins to change, and this process sends out valuable signals, such as a stench and discoloration of its flesh. I did not note these clues and would not have normally thought that the victim had been dead for more than two days. However, when I heard a report that the bedroom, when first entered, had been extremely cold, my estimates on the time of death immediately were put on hold. A corpse which is in a very cold environment, such as in a refrigerated room, will decompose at a much slower rate than a body which is in normal summer temperatures. (See the end of this chapter for medical forensics on establishing the time of death.)

As I looked very carefully at the sheets, I noted urine, saliva, and mucus stains. Some of the saliva stains were under the body, as it lay supine. I also had observed a white frothy foam which had come out of her nose and mouth. The upper satin sheet contained forty stains which appeared to be semen, yet there was no evidence of any sexual assault. In studying the body itself, I found that the victim was still in rigor. (See the medical forensics discussion on this phenomenon at the end of this chapter.) It became apparent to me that the victim had probably been strangled at least once from behind, with her face down, directly leaving the saliva and mucus on the sheets, and her body had been turned over by someone following her death. Upon closer examination, some of the many semen stains appeared to have been washed. Thus, the semen could have been deposited on the sheets over a long period of time and some could have even been the result of masturbation. During the trial, defense lawyer James Wade asked me "are those semen stains from one person?" My answer to him was "I cannot do it, maybe you can, Mr. Wade."

At seven the next morning, Dr. Catherine Galvin, then the former state's chief medical examiner, arrived and conducted her own murder scene investigation. Dr. Galvin's first estimated time of death was between 10 P.M. Friday, August 2, and 7 A.M. Sunday, August 4. However, after a lengthy discussion with her regarding the extremely cold temperatures in the murder scene and her subsequent autopsy, and weighing this question for several months, Dr. Galvin would revise this estimate to cover a timespan from 7 A.M. Thursday, August 1, to 7 A.M. Saturday, August 3. This would mean that Edward Sherman had ample time to commit the murder. During her autopsy, Dr. Galvin would find the victim's last meal undigested, the linguini and seafood sauce mentioned earlier. This indicated that, under normal room temperatures, Ellen Sherman would have eaten her last dinner less than five hours prior to her death. That is the time normally needed for the ingested food remains to move into her small intestines. (See the forensic medicine discussion at the end of this chapter.) Initially, Dr. Galvin also thought that the victim's bra had been the murder weapon, an opinion she would later revise. As new evidence comes forward, revisions are not unusual.

The state police's Eastern Major Crime Squad was called in to assist the East Lyme police to investigate this case. Detectives took photos and thoroughly searched the Sherman house and grounds. Among the items seized were a pair of tinted, aviator-style sunglasses. Police also found a copy of a local newspaper, the *Black Pointer*, rolled up for delivery inside the front screen door's handle. This paper had been circulated on Friday evening. Early Monday morning, Edward Sherman was contacted at sea, and his boat was ordered to proceed by engine to the Coast Guard station at Wood's Hole, in Massachusetts. Sherman broke the news of his wife's death to his shocked crewmates. The boat docked around nine that Monday morning, and Sherman was taken by state police detectives to a room there where he was questioned.

State police Lieutenant William Sydenham and Detective Michael Malchik conducted this initial interview. Malchik asked Sherman, hypothetically, what he would say if investigators found his skin tissue under his wife's fingernails. Sherman replied that he'd forgotten to tell the police that Ellen had scratched his back. The two investigators saw two deep scratches on Sherman's wrist, lacerations which had previously been covered up by the two long-sleeve shirts he wore for the sailing trip. Both investigators made note of the fact that Sherman knew his wife had been strangled, a fact they had not shared with him. Sherman's four crewmates were soon released and allowed to continue sailing their boat down toward New London. Sherman was next taken by helicopter to the Groton airport and then to his home. State police continued to question him, and it was clear, from the outset, that he was a prime suspect, whether he had been sailing for the weekend or not.

Back in the Black Point section of Niantic, police investigators were looking through garbage cans throughout the neighborhood, and they discovered two items of Sherman's in the garbage of the house next door: a bill of sale for the Shermans' new sailing boat and a voided check Edward Sherman had made out to an orthodontist for $550. This amount would have paid off the remaining charges for Jessica's braces. Sherman had disposed of the check, dated August 2, police hypothesized, since he realized he wouldn't have to make good on this bill after his daughter later moved to Florida to live with Mrs. Rose Cooper, her maternal grandmother. This is, in fact, where Jessica went soon afterward. On Monday, August 5, Edward Sherman did not bother going to see his daughter at camp or calling to console her on her mother's death. Jessica Sherman was independently notified the Monday morning after Ellen Sherman's strangled body had been found. Sherman, however, called his mother in Florida and, according to him, she did not mention her Sunday evening call to his home and her truncated conversation with a strange, male voice.

The police gave Edward Sherman the use of his house late that Monday afternoon. However, Detective Malchik executed a search warrant on Thursday and seized food from the refrigerator and dishes from the dishwasher. This three-day gap provided the defense with the argument that the chain of custody for evidence had been broken and, thus, the linguine and red clam sauce found in the refrigerator, for instance, could not be introduced as evidence, since it might have been placed there after the body had been discovered. This would become a legal battleground in the eventual trial. The police searching the house were unable to find Sherman's address book and his files, though the files turned up later.

All of the state's major media played up Ellen Sherman's shocking

death, covering the case in great detail. As they were completing their
sailing trip, Sherman's four boatmates talked about the possibility of
him being the killer. On August 22, Sherman retained the services of
attorney James A. Wade of Hartford, one of Connecticut's most preeminent defense lawyers. He would be ably assisted by his colleague,
Daniel Sullivan. The police worked this case very hard, questioning as
many as two hundred potential witnesses. The couple's stormy marriage became a key issue. Meanwhile, detectives came to my office in
the Meriden Crime Laboratory to discuss the case and requested a
crime scene reconstruction. When I reviewed the case and pondered
the fact that Ellen Sherman had been pregnant, I raised the question as
to who was the father of the fetus. However, no fetal tissue had been
collected during the initial autopsy. After a meeting with the New
London County chief state's attorney, C. Robert Satti, a decision was
made to conduct a serological typing of the fetus to enable us to conduct a paternity test. On October 11, Dr. Galvin had Ellen Sherman's
body exhumed, and she performed an autopsy on the victim's dead
fetus. She found that the fetus had undergone some decomposition and
the tissue became dissolutive. I was at the autopsy to collect bones
from, and examine the fetus. Those bones were taken back to my laboratory for further serology analysis to determine the paternity.

The prosecution team, which would be headed up by Robert Satti
and his senior assistant state's attorney, Kevin T. Kane, now debated
whether to charge the murderer with two killings, that of Ellen
Sherman and also the fetus she was carrying. This was extremely relevant since the two convictions could mean the death penalty or life in
prison. Since the age of the fetus was less than six months, the determination was made that it could not have survived on its own and,
thus, the second charge was not applicable.

Ellen Sherman's mother would later say that Edward Sherman did
not seem grief-stricken during her daughter's funeral a few days after
her death. Indeed, Sherman would soon be living with his mistress and
her two children. In 1986 the mistress would sell her house in Groton,
and Sherman and she then would buy a house in Old Saybrook, a

graceful and old town on Long Island Sound, just across the mouth of the Connecticut River from New London County. They would eventually buy a second home there. This kind of behavior by the case's prime suspect only energized the police and prosecution team investigating the murder. Also in 1986, Sherman, who was the executor of his wife's estate, would inherit $173,000, their combined assets, as well as receive $76,500 in life insurance death benefits. After some negotiation, Sherman would agree to pay Mrs. Rose Cooper, Ellen's mother, $15,000 from these amounts.

The investigation into this murder was sent to a one-man grand jury in 1986. This grand jury probe was to be conducted in absolute secrecy. Judge Joseph J. Purtill would conduct this exacting investigation, and he would have to call dozens of witnesses to testify, myself among them. All of this work on the grand jury probe had to be scheduled around Judge Purtill's busy court schedule since he was a sitting jurist. This added to the delays, and this probe would end up taking nearly two years.

In 1986, Sherman refused to sell the business, defying the agreement his wife and he had signed with the broker. The broker then sued Sherman and won. On appeal, though, Sherman would have the decision overturned. Eventually, in 1991, Sherman sold Ad Graphics. The agreement to sell the business was not the only time that Edward Sherman would find himself in more trouble with the legal system. During the grand jury probe, which went on through all of 1987, Sherman approached his former sailing buddy, Stanley Mueller, just as he was to testify. Sherman asked Mueller to say that the living room blind in the Sherman house was up when he had stopped in front to pick him up. Sherman also asked Mueller to say that he did not hear the air-conditioning unit running. Oddly enough, this last piece of testimony would not, on its face, be false, since Mueller did not get out of his car and would never have been close enough to the house to hear the air conditioner. Mueller reported Sherman's attempts to tamper with his testimony, and Sherman was sternly warned by Judge Purtill that he had better cease any attempts to tamper with any other witnesses.

In 1988, Michael Malchik left the state police to go to law school. As a detective Malchik had come under severe criticism by some of his colleagues for not taking the master bedroom's temperature when he first arrived at the crime scene. There was a thermometer in the room, one which showed a normal indoor temperature when investigators arrived at the scene and noted it. Given the aerodynamics of a very cold room in a normally warm house in summer, any temperature reading taken after the bedroom door had been left open for any length of time would prove invalid. Malchik continued to work on this case for the next several years. He was one of the most dedicated and smartest detectives on the force at the time of the murder. Detective Malchik also received a lot of credit and favorable publicity for his work in solving the string of sexual assaults and murders of teenage girls in New London County committed earlier in the eighties by serial killer Michael Ross.

The defense attorney, James Wade, is one of the best defense lawyers in the state. He is extremely seasoned and very smooth. The case's prosecutor, Robert Satti, who is now enjoying his retirement from a long and distinguished career in public service, is a very careful and cautious attorney. Some courtroom observers coined the nickname "Bull Dog" to describe his passionate and determined efforts in his pursuit of justice. Bob Satti is a good friend of mine, a bond forged through years of working together. His principal assistant, Kevin Kane, is another extremely hardworking, excellent lawyer and is also a close friend. Working with their chief investigator, Thomas W. Viens, the prosecution pursued the Sherman case for two more years. Then on March 20, 1990, the prosecution team issued an arrest warrant for Edward R. Sherman for the murder of his wife. Judge Robert Burns initially set bail at $150,000, but would reduce that amount to $75,000 the next day, at the urging of defense counsel Wade. Sherman would post bail that day and would be free, though he would take a leave of absence from his teaching position at Mohegan Community College.

Shortly after Sherman's arrest, Jamie Albright heard the news on a car radio as she rode with her family. She told her father and her stepmother that she thought she had some evidence in the case and narrated her recollections of the strange, one-way telephone call she'd heard Sherman make on the evening of August 2, 1985. This development strengthened the state's case and hardened the resolve of the prosecution team.

Judge Joseph Q. Koletsky would preside over a probable cause hearing in June 1990. Held at the New London County Superior Court House, a short distance from Long Island Sound, this forum would determine if Sherman should be tried before a jury for his wife's murder. I would testify on June 19, early in the fourteen days the hearing lasted, and present thirty-six color slides of the murder scene, the victim's torn underpants, and other case evidence to reconstruct what had happened, when it had happened, and how it had happened. Sherman would not look at these slides, since, as defense attorney James Wade argued, he had never seen them before. During my six hours on the stand, I gave my opinion that the underpants had been ripped off of the victim and then used as a ligature in her fatal strangulation. The slides clearly showed three long, narrow, and red abrasions on Ellen Sherman's throat. I then compared the zig-zag and scalloped patterns on the elastic waistband around the underpants with the similar pattern which we found etched in the victim's neck. My top assistant, Elaine Pagliaro, and I conducted a microscopic study and made detailed measurements. We concluded that the torn underpants, in fact, were the ligature used for strangulation.

Defense attorney James Wade objected to my testimony and cited Dr. Galvin's 1985 opinion that the murderer had strangled Ellen Sherman with her bra. My response to this was that all forensic experts are entitled to their own opinions. Whether or not their opinions are believed depends on the court and the jury which evaluates them. What are presented in court are my scientific findings, which represent my opinion. I also noted semen stains on the bedsheets and on the victim's underpants, but said that there was no evidence of a sexual assault. Later that day, former state police detective Michael Malchik used a crime scene videotape to show the piles of dog feces on newspapers strewn about the home's floor and dirt from an overturned flowerpot. During the hearing, dozens of other prosecution witnesses would testify. Judge Koletsky then adjourned the public forum, considered the matter, and ultimately ruled that Sherman should be tried for murder in the first degree.[1]

THE SHERMAN TRIAL

Edward Sherman's trial for murder would begin on Monday, November 4, 1991. Judge Robert C. Leuba would preside. Judge Leuba had a strong reputation for being fair-minded, meticulous, and conscientious. The jury would initially consist of eight men and four women, with four alternates. During the *voire dire*, or jury selection process, both sides were careful to choose jurors who had not been influenced by the case's considerable media attention. The prosecution was most interested in finding prospective jurors who would be willing to find an individual guilty in a murder case, while the defense was concerned about seating jurors who would not be prejudiced against a husband who had engaged in marital infidelities. Most courtroom observers thought the trial would take about four weeks, a forecast that underestimated the case's complexity.

Judge Leuba would rule out the evidence of Edward Sherman's arrest in 1988 for assaulting his mistress, with whom he had lived in Old Saybrook until several weeks before the trial started. Robert Satti, the lead prosecutor, had photos of the battered woman he had wanted to introduce, as well as evidence that she had told the local police that Sherman had murdered his wife. He also would not admit into evidence Sherman's assault of another lover in the mid-seventies. In making his ruling, the trial judge said that, in his opinion, this evidence would be more prejudicial to the defendant than helpful to the prosecution when it made its case. Judge Leuba also ruled against admission of any evidence of the delivery of the Niantic neighborhood's newsletter, the *Black Pointer*, since the defense had not received prior notification on this piece of information. The newsletter, delivered to the Sherman home on the Friday prior to Ellen Sherman's body being discovered, was visible in a police videotape made on Monday, August 5. Finally, Judge Leuba would reject a defense motion to dismiss the case based on the five-and-a-half-year period which had elapsed from the murder until the trial.[2]

The prosecution would call me to the stand on December 7, and I would testify on direct examination for three days and would be cross-examined for another full day. As I had at the probable cause hearing, I showed slides of the victim and the crime scene. Carefully explaining to the jury and the court what I considered my key points, I reconstructed the crime scene. Ellen Sherman had been strangled two times, once by her assailant's bare hands and once by her torn blue underpants, which had been ripped off of her. One of my slides showed the three long and deep abrasions on the victim's neck. I then analyzed the pattern I had observed in a wound on her neck and compared it to the pattern I had found on the underpants' elastic waistband.

In his cross-examination, the seasoned defense lawyer Wade challenged me again with the fact that Dr. Galvin had thought that the murderer had used the victim's bra as a ligature. I again said that this was her opinion. The bra was simply not long enough to go around the victim's neck and then leave a set of three uniform and narrow grooves. Wade then decided to conduct an experiment to see whether or not the elastic band from the underpants could stretch far enough to actually strangle someone. I asked him to put the underpants around his neck, which he did. Then I asked Wade to double the band around his neck, which he again was able to do. I demonstrated that the waistband could be stretched to a length of fifty inches. Wade then objected to this demonstration, an objection which was overruled. I think it will be a long time before he and I will forget the image of this distinguished gentleman standing in front of the court, his hair slightly mussed, with three loops of the underwear around his neck. The following morning's newspapers used this demonstration for their headlines.

My testimony on the room's temperature was very minimal. I

pointed out that there appeared to be ice accumulated on the air conditioner. As far as the room's exact temperature went, I testified that I did not know. We all have to know the limitations of science. The defense would ultimately introduce an expert witness on air-conditioning, who would testify that the unit should have had an automatic shut-off feature which would prevent the room from becoming very cold. Wade would also challenge a prosecution witness, a state policeman who testified that he had seen frost formed on the unit's interior side. Frost and ice could form, the defense expert testified, but on the exterior side of the air conditioner. The state investigator had probably observed beads of moisture, the expert concluded.

Ellen Sherman's time of death would prove the critical battleground in this trial. Wade would attempt to spotlight Dr. Catherine Galvin's initial estimate of a much later time of the murder. Dr. Galvin explained to the crowded courtroom her reasons for revising her estimate to an earlier time frame, one that would have enabled Sherman the time to kill his wife. Once Dr. Galvin established the impact the

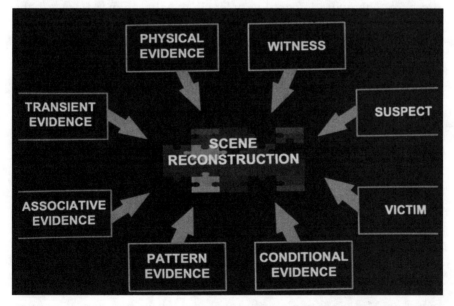

The diagram shows the elements of
crime scene reconstruction

colder air would have had on the decomposition process, she then shifted her testimony to focus on the victim's undigested supper of linguine and a seafood sauce, as found in her autopsy. This analysis dovetailed with the leftover plate of linguine and red clam sauce found by the police in the Shermans' refrigerator.

Young Jamie Albright, a teenager at the time of the trial, would lead a series of prosecution witnesses who testified to Edward Sherman's peculiar behavior, particularly with the telephone, both on the Friday evening the prosecution charged that his wife had died, and on into the next two days.[3] Charles VonKrack, the summertime neighbor in Black Point, would prove a particularly effective witness. Why had Sherman decided to finally recognize his existence, stop his car in a blocking maneuver, and talk to him that evening? Also, Sherman would, during his own testimony later in the trial, directly contradict VonKrack's testimony on seeing Ellen Sherman wearing khaki shorts when she walked the family dog at four that Friday afternoon. Sherman would tell the jury his wife was still wearing her blue dress from her workday until very late in the afternoon. Afterward, the jurors would, interestingly enough, say they largely discounted Jamie Albright's testimony, but were particularly impressed with what VonKrack had to say.

Testimony on the Shermans' marital difficulties was also important. Sandra Wright would detail the horrible fight the couple had had on Father's Day. Evidence of Sherman choking a high school student was also introduced. June Rossiter spelled out, in one of the lengthy trial's most colorful episodes, Edward Sherman's bullying and angry behaviors toward his wife. Wearing braided, white leather slacks and looking a lot more like Melissa Taft, her stage name, the blonde and emotional friend of Ellen Sherman came across to the courtroom full of lawyers, jurors, press, and spectators as extremely sincere. The jury and courtroom also watched the entirety of the HBO film *Blackout* after James Wade objected to only portions of it being shown. Testimony on Mrs. Sherman's own novel, a work in progress, was ruled inadmissible by Judge Leuba.

Edward Sherman's own testimony, a keystone to the defense's case, proved to be climactic. Under direct questioning by Wade, Sherman denied killing his wife, said he loved her, and that Ellen had never discussed getting a divorce. He also denied that the couple was trying to sell Ad Graphics and their magazine. Sherman admitted to having affairs with other women and expressed remorse for the life-style he had chosen. Sherman went on to discuss future plans for the business he had shared with his wife, such as starting up a companion health magazine, called *YOU*, and otherwise expanding their business. Sherman wore his tinted sunglasses during all of his testimony.

Robert Satti cross-examined Sherman for ten days. Satti attacked Sherman's account of how he spent his hours before leaving Ellen on that last Friday of her life. Satti very carefully probed the nature of Sherman's stormy relationship with his mistress and the fact they had gone house hunting together in New London in June 1985. He also bore down on Sherman's assertion that his wife had never discussed getting a divorce, using statements from prosecution witnesses. Satti grilled Sherman about the testimony from his wife's coworkers on how she looked and acted the day after his violent Father's Day out-burst. On the stand, Sherman seemed to fumble for answers under this withering barrage, according to jurors who were interviewed after the trial. Satti zeroed in on Stanley Mueller's testimony about how Sherman had acted when he'd been picked up and how Mrs. Sherman had uncharacteristically not come out to see the two men off on their sailing trip. He reminded Sherman of what his daughter, Jessica, had said about her never having seen the living room blind down before. And then there were dozens of questions about all of those phone calls. Kevin Kane, Satti's cautious lead assistant, sat and watched all of this intently, wondering when Satti would finally let up. Kane wor-ried that the grilling could possibly verge on overkill. Yet, more than anything else, this masterful cross-examination seemed to set the stage for the verdict which followed.

After receiving their instructions, the jury, which now consisted of nine men and three women, because two jurors had to be dismissed for personal reasons, began deliberating Tuesday, February 4, seven weeks after the trial had started. During the next four days, the jurors asked to rehear testimony from several witnesses, and they seemed particularly interested in evidence on the time line and the expert testimony establishing the time of death. At 3:40 P.M. Friday, February 7, the jury returned its verdict of guilty.[4] James Wade asked that the jury be polled, and each stood and spoke out the word, "guilty." When the jurors had first begun their deliberations, they had taken a preliminary vote. Four had voted guilty and the other eight were undecided. Before the jury members finally broke to file back into the courtroom and render their decision, they gathered themselves and spoke a prayer for Ellen Sherman and the unborn son who died along with her. This occasioned one last objection from Wade, which was overruled. Sherman was taken to the Montville Correction Center, and Judge Leuba set his appeals bond at $250,000, an amount he would not make.[5]

On March 17, Edward Sherman was sentenced by Judge Leuba to fifty years in prison for the murder of his pregnant wife. Mrs. Rose Cooper said she had "mixed feelings" about the verdict because it was very hard for her to accept that her son-in-law had actually murdered her daughter. She was happy, though, that justice for her daughter had been done. Mrs. Cooper had high praise for the police and prosecution teams and also said that she hoped "there would be no more victims." James Wade would appeal this conviction on a number of counts, but Sherman's verdict would stand. Jessica Sherman went on to college. She would remain steadfast in her belief that her father was innocent of this crime. Upon his conviction, Edward Sherman would officially be terminated from his $42,000-a-year position at Three Rivers Community College, the new name for that institution of higher learning, but he would remain eligible for his state pension.[6] Edward Robert Sherman died in prison on January 6, 1996.

THE CASE'S SCIENTIFIC FACTS

The Edward Sherman case presented a number of compelling forensic issues, most of which fell into the field of medical forensics. In preparing the scientific portion of the case, my old friends, Dr. Michael Baden, director of forensic science for the New York State Police, and Dr. Romeo Vidone, the chief pathologist at the Hospital of Saint Raphael in New Haven, have provided some of the reference materials and otherwise assisted us.

In 1985, Dr. Catherine Galvin was the chief medical examiner for the state of Connecticut. Her determination of the timespan in which Ellen Sherman actually died was critical to this successful prosecution. Dr. Galvin's initial estimate of the time of death (TOD) did not reflect the murder scene's unusually cold temperature. This was natural since the bedroom's temperature was a normal sixty-eight to seventy degrees Fahrenheit when Dr. Galvin arrived at 7 A.M. the morning after the body had been discovered. Only later, after learning what the room felt like in the words of Len Fredriksen, Dr. Galvin was courageous enough to admit that her initial estimate of the time of death was wrong and that she needed to reassess her estimates. She based her reassessments on two major after-death phenomena: the body's still being in partial rigor and the undigested food left in the victim's stomach.

Before going into a more detailed discussion of these two phenomena, I want to emphasize that even today, with the advances in forensic science, we still struggle to narrow down the exact TOD, and we ultimately rely on the time when the decedent was last seen, all of the body's indicators, as well as the educated guess of a qualified forensic pathologist. This point is well stated in the text *Forensic Pathology* by a father and son team, Doctors Dominic J. Di Maio and Vincent J. M. Di Maio. Both of these gentlemen are excellent forensic pathologists and both are my good friends. Dominic was the former New York City chief medical examiner, whereas Vincent is the chief medical examiner for Bexar County, Texas.

Death is often defined as "the cessation of life." There are many

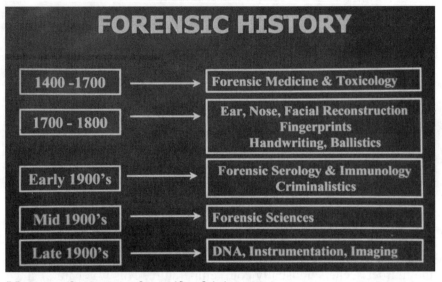

FORENSIC HISTORY

1400 -1700	→	Forensic Medicine & Toxicology
1700 - 1800	→	Ear, Nose, Facial Reconstruction Fingerprints Handwriting, Ballistics
Early 1900's	→	Forensic Serology & Immunology Criminalistics
Mid 1900's	→	Forensic Sciences
Late 1900's	→	DNA, Instrumentation, Imaging

Major milestones show the history
of the development of Forensic Science

types of biological and physiological changes after death. These changes can be used to estimate the time of death. Many renowned forensic pathologists have written excellent treatises on this subject area, such as Dr. Cyril H. Wecht, with his Matthew Bender series *Forensic Sciences: Law/Science Civil/Criminal*; Dr. Werner Spitz, with his *Medicalegal Investigation of Death*; Dr. Michael Baden, and his new book, *Dead Reckoning: The New Science of Catching Killers*; and Vernon Gerberth and his book *Practical Homicide Investigation: Tactics, Procedures, and Forensic Techniques*. They all reach the same conclusion that all the methods and techniques now in use to determine the time of death are just an estimation. A forensic investigator should consider all of the factors, not just the body changes.

However, using modern knowledge of forensic medicine and techniques, a great deal can be utilized to establish a more accurate TOD estimate, especially when the forensic pathologist is able to take into account the existing temperature and other conditions in which the body has been located. "Temperature is the most important variable influencing the 'dwell time' in a particular [decomposition] stage," writes Dr. H. Gill-

King in the text, *Forensic Taphonomy: The Postmortem Fate of Human Remains*, edited by William D. Haglund and Marcella H. Sorg. By "dwell time," Dr. Gill-King refers to the body's processes remaining intact and functioning after a human being becomes clinically dead. And here it's timely to point out that death is most often not a single event, but a pathological process. Other critical factors influence the rate of decomposition after death, such as a body being submerged in cold water, at a high altitude, or in a hermetically sealed environment such as a submarine. In all of these cases, body decomposition will proceed at a slower rate.

In the Sherman case, the body was in a room which was abnormally cold. This meant that the processes normal to decomposition moved forward, but at a slower pace. The warmer an environment, the more quickly the cellular energy within a body will break down. The basic principle, known as the "rule of ten," holds that the speed of the body's chemical reactions increases two or more times with each ten-degree Centigrade rise in temperature.

To determine the time of death, besides studying the postmortem changes in the body, the forensic investigator should always consider the environmental factors, witness statements, and physical evidence at the scene. The best determination of the time of death is still the witness's direct observation of the crime while it was taking place. Next best would be physical evidence which can indicate the time of death. For example, in 1986 a young lady was run over by a vehicle and the body was moved to a deserted park. We had found her watch, which was crushed. The time on the watch (12:15 A.M.) established the exact time of her death. In the absence of direct witness statements or physical evidence, then the postmortem changes and entomological evidence will become a postmortem clock to help investigate and establish the time of death. (See Table 1.)

The early postmortem changes include the cooling of the body, skin discoloration, rigidity, lividity, a drying of the ocular bulbs, changes in the retinal layers of the eyes, fluctuation of the blood glucose levels, changes in potassium concentrations of the eye fluids, and so forth. The most frequently used changes are:

TABLE I EARLY POSTMORTEM CHANGES		
Indications	Start	Changes
cooling of body	at death	2° F per hour in the first six hours, 1–1.5° F each hour afterward
livor mortis	1–2 hours	6–10 hours maximum 10–12 hours—partially fixed 24–48 hours—moveable 3–5 days—permanently fixed
rigor mortis	2–4 hours	12–16 hours—complete 35–48 hours—starts abating

- **a cooling of the body**—Immediately following death, the body temperature gradually falls from its usual 98.6° Fahrenheit until it reaches the ambient temperature. The rate of cooling varies from one to two degrees Fahrenheit per hour. The body mass, the environment temperature, conditions, ventilation, clothing, and humidity all affect the configuration of the cooling curve.
- **livor mortis—postmortem lividity**—The lividity (the discoloration of human skin to a pinkish color) is produced by the gravitational movement of the blood cells and their settling in the small blood vessels of the dependent skin and tissues. Lividity will show on the back of a person lying supine; lividity will show on the front of a person lying prone. Lividity will show on the legs and lower parts of the body of a person in a standing position. Lividity will start one to two hours after death and initially is totally or partially moveable and later on will become permanent.
- **rigor mortis**—Postmortem rigidity occurs soon after death. At first the body and its extremities are very flaccid. However, within two to four hours after death, the body and the extremities exhibit progressive stiffness. This stiffness results from chemical changes of the muscular tissues. Rigor remains unchanged for about twelve hours, then disappears gradually,

and the body becomes flaccid again. Rigor is also affected by the body mass, environment, and, especially, temperature; in cool or freezing temperatures rigor will be substantially delayed.

- **late postmortem change**—This includes green discoloration of the skin, a foul smell, decomposition of the body, putrefaction, mummification, and other changes.

Studying the contents of the victim's stomach is also a means for establishing an accurate estimation of TOD. This is particularly so if the time the deceased ate a meal is known. There was no evidence introduced to establish the time at which Ellen Sherman ate a dinner of linguine with a red seafood sauce, probably clam sauce. Forensic textbooks provide parameters for determining the length of time needed to digest meals of varying sizes. A heavier meal, such as linguine and a rich sauce, would take from four to six hours, according to the experts. A light meal, such as a sandwich, would take one to two hours to digest. The digestion process is defined as the gastric emptying of the food from the stomach into the small intestines. Ellen Sherman's stomach still contained her last supper, a sharp contrast to the fact that her body was in rigor mortis, indicating the importance of considering the effect that the frigid room temperatures had on her decomposition process.

THE SUMMARY OF THE CASE

The Ellen Sherman murder is a classic example of a crime being solved and the murderer being brought to justice through careful scientific and forensic work, combined with a determined and resourceful police investigation. The time of death showed that Edward Sherman had ample time and opportunity to strangle his wife to death, prior to leaving on his sailing vacation.

The objective of a forensic death investigation is not only to establish the manner and cause of death, but also to find all the facts relevant to the death. The manner of death is the legal cause of death, be it natural, a suicide, an accident, a homicide, or undetermined. With the death of Ellen Sherman, it is clear that her death was a homicide. As for the most common causes of unnatural death, these include blunt force injuries, sharp instrument injuries, gunshot wounds, drugs and poisons, death by asphyxia, electrocution, drowning, and fire-related death. The two most common types of asphyxiation are hanging and strangulation. The autopsy report should mention any evidence of asphyxia, including: dimensions of pressure marks, discoloration of the face, the presence of petechia hemorrhages, fracture and/or dislocation of neck cartilages and bone, the degree of hemorrhage in the muscles and soft tissues of the neck, and other physical evidence and pattern evidence on the body.

Asphyxia is defined as the condition in which free flow of air to the lungs is cut off or markedly reduced. The actual mechanism of death in asphyxia may be one or a combination of the following:

1. Oxygen starvation of the brain as a result of pressure and closure of the respiratory passages in the neck.
2. Compression of the major blood vessels in the neck (carotid arteries and jugular veins), with the resulting slowdown of the blood supply to the brain.
3. Pressure of the nervous system in the neck (carotid sinuses and vagus nerves) which induces a very fast reflex action with cardiac arrhythmia or arrest.

Manual strangulation as the manner of death is always homicide. Ellen Sherman's death was determined to be a combination of ligature strangulation and manual strangulation. During the trial, one of the most heated arguments was over the ligature itself. Dr. Galvin first determined that Mrs. Sherman was killed by her bra. With our subsequent examination of the pressure marks on her neck, we were able to determine those impressions were actually made by the waistband of the victim's underpants.

This case also illustrated the importance of the identification and examination of pattern evidence found on the victim's body. Physical evidence related to a homicide investigation can be extremely important to the solution of the case. Those patterns on Ellen Sherman's neck, with their zig-zag type of design, their diameter, and their measurements, all indicated that they were made by the waistband on her torn underpants.

James Wade, Sherman's very capable defense attorney, made much about the lengthy timespan between the 1985 murder and his client's arrest in 1990. This was due to the complexity of the case, one that relied almost exclusively on circumstantial evidence. Prosecutor C. Robert Satti, and the chief assistant district attorney, Kevin Kane, moved in an extremely methodical way in this case, and their excellent work resulted in a conviction. The Connecticut media also did an excellent, responsible job of covering this case, particularly the region's principal paper, the *Day of New London*, whose reporting was headed by Rosanne Simborski.

Though a college professor, Edward Sherman had displayed, over the decade leading up to his wife's murder and beyond, a violent side, one particularly directed toward women. His conviction should serve as a benchmark in placing domestic abuse in the proper perspective. This is a profoundly serious genre of crime, one which authorities today take very seriously. Perhaps, if Sherman had been dealt with earlier in his life, Ellen Cooper Sherman would still be alive and the mother of a second child, the convicted man would not have died in prison as a disgrace, and the couple's daughter would never have been orphaned at so tender an age.

chapter
five

THE MacARTHUR CASE

A lie is as good as the truth, if someone believes it.
—Police Sergeant Theodore MacArthur

Like several other homicides we have covered, solving the Theodore MacArthur case relied heavily on teamwork among several branches of the law enforcement agencies we have already described. In the vast majority of cases, police investigators, supported by thorough expert scientific and medical forensics work and a diligent and earnest prosecution team, are able ultimately to provide justice for the murder of a loved one. The MacArthur case brings to light once again the contemporary social problem of spousal abuse, though in this instance the battering in its earlier stages is psychological and not physical. Finally, this is another case complicated by the fact that the defendant was an experienced homicide detective.

Law enforcement personnel, due to a professional dedication to the law, would seem less likely than most to commit a homicide; however, because the police are more experienced with crime fighting techniques, those cases where they have committed a murder can pose more of a challenge to the criminal investigator. That reality is a major reason why three of the five cases presented in this book involve police professionals (though one was only a part-time policeman). As we've seen, the successful outcome of any case is also very dependent on the preservation of the crime scene and the physical evidence. Blood evidence plays a crucial role in this case's investigation and prosecution, as do gunshot residue detection and the establishment of a bullet's trajectory. From my own perspective, the absence of bloodstains in certain crucial areas is as important as what investigators find at a murder scene. The investigator's common sense quotient came into play at a very early point in this prosecution. Medical forensics experts were able to apply their insights into a number of peculiar clues which a very confident murderer left behind as a calling card. Let us return to 1989 in North Miami in Dade County, Florida, where a husband and wife who are both employed in law enforcement have been encountering marital and financial difficulties.

THE FACTS OF THE CASE

On the morning of Tuesday, August 1, 1989, Theodore "Ted" MacArthur was thirty-eight and Pilar, his wife of twelve years, was thirty-five. MacArthur, originally a policeman from the Boston area, had lived in the Miami area since 1981 when he had become a member of the police force there. Within the year he would be joined on the force by his wife of four years, after she had given birth to their first son, Christopher. Pilar Sones had been born to poor, proud, and loving parents who lived in the seaside Spanish fishing village of Cullera on the Mediterranean Sea near Valencia. While these two products of struggling families would appear to have very similar backgrounds, their formative, family nurturing appears to have been in stark contrast.

MacArthur was raised in Malden, Massachusetts, a blue-collar town a few miles north of Boston. His father was an itinerant merchant seaman who divorced his wife five years after his son was born. MacArthur's mother was a Cuban-born nurse who also would purchase and operate a boarding house. Pilar Sones moved to Paris with her family when she was fourteen since her father was not able to support his four children on the meager amount of money he made as a commercial fisherman. In France, he would obtain a much more lucrative position working as a gardener for the city of Paris, and Mrs. Sones would continue her work as a maid, but for much better wages than she had earned in Spain. Pilar and her siblings would also receive a free education in the French public schools. With an aptitude for language, Pilar would quickly become trilingual, learning some English as well as mastering French. At the age of eighteen, Pilar decided to leave her family and go to Boston to work as a nanny, where she would be close to her older sister, Carmen, who had preceded her to America.

Quickly settling into her new surroundings, Pilar found she liked to hang around Harvard Square in Cambridge to talk with students from France or from the Spanish-speaking countries. She enrolled in a community college in Newton and took courses to improve herself, including one in English composition. Pilar, who had beautiful, very black hair, now saw herself becoming a flight attendant and talked of falling in love with and marrying an American man. After two years in America, Pilar met Theodore MacArthur, a young motorcycle policeman, through her sister, since his mother owned and operated the boarding house where Carmen Sones lived.

MacArthur, at twenty-three, already had been through several seminal life experiences. After his parents had divorced, he was supposed to live with his father, but that proved impossible since he was away at sea so much of the time. Instead, MacArthur would be raised by his grandparents, and he would later say that this couple instilled in him a solid set of values. MacArthur would write years later that his boyhood taught him several lessons about the opposite gender, including "You don't hit girls," and "At this point I decided that it would be to my advantage to stay well clear of females." MacArthur went to Malden High School for a couple of years, where he was an indifferent student. At fifteen, he dropped out to become a merchant seaman, going to sea as his father had before him. He quickly became bored with the dissolute lifestyle that career seamen seemed to live and, at seventeen, joined the air force. When he was eighteen, he married Betty Lou Williams, a nurse who was a year older than

MacArthur. After an uneventful tour in Vietnam, he received an honorable discharge in 1975 and was able to land a job as a part-time motorcycle policeman with the police department in Rowley, a town of two thousand not far from Malden. He also took some classes at a community college at this time, having obtained his high school diploma through the military's GED program.

When he first met Pilar Sones, MacArthur was living in his mother's basement, recuperating from a motorcycle accident. He immediately set out to woo this lovely and impressionable young woman. He did all of this without bothering to tell Pilar that he was still married, though separated from his spouse, and the father of a small child. MacArthur's first wife had found that her policeman husband was cheating on her with a waitress from a nearby rock 'n' roll bar and had taken steps to divorce him.

MacArthur intrigued Pilar with his constant stream of presents and flowers, his free-flowing use of cash and credit cards, and his other quick-witted American ways. Her English linguistic skills increased to the point where she took a job as a secretary. The couple courted for two years. MacArthur often took Pilar riding on a motorcycle on jaunts throughout New England with the Blue Knights, a social club of police officers. In 1977, Pilar's family would arrive for their wedding, which took place only a few days after MacArthur first told Pilar about the first marriage and the existence of a child by it. This disclosure came just before the divorce was finalized and a few days before the marriage to Pilar.

Theodore and Pilar MacArthur did not have children for their first few years together in Massachusetts. MacArthur, now with the Malden Police Department, was building up a reputation as an extremely thorough and energetic officer. Some of his fellow police had nicknamed him "General MacArthur," and others said that when they saw graffiti on a wall that targeted the police, they could be sure MacArthur's name would be the one mentioned. He was thought to be fair, but he would stop and give a motorist a ticket if there was so much as a small crack in a tail light. If there was an arrest to be made, one said, MacArthur wanted to be in on it.

Meanwhile, Theodore MacArthur dreamed of moving on to big-time police work, and he also wanted to leave Boston and its New England weather behind him. He began applying for police jobs in other parts of the country and was soon hired by the Miami-Dade Police Force in Florida. Moving south in 1981, MacArthur decided to initially go it alone on his new job, leaving his pregnant wife behind to have their first baby. Their plan was that Pilar's sister, now Carmen Sones Barraford, would help her through the birth of their first child. This separation made Pilar nervous and she consulted a psychic, a session which she tape-recorded. In their dialogue, Pilar said that, while her husband had never struck her, "He is unpredictable, nervous, and demanding." The meeting concluded with Pilar being told, "Your husband will never divorce you," and she was reassured that, "He loves you very much." This drove Pilar to tears. Still, MacArthur was a very controlling person, Pilar confided to the psychic. As an example, he was a husband who was also very suspicious of his wife's relationship with her older sister, Carmen. The two Sones sisters had vowed that they would never let him divide them, one against the other.[1]

After Christopher was born in 1982, Pilar and the baby moved to the Miami area to join her husband. They decided to rent a home in Keystone Point, a comfortable suburb in North Miami. Pilar soon went to work in the county's criminal justice system, starting out as a records specialist for the Miami-Dade department's traffic police, handling videos made in cases charging the motorist with drunken driving. She was able to put her native Spanish to very good use in her professional career and, with her gift for languages, quickly mastered the Cuban dialect, a dominant vernacular in Miami. In 1984, Mrs. MacArthur gave birth to another boy, Philip. In 1987 Pilar was promoted to a higher post as a Miami-Dade corrections officer, working at "the stockade," the county's main detention center.

Meanwhile, Theodore MacArthur's police career was skyrocketing. Starting off as a patrolman, he worked in the region's central district, encountering a great deal of street crime and often working with minorities, many of whom were Cuban or from another Spanish-speaking country. If anything, he was taking his police work even more seriously, and, given his outgoing personality, he'd even managed to turn his pronounced Boston accent to his advantage since his speech patterns helped break the ice with strangers. He was promoted to detective within his first year, working general investigations, and in 1985 landed himself a job in the homicide division. Noting the trends in America, MacArthur seized on his mother's birthplace, having his racial status changed from Caucasian to Cuban, making him a minority. He also became quite active in the department's huge and powerful police union.

MacArthur's best times as a police detective were just ahead of him. Over the course of several years, nine middle-level drug dealers had been murdered. These homicides appeared to be the work of a professional, one who had shot his victims through the head. Assigned to the case, MacArthur worked night and day. Manny Pardo, a policeman from nearby Sweetwater who had a sour reputation, had emerged as a primary suspect. Pardo, who was known for shaking down drug dealers for protection money, had kept a diary. This journal contained a listing of numbers which no one had been able to decode. MacArthur recognized the numerical sequencing as firearm serial numbers and went to work. A gun manufacturer, Sturm, Ruger & Company, Inc., of Southport, Connecticut, had sent six guns to a Miami weapons dealer, where Pardo had purchased them, using the identification of a murder victim. This helped convict Pardo, and he was sentenced to death. His superiors called MacArthur's work in this case brilliant and the media agreed.

MacArthur's personnel file was now bulging with favorable reports and commendations. Prosecutor David Waksman, in particular, was impressed and insisted that MacArthur be kept on the Pardo case through its trial stages, an unusual move since detective sergeants are normally rotated back to work on other investigations once the defendant is headed for trial. Sergeant MacArthur and his family also became Waksman's prized tenants, moving into his three-bedroom, two-bath house in Key Point, one which featured a swimming pool, for only $750 a month. In addition to the Pardo conviction, MacArthur also led the successful hunt for the killer of a Miami grocery store owner.

Things never looked better for the MacArthur family. Pilar was very supportive of her husband's work. She lined their home's front hallway with his commendations and awards. Pilar was good-natured and patient when her husband would bring his squad home at four in the morning after a night at a sports event and nightclubbing. Usually she would get up and serve them all breakfast. Still a member of the Blue Knights, MacArthur and she would attend conventions, and Pilar would laugh off the rough terminology the police colleagues liked to use, such as asking her if she were Mrs. MacArthur or her husband's "whore." At a police party in Massachusetts, Pilar and most of the other guests who were not in the know watched in horror as another policeman pulled out a gun, aimed it at his own wife, and then fired off a blank. As someone who carried a weapon on the job, Pilar liked to engage in the horseplay. At another police party, she pulled out a toy derringer pistol, and, paraphrasing a line from a Mel Brooks movie, put the gun to her head, shouting out, "Nobody moves. . . . Or the Spic gets it." To her close friends, though, it seemed Pilar found most of this ghoulish humor childish at best and vulgar at worst.

As much as Pilar tried to please her husband, she became increasingly convinced that she was failing in doing her part to make their relationship stronger. MacArthur had been an active social drinker, but with his success and the pressures it carried, he began to drink very heavily. He also began to spend the couple's money. He would take out heavy credit card cash advances, and soon their bank account could not cover his spending; this resulted in a steady stream of bounced checks. Mrs. MacArthur never pressed her husband too closely when he did not return home for a couple of days at a time, nor did she speak up when all of her own paycheck went into their joint bank account and only a part of his did. Pilar would also listen attentively when he would describe a work situation, and at times when she would spontaneously cry out in Spanish, MacArthur would quickly correct her, snarling, "This is America. We speak English here." MacArthur kept a running list of personal improvement projects he expected his wife to work on, such as not smoking, losing weight, and stop spoiling the children. Pilar was even good-natured when her coarse father-in-law would show up at their doorstep, unannounced, and become a house guest for three weeks at a clip. The elder Mr. MacArthur repaid his daughter-in-law's kindness by referring to Pilar as, "Ted's doormat," since she was so conscientious as a wife and homemaker.[2]

On the job, as Sergeant MacArthur's star continued to rise, he increasingly came to the attention of the Miami media. And one member in particular. A married young woman who had worked for the *Miami Herald* as a high school intern in the early eighties, she had been bitten by the news bug and had returned in 1987 as a full-time employee. (As in other chapters, I have chosen to omit a name which is not relevant to the case discussion to protect the person's privacy.) This journalist, who was in her mid-twenties, worked on the police beat for the area's largest paper and was assigned the chore of sitting each night in a room full of police scanners, then letting her editor and the other appropriate reporters know when and where something was happening. A recent graduate of Miami University, she would occasionally write a story for the paper and get a byline. As a way of getting ahead in her profession, this reporter would hang out in bars and clubs which the police frequented, trying to ferret out news tips and leads for stories on what was happening inside the Miami-Dade police establishment.

The journalist had first noticed the burly MacArthur at one of these police bars. She had noticed that he always dressed well, seemed to have money to spend, and carried his star status on the force as though he were used to it. She even liked his arrogance. After a few weeks, the two began talking and then quickly moved on to a sexual affair. Soon, the journalist was getting solid news leads, ones that were helping her at the paper. Her new lover was also eager to spend considerable amounts of time with her and to buy her lavish presents. Before long, Sergeant MacArthur was talking to fellow policemen about his new relationship with a hot, younger woman, often bragging about the couple's sexual exploits. Many of the police around MacArthur had known Pilar for years, and they all liked her a good deal. Some of the other police also wondered if MacArthur was giving up too much information to this reporter with whom he was sleeping. Several openly resented it when MacArthur brought her into the homicide division bureau, a kind of safe haven for homicide detectives only, where even wives were not welcome.[3]

Pilar began to suspect her husband was having an affair, especially when his absences became more prolonged. Expected for dinner at 7 P.M., he would arrive home at midnight, with nothing to say. He was also spending less and less time with his sons. Pilar worried that she had not been everything a wife should be, concerns she shared with friends. To remedy matters, Pilar went on a crash diet, lost ten pounds overnight, began to experiment with a new hairstyle, and otherwise tried to rekindle her husband's interest in her. Meanwhile, MacArthur and his "mistress," a term he began using when he introduced this new woman to other police and acquaintances, even made an expensive 1988 trip to Boston to spend several days in a hotel room together, where he took her photo in a sexy red negligee.

This snapshot would eventually sharpen his wife's concerns over his infidelity and overall conduct. Pilar had many friends, and many of them now knew about the mistress but were reluctant to tell her. Things finally came to a head in March when MacArthur and Pilar had gone to a Police Benevolent Association dance. This was about a month after the discovery of the mistress's photo. Pilar sat chatting at the bar while her husband circulated. Soon she saw him slow-dancing with an auburn-haired young woman who wore a black leather skirt. Pilar could not quite match this alluring dance partner with the snapshot she'd found a month earlier. Later when she slow-danced with her husband, Pilar asked MacArthur about this and he brushed it off, saying she was another policeman's girlfriend and he'd been covering for the guy, since the guy's wife was there. Pilar flatly told MacArthur she did not believe him. Then the young journalist went into the ladies' room and was confronted there by some of the police wives who knew about her. This caused a scene, with the woman asking MacArthur, in front of Pilar, if he wanted her to leave the dance. MacArthur then spent the remainder of the night dancing with the mini-skirted young woman. Pilar ended the evening by driving home alone.

Pilar MacArthur had come to America as a young adult who had deep-seated and proud traditions. Prominent among these were a wife's need to believe in her husband and to, above all, keep private whatever difficulties the husband and wife might encounter in their marriage. Pilar was also liked and respected by a wide circle of individuals with whom she came in daily contact. Later, Susan Dannelly, the case's lead prosecutor, would speak with wonder about the fact that, in three years of investigating Pilar's background, she had never encountered a single person who had a bad thing to say about her, a first in years of digging up dirt on people.[4]

However, Pilar's old-world pride and stoicism were wearing thin, and she began to share some of her difficulties with a select circle of close friends. And by February 1989, two of her closest friends, fellow correction officers Marilyn Marcusson and Jenny Alverez, had become impatient with Pilar's apparent inability to see what was going on. This sexy, young dance partner from the PBA dinner had a name and was a news reporter. Marcusson and Alverez, a month earlier, had accompanied Pilar to the MacArthur house when she began looking through her husband's suit pockets and other belongings. Pilar had pulled out of a jacket pocket the provocative photo MacArthur had taken of his mistress. There was a police case number jotted down on the back of the photo. Pilar then checked out this number at the court house and found it was for only a traffic violation. Thus, she was ready for MacArthur's lie that the photo was associated with a homicide case when she confronted him that evening. Caught in the lie, MacArthur then admitted the photo was of a girlfriend and said he had been going through a midlife crisis and would drop the relationship. Pilar was eager to accept this as an answer, telling her friends, "But I love him."

Still distraught, the next morning Pilar called work to take a personal leave day so she could go see Linda Saunders,* an old friend of theirs from the Boston area who was now a police aide in Fort Laud-

---

*denotes pseudonyms

erdale. Meg Laughlin's excellent later summation of the MacArthur case in the *Miami Herald* reports how Saunders let Pilar know the facts about her husband. She told Pilar how MacArthur had bragged to her once about a house he'd pointed out that, according to him, he and his friends rented to use for going to bed with their "whores." Saunders also told Mrs. MacArthur her husband had once asked her, at a Blue Knights enclave, to sleep with him and, once she had turned him down, she had been pretty sure he'd found someone else. Saunders reminded Pilar that she'd once told Saunders that, if confronted with the knowledge that her husband was cheating on her, her European background would get her past that problem. "That was then. Now I've become Americanized," Pilar had replied to Saunders.[5]

After her conversation with her husband, Pilar MacArthur began to take steps, MacArthur's promise to change notwithstanding. Friends saw her writing in a notebook, and when they asked her about it, Pilar dismissed it as simply her diary. She also took what was a very extraordinary step for any wife, let alone one who had been so compliant with her husband's selfish and unfaithful conduct. Pilar called her husband's boss, Captain Wayne McCarthy of the homicide division and complained to him about the way her husband had been behaving. When MacArthur learned about the phone call to Captain McCarthy, he was astounded. Initially, he said he would not change his conduct, that he needed this other woman in his life. Pilar, meanwhile was having a great deal of difficulty sleeping and eating. A few weeks later, she went back to Captain McCarthy and told him that her husband was spending enormous amounts of money pursuing this affair and that they were threatened with bankruptcy. This time Pilar's words had their intended effect.

MacArthur was now hearing about his indiscretions and bad conduct from his boss, and all of this was causing him serious job problems throughout the homicide division. In later spring, MacArthur took his mistress on a ten-day motorcycle jaunt through Florida, and the two of them decided that the best course of action would be for him to appear to give up the relationship, try to put his marriage back

on track, and then, when these efforts had all failed, he would file for
a divorce under honorable circumstances. The two plotted a reunion in
early August and, in the meantime, they could still see each other
when no one was looking.

From all appearances, MacArthur seemed to have decided to
remain married to Pilar. He no longer was gone for days at a stretch
and was home most evenings. MacArthur announced ambitious plans,
saying he'd put $1,000 down on a $200,000 house in a swanky new
subdivision, using a stash of money he'd secreted away over the years.
MacArthur also told Pilar that he wanted to put their marriage back
together again. He promised a time in the summer when their two sons
would visit their grandmother in Massachusetts. This would give the
couple a chance for a second honeymoon. In early August, they would
use vacation time to travel up north, pick up their sons, and all of them
would take a nice family trip into Canada before returning home. He
seemed to have changed.

MacArthur's new behavior seemed to reassure Pilar, and she hap-
pily told her friends and a marriage counselor she'd consulted that she
thought she had her husband back and she again trusted him. Pilar did
not take any real notice when MacArthur, responding to what he
would later claim was her demand, took out a considerable amount of
life insurance on the two of them. The policy's monthly premiums, he
told Pilar, would be more than $325. In the event of his wife's acci-
dental death, MacArthur would receive $471,000. When Pilar did ask
if these policies had already gone into effect, MacArthur evaded
answering, citing the fact that neither of them had yet taken the
required physicals.

Then, in late July, an event occurred that shocked Pilar as never
before. MacArthur had warned his wife about the importance of
keeping electrical appliances safely away from a filled bathtub or any
other water sources in the house. One morning, with the two boys
already in Boston, he invited his wife to take a bath with him and carefully placed a small television on a safe ledge at the foot of the filled
tub they would use. Once Pilar was settled in for this romantic inter-

lude, MacArthur then decided to get something in the bedroom. As he stepped out, his foot caught on the set's electrical wire, and his leg yanked the TV off its shelf. Pilar averted the accident by instantly stopping the appliance's fall with her outstretched feet, wrestling the television over the tub's side with her legs, and sending it crashing to the floor. At that instant, more than the TV set was shattered. "Are you trying to kill me," Pilar screamed at her husband, who proceeded to shrug off this nearly fatal accident.

The next day at work, Pilar MacArthur seemed badly shaken by this incident, one which she described in detail for Alverez and Marcusson. She then told another close friend, court bailiff Victoria Aguilera, that she was going to divorce her husband and take her two boys to Spain where she would raise them herself. Aguilera would later say that Pilar was visibly upset. "She was scared. She was crying."[5]

THE INVESTIGATION OF THE CASE

At 8:30 A.M., Tuesday, August 1, 1989, Sgt. Theodore MacArthur phoned a North Miami police dispatcher and said that his wife had accidentally shot herself in the head. When an ambulance arrived a few minutes later, the paramedics who first responded found Pilar MacArthur, clad in a nightgown, lying on the floor at the foot of the couple's waterbed, a bullet wound in the upper left side of her head. MacArthur was slumped in a chair, holding a bloody towel and in a very emotional state. A Magnum .357 pistol lay on the floor next to the bed, and there were five unused rounds on a bed table next to the bed. There was a second bloodied towel strewn on the bedroom floor.

The paramedics vainly tried to revive Pilar MacArthur but were unable to do so, and pronounced her dead at the scene. North Miami police and homicide detectives arrived a short while later. A distraught MacArthur described how he had tried to wake up his wife to get her to go to work, but that she had dallied, insisting on a little more sleep. To get her up, MacArthur had then playfully used a water pistol on

Pilar. His wife had responded by grabbing a gun from the bed table drawer, emptying the five rounds out of it, but leaving a sixth round in the firing chamber. To MacArthur's shock, Pilar then put the weapon to her head and discharged the sixth round into her left temple. This had all happened before MacArthur could get a word out to warn his wife of the last, loaded round. MacArthur blurted this story out between his sobs. The gun, he said, was his personal property, and he had it in the house for the family's protection.[6]

Not everyone who walked into the MacArthur home that morning was willing to buy Sergeant MacArthur's story at face value. Miami-Dade County Prosecutor Susan Dannelly had known Theodore MacArthur for some time, and the two had not always agreed on police procedures. Dannelly recalls arriving at the MacArthurs' home that morning, around 11 A.M., and seeing a number of TV cameras, reporters, and photographers out front. Reports later circulated that Dannelly, as she approached the house, was overheard telling a companion, "I'll just bet you the son of a bitch did it himself," a charge she categorically denies, especially in light of the high number of media people outside the front door. I have been privileged to get to know

Overall view of the master bedroom
at the MacArthur residence—
scene of the homicide.

Susan very well, and I trust her version of the facts completely. This falsehood about her saying those words is a good example of how a rumor can fester into fact if it is repeated enough. That quote actually showed up in several news stories on the case. North Miami Homicide Detective Donald Slovonic, who knew MacArthur, arrived shortly afterward and began his investigation. He would note that the victim did not have any blood spatter on her left hand and would later learn that Pilar MacArthur had been right-handed.

This death immediately caused a sensation in the Florida media. Theodore MacArthur was not simply a sergeant in the Miami-Dade Homicide Bureau. He had taken a lead role in solving the Pardo drug killings, a case which had received national attention. Many in the Miami-area criminal justice system knew both the victim and her flashy husband. As MacArthur had risen to stardom, some in the Miami-Dade police establishment had grown concerned about his private life, especially the well-known affair he'd openly carried on with the young newspaper reporter. Others in the homicide bureau would remember MacArthur's penchant for playing with the truth. Several would quote one of his favorite expressions: "A lie is as good as the truth, if someone believes it." Sergeant David Rivers, one of MacArthur's colleagues and a veteran detective with an excellent reputation, later commented, "It was unspoken, but from the first day, there were sidelong glances across the office. We knew he did it."

In the summer of 1989, I was the chief criminalist for the state of Connecticut and the director of the state police forensic lab. The fact that I was working seven days a week, fourteen to eighteen hours a day, meant that I was scaling back my course load at the University of New Haven, where I had started teaching as a professor in the mid-1970s. The competing demands for my time now included a growing number of speaking engagements and case consultations. I developed several lectures on various forms and topics, utilizing a slide projector. As I improved my presentations and grew into this role, the invitations to speak escalated. My ego is not so big, though, since I also recognized the fact that I was donating my honorariums for public appearances to charities and scholarship funds made me a popular candidate for civic gatherings. These appearances, of course, were added to my regular workload at the forensic lab and the additional casework for police departments around the world.

A week after Pilar MacArthur's body was found in her master bedroom, Susan Dannelly called me to ask that I come down to help with the investigation. She was particularly concerned that the case involved one of the Miami-Dade department's rising homicide sergeants. This was obviously going to be a very high profile case and one that was going to be the talk of the entire Miami area. If Susan was particularly convinced that Sergeant MacArthur was behind the crime, she did not share that with me that day. This highly capable prosecutor also disclosed to me, during this first call, two other pieces of information which I found intriguing: Absolutely no gunshot residue had been found on Pilar MacArthur's left hand, and there were no fingerprints whatsoever found on the gun. This did not compute at all. "Something is wrong here," again went through my head. (See the forensic evidence section at the end of this chapter for a discussion of gunshot residue.)

I had been getting an increasing number of calls for assistance from law enforcement jurisdictions, especially after the 1986 Woodchipper murder, which was still pending in court at that time. However, on the face of it, this case stood out as one where I felt I should assist the North Miami authorities in their investigation. After a brief conversation with Susan Dannelly, I asked her to send me copies of the crime scene photos, reports, and documents. I told her I thought we could be of some assistance, and I would get back to her.

When I arrived in Miami ten days later, the MacArthur case was still big news. The media carried stories indicating that the death was initially being called accidental. MacArthur told the press that he could not understand why the investigation had not been concluded and the homicide declared an accident. There was a growing list of solid reasons why this case was still very open. I met Assistant District Attorney Dannelly and detectives working on the case and, using the crime scene photos taken on August 1, was able to picture what the bedroom looked like when the police and paramedics first arrived. MacArthur had insisted, from the very outset, that he had initially called 911 and then pulled his wife's body from the waterbed to the floor, where he began to administer cardiopulmonary resuscitation.

From the very large amount of blood on the bedsheet and on the pillow of the bed, I could see that Pilar MacArthur had been dead in that room for longer than her husband had said. Blood flows from certain kinds of wounds in uniform ways. A gunshot to the head causes a blood mist to first emanate, and this blood flow then turns to a steadily diminishing stream. Following the high-speed mist, this stream of blood is quite strong, almost like water out of a hose. As the amount of blood left in the body decreases, the blood flow continues but at a slower rate. Also, the left side of the pillow and bedsheet were thoroughly soaked with blood. The fatal wound must have occurred earlier than the fifteen minutes prior that MacArthur said it did. Dr. Charles Wetli, the Miami-Dade chief medical examiner, also came to the same conclusion about the high volume of blood evidence showing an earlier time of death than MacArthur was alleging.

Dr. Jay Barnhart, the Miami-Dade associate medical examiner, performed an autopsy on the remains of Pilar MacArthur the day after the murder. In analyzing the bullet entry wound the .357 round had made in Pilar MacArthur's left temple, Dr. Barnhart discovered that the gun which killed her had been fired from above, at a downward angle, as the round entered the victim's head. In cases of suicide by a gunshot wound to the head, generally the victim holds the gun barrel evenly toward the head, or holds the gun at an angle pointing upward. It was highly unlikely that there would be a self-inflicted gunshot wound in a suicide where the gun was held at a higher angle, with its barrel pointing downward. This was a critical forensics finding for the prosecution and one that tied in directly with the hypothesis that Sergeant MacArthur had shot his wife and then delayed calling in her death for ten minutes so he could: Clean her blood off of his hands, remove the gunshot residue from his hands, and wipe his fingerprints off of the gun. These findings were analyzed in light of the fact that right-handed suicide victims do not customarily shoot themselves with their left hand. Finally, what could explain the fact that there were no fingerprints found on any part of the gun?

To the outside world, the police were now only saying that the case remained open. Pilar MacArthur's funeral, held Saturday, August 5, was well-attended, with many of her friends and family coming from as far as Boston and Spain. Meanwhile, neither the police nor the coroner's office would publicly comment on Pilar's death. Susan Dannelly did say that the case was being investigated "very actively." Within the police establishment, more than a few of MacArthur's colleagues were expressing doubts about what they really felt about him and how his wife had died. The existence of a young and ambitious mistress who happened to be a newspaper reporter only intensified this speculation. The case was being very actively discussed throughout the Miami-Dade court houses and police departments. Within a few weeks of his wife's death, MacArthur's mistress had moved into his home. Word circulated that she was actually seen wearing his late wife's clothing and had already become a surrogate parent to the two boys, now eleven and nine.[7]

Things began going sour very quickly for the other woman in MacArthur's life. Her editors at the *Miami Herald* were soon reading her name in their own paper, as news of her affair with MacArthur leaked out. This initially caused her editors to transfer her out of her police beat and to a suburban bureau. In a few weeks, though, the paper discharged her. Instead of finding MacArthur sympathetic to what had happened to her, the mistress began to feel the same kinds of pressure applied by her lover that Pilar MacArthur had complained about. The fired reporter got another job working as a secretary and attempted to rebuild a good home for the children. The two MacArthur boys had, indeed, turned to her for help and nurturing, and she seemed to relish this role. She also nurtured deep-seated doubts about how Pilar MacArthur had died. These misgivings deepened in March 1990 when the story about the television set almost falling into the bathtub and electrocuting Pilar made the papers. The mistress would eventually get another newspaper job, with a suburban paper. MacArthur and she would live through very stormy times. The boys quietly told her that their father was seeing a new woman; they knew since they'd all had lunch together. Three Christmas seasons after Pilar's death, MacArthur would place a knife to the reporter/mistress's throat during an argument one day that erupted as she and the children were decorating the family's tree. She would then leave him and would eventually tell Susan Dannelly her whole story and agree to become a prosecution witness, an offer Dannelly eventually decided to decline, due to the amount of baggage she brought to the case.

Susan Dannelly doggedly kept pursuing the MacArthur investigation, and in late 1989 the case was referred to a grand jury. Susan then contacted me and asked me to conduct an independent evaluation and make recommendations on the case. I was extremely busy, as I have said, and was reviewing several serial killer investigations, as well as hundreds of other murder cases. This was all on top of my teaching responsibilities at several police academies, the FBI Academy, and at several universities. I told Susan that it was almost impossible for me to take any new cases. I recommended a couple of my forensics colleagues to her. I have to give a lot of credit to Susan for her persistence and her persuasive powers. Finally, I caved in and told her I would take the case.

On the late afternoon of a fall day in 1989, I was in Hartford at a meeting, and my assistant, Sergeant Robert Mills, and my secretary, Barbara Martin, informed me that Susan Dannelly and two North Miami detectives, William Craig and Don Slovonic, had shown up at my office at the Meriden lab with all kinds of evidence. I rushed back to the laboratory and looked at the piles of evidence. It was almost 6:30 P.M. I called my wife, Margaret, and informed her that we would have three guests from Miami for dinner that evening. Margaret is such a good sport. She said, "I hope they like Chinese food." After our dinner, we went to my basement where I have a laboratory set up. This is there for a reason. Many times police and detectives from local or state police forces will show up in the middle of the night to ask me to examine evidence to provide them with a preliminary evaluation of a case.

Susan, Detectives Craig and Slovonic, and I examined each piece of evidence, including the .357 Magnum revolver, Pilar's nightgown, bed sheets, pillow cases, and the like. Subsequently, we reenacted the possible scenarios to determine which one was most likely and which ones were impossible. Detectives Slovonic and Craig of the North Miami Police Department are two seasoned and very devoted criminal investigators. We all worked through the night to test all the possibilities and to reexamine each piece of physical evidence.

By dawn, we determined that there were several questions that had to be answered and several experiments would have to be conducted to resolve the crime scene reconstruction issues:

1. How much blood was deposited on the left side of the bed?
2. What kind of bloodstain patterns can be observed?
3. How long does it take for that amount of blood to coagulate?
4. Are there any high-velocity blood spatters?
5. Are any of those blood spatters the result of blow-back action?
6. Were any of these blood spatters found on the tip of the gun barrel?
7. Was there any gunshot residue (GSR) produced by the .357 revolver? (No GSR was found on the GSR kits collected from both Pilar's and MacArthur's hands.)
8. Was there sufficient physical evidence to prove that the death of Pilar MacArthur was a homicide and not a suicide or accidental shooting?

In the winter of 1989, we conducted some experiments to find a way to estimate the amount of blood at a crime scene. The results of my study were subsequently published in the *Journal of Identification News* (an official publication of the International Association of Identification or IAI). We know that blood is a two-component system; a liquid fraction, commonly referred to as *serum*, and a cellular fraction, which consists of erythrocytes, leucocytes, and platelets. After the blood dries, the majority of the liquid portions of blood will evaporate and will leave the cellular fraction behind. We also learned that 55 percent of the blood is liquid and 45 percent is solid materials. The weight of liquid blood equals the weight of serum plus cells. After the blood has dried, the weight of the same amount of blood equals the remaining solid cells. Therefore, we would be able to estimate the amount of liquid blood by weighing the blood crust at a crime scene, then multiplying by the evaporation factor of the blood, using the following formula:

total weight of blood crust × 4.167 ml/mg = original volume of blood

We were able to determine by weighing the blood crust found on the bed that a minimal amount (1000–2000 cc) of blood was deposited on the bedsheet when Pilar's body was removed from the bed.

The majority of the bloodstains found on the bed were deposited from the gunshot wound on Pilar's left side of her head. Since these bloodstains were located on the right portion of the left side of the bed, she had likely slept on the left side of the bed in a supine position. In other words, Pilar's body was face down on the pillow when she was shot. It would be very difficult for someone to shoot oneself when in such a position, using the right hand. In addition, Dr. Barnhart and Dr. Vincent Di Maio found the orientation of the gun was such that it was impossible to produce such an angle. Upon the detailed examination of the photographs taken by the crime scene investigators, it was clear to us that there was no blow-back type of high-velocity blood spatters to be found on Pilar's hand. If she had shot herself at the described angle, we should have seen blood spatters on the alleged shooter's hand. In addition to these facts, there was no GSR detected on her hands. Therefore, the physical evidence in this case clearly showed that Pilar MacArthur's death was inconsistent with suicide and more consistent with homicide. It is also clear that Pilar's body was, in fact, dragged off of the bed after her blood had coagulated.

According to the North Miami police radio communication log, the first officer arrived at the scene approximately fifty-six seconds after MacArthur's phone call. This officer observed that the blood-stains on the bed were coagulated. The crime scene photographs also clearly showed the blood smears were serum smears with small amounts of blood crust. This is an indication that the smear pattern was produced after the blood was coagulated.

In order to determine the blood coagulation time on the bedsheet, we needed 1000–2000 cc (ml) of fresh blood to place on the exact same type of red-colored bedsheet, under a similar set of environmental conditions. Over the years, I have been extremely lucky to have so many dedicated scientists and loyal friends work with me. When they heard that I needed some fresh blood to conduct an experiment, many of them volunteered, but when they learned I needed 1000 cc of fresh blood, they told me, "Friendship and loyalty have a limitation." The only solution was to use my own blood. Later, I was challenged in court by a defense attorney on how I would know that Oriental male blood would have the same characteristics as Caucasian female blood. But the presiding judge let the evidence in. We were able to prove that it takes much longer than fifteen minutes to produce such an amount of coagulated blood on that bedsheet.

Theodore MacArthur had initially retained Kieran Fallon as his defense lawyer. On instructions from his client, Fallon vehemently had denied any marital problems and that there was any other woman in his life. Eventually, MacArthur would settle on Edward O'Donnell as his defense attorney. I testified in the fall of 1992 before the grand jury for a full day about crime scene reconstruction, especially emphasizing that one essential issue: The time involved in blood coagulation. In early 1993, after calling nearly one hundred witnesses, many of them MacArthur's fellow police officers, the grand jury announced that it was indicting MacArthur for first-degree murder. The day he was indicted, Sergeant MacArthur was suspended from active duty, with pay, pending the case's outcome.

THE MACARTHUR TRIAL

More than four years after his wife's tragic death, Theodore MacArthur would be brought to trial for her murder on Monday, October 24, 1993. Miami-Dade County Circuit Judge W. Thomas Spencer would preside. After a great deal of exposure in the region's media, both the prosecution and defense had taken great pains to assure themselves of a jury who would hear a vast amount of evidence, much of it scientific and medical, and then render a fair verdict.

Susan Dannelly and her prosecution team were concerned about jurors who appeared to be erratic or out of the mainstream. Their side would be interested in intelligent individuals who believed in right and wrong in life and the legal processes that were in place to protect that kind of governmental and social system. The defense, on the other hand, was particularly interested in any prospective juror who had experienced a difficult time with the police or who had family members who did. The defense attorneys were also interested in ferreting out any juror who attached great onus to someone who had been unfaithful to a spouse. After three weeks of the *voir dire* process, a jury of seven men and five women was seated, along with six alternates.

The prosecution's case relied very heavily on the medical and forensic testimony. To prepare the jury for this, Susan Dannelly had to frame the events which led up to the morning of August 1, 1989. This required that the prosecutor call several members of the Miami-Dade Police Department who testified about Theodore MacArthur's lack of honesty and his fast-lane lifestyle. One officer said that MacArthur was a habitual liar and was willing to say anything to get his way. Another cited an expression favored by MacArthur, "Lie, lie, deny, demand proof, and make counterallegations." A police witness calmly testified, "I knew him as a liar."[8]

Susan Dannelly also introduced evidence of MacArthur's extramarital affairs, focusing on the strain caused by his long-running relationship with the news reporter. She then put Pilar MacArthur's friends on the stand who outlined the couple's disintegrating marriage.

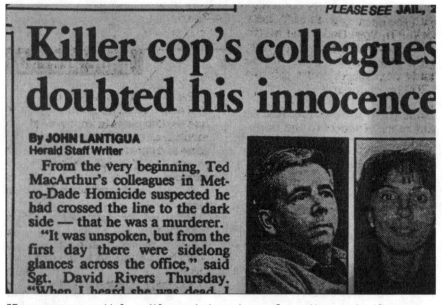

PLEASE SEE JAIL, 2

Killer cop's colleagues doubted his innocence

By JOHN LANTIGUA
Herald Staff Writer

From the very beginning, Ted MacArthur's colleagues in Metro-Dade Homicide suspected he had crossed the line to the dark side — that he was a murderer.

"It was unspoken, but from the first day there were sidelong glances across the office," said Sgt. David Rivers Thursday. "When I heard she was dead, I

Newspaper article with an interview of a witness in the case.

Dannelly then introduced testimony about the instance when Pilar's husband had almost pulled a turned-on television set into her filled bathtub. Evidence was also introduced on the $471,000 life insurance policy which MacArthur had purchased on his wife in the last spring of her life. Thus, the stage was set for the forensic testimony of Dr. Jay Barnhart and Dr. Charles Wetli, from the Miami-Dade Coroner's office; Dr. Vincent DiMaio of Texas; and myself.

There was no gunshot residue on Pilar MacArthur's hand, as there would have been if she had fired the fatal shot into her head. Pilar was right-handed, and individuals who commit suicide by shooting themselves characteristically fire with their primary hand. There were also no fingerprints found on the gun at all, raising the question of whether someone had cleaned the weapon after it had fired the fatal shot. Finally, during his autopsy, Dr. Barnhart had measured the entrance angle in the victim's skull and was able to determine that the weapon had been fired at a sharp angle from above, with the barrel pointing downward. Dr. Vincent DiMaio also testified that the angle was inconsistent with suicide but consistent with homicide. During my day and a half on the

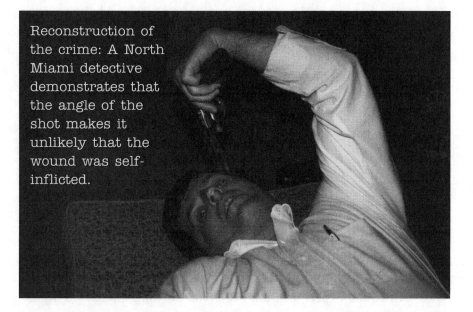

Reconstruction of the crime: A North Miami detective demonstrates that the angle of the shot makes it unlikely that the wound was self-inflicted.

stand, I testified to the large amount of blood I had seen in photos of the couple's bedsheet and pillow. We estimated that there was approximately 1000–2000 cc of blood deposited on the bed. All of this blood meant that the victim had been dead for at least ten to fifteen minutes longer than Theodore MacArthur had reported to the police after they had arrived. I also testified on the lack of any GSR, blow-back, and blood spatters on Pilar MacArthur's hand. This was inconsistent with her shooting herself. The blood coagulation time also proved that her body was removed from her bed after this coagulation process.

Theodore MacArthur seemed very relaxed during most of this trial. He had testified in court himself hundreds of times, and he breezed through his time on the stand when the defense presented its case. His defense lawyer, Ed O'Donnell, questioned his client about having a mistress, and MacArthur's response was, "I was weak." This strategy seemed to place him on trial for being an unfaithful husband, not a murderer. At one point, O'Donnell asked MacArthur what he saw after he had heard the fatal gunshot. His client's answer was gruesome: "I saw smoke coming from her eyes." A total of seventy-five witnesses were called during the seven-week trial.

The jury began its deliberations on Tuesday, December 7, 1993. That evening, MacArthur was supremely confident of his acquittal and even held a news conference predicting this outcome and promising legal action against his accusers. The Miami media showed up for this bizarre event. After nine hours of deliberations, the next day this jury filed back into the court room at 3:15 P.M. and pronounced Theodore MacArthur guilty of first-degree murder. The courtroom burst into applause as this verdict was announced. Judge Spencer sternly said, "Theodore MacArthur, you have disobeyed the commandments of God, violated the laws of man, disgraced your profession, and left your children without a mother." After court had been adjourned, Susan Dannelly was embraced by her friends and her peers. The next day's *Miami Herald* noted that Dannelly had worked the case since the day of the murder. One female juror, when questioned by the press, said, "All of the expert testimony was the deciding factor."[9] I would add that all of the excellent police and prosecution work meant that the expert testimony could have this kind of effect.

THE CASE'S SCIENTIFIC FACTS

Crime scene reconstruction is the process of determining or eliminating the possibility of any events and actions that may or may not have occurred at the crime scene, through the analysis of the scene's patterns and physical evidence. The location and condition of each piece of evidence gives the investigator information on the history of the scene, the actions of the suspect, and the location of the victim. The results of laboratory examination of the physical evidence will provide the crucial linkage between the crime, the victim, and the suspect. They also can be important in providing or disproving an alibi provided by the suspect.

It is often useful to determine the actual course of a crime by limiting the possibilities that resulted in the crime scene, its location, and the condition of pattern evidence, such as blood-spatter patterns, gunshot-residue patterns, bullet-trajectory patterns, footprints and tire trails, and glass-fracture patterns. These are all important for crime scene reconstruction. The MacArthur case is a typical example of thorough crime scene reconstruction. The prosecution was able to show the jurors that Sgt. Theodore MacArthur was lying about the death of his wife, Pilar. This was based on forensic evidence which showed that the death of Mrs. MacArthur was not a suicide or an accidental death, but a homicide.

A successful reconstruction is dependent on the ability: To make observations at the scene using logical approaches, to examine evidence scientifically, to develop a theory on the crime, and to formulate a conclusion. There are basic principles used in the forensic examination of the physical evidence. They are applied to the many types of reconstructions, depending on the nature of the crime; the questions which need answers; the types of crimes that have taken place; and the issues related to the case.

The utilization of bloodstain patterns for a crime scene reconstruction has been described in the Mathison chapter. In the MacArthur case, bloodstain patterns were used to identify the facts surrounding the investigation by knowing the physical nature and biological characteristics of bloodstains.

The physical pattern of the bloodstains in the bedroom demonstrated that Pilar's body had been moved from the bed to the floor. However, this issue was not contested by the defense. The issue was *when* the victim's body was moved from the bed to administer first aid. According to MacArthur, his actions in trying to save Pilar's life explained the transfer of her blood onto his hands and clothing. It also explained the changes of the bloodstain patterns on the bed and at the scene. However, the observations by police officers and the scientific facts were able to prove that Pilar's body was moved from the bed *after* the blood had coagulated, that is, much later after her death. The removal of her body from the bed was just another part of MacArthur's staging of the crime scene.

The presence or absence of gunshot residue on a person's hands and the target surfaces provide scientific data used to determine whether or not somebody touched or fired a gun and to determine the target-distance information. This data has been used by forensic scientists and medical examiners for many years to determine the possible manner of the death—whether it is suicide, homicide, or an accidental shooting. When a firearm is discharged, the rapid oxidation of the gunpowder creates a tremendous amount of energy associated with hot gases, soot, and partially burned gunpowder. These materials are generally referred to as gunshot residue (GSR). GSR originates from the detonation of the primer, gunpowder, and other components of the ammunition. Some of these materials are propelled forward with the projectile toward the target as well as backward onto the shooter's hands and clothing. The components of GSR may be detected if samples are collected from the hands or clothing of the shooter, before washing or removal by other means. GSR also can be found on the target, such as the victim's body, clothing, or other target surfaces, if the gun muzzle is close enough in range. Therefore, detection of GSR has two primary objectives: to determine whether an individual fired or handled a recently discharged firearm and to determine the muzzle-to-target distance. Distance determination can play a vital role in helping to distinguish between a self-inflicted gunshot wound and a distance shot attributable to a murder.

There currently are several tests used by forensic laboratories to determine gunshot residue data, such as: Diphenylamine (DPA) testing, the Modified Griess test, the atomic absorption spectroscopy (AA) test; the induced couple plasma spectroscope (ICP) test, and the scanning electron microscopy (SEM) with elemental analysis method. The first two of these, the DPA and Griess tests, are considered screening tests (providing general information) and are used for field test or examination of GSR pattern analysis, while AA, ICP, and SEM are considered more specific laboratory tests.

AA, ICP, and SEM are currently the methods of choice by forensic science laboratories. AA and ICP are instrumental analyses for the detection of barium, antimony, and lead. These are elements that commonly appear with gunshot residues. The presence of these residues could indicate one or a combination of the following:

1. That a person fired a firearm.
2. That a person handled a recently discharged firearm.
3. That a person was close or next to a discharged firearm.
4. That a person worked in an environment with a combination of those elements.

The scanning electronic microscopy–energy dispensive x-ray spectrometry (SEM-EDAX) technique provides the advantage of combining particle-pattern recognition and elemental-composition determination. Therefore, it is a more conclusive type of test. With the number of GSR particles present and the distribution of those particles, the forensic scientist can reach a more definitive conclusion about the presence of GSR; for example, the morphological identification of the spherical shape of the gunpowder particles and the elemental composition of those particles. The SEM test will enhance the specificity of GSR test results.

THE SUMMARY

Theodore MacArthur had put himself above the law when he decided to murder his wife, Pilar. For this crime, MacArthur will stay in prison until at least the year 2018, when he will be sixty-three. This conviction was achieved because honest police, individuals who silently resented Sergeant MacArthur's cynical and manipulative methods, quietly went to work and successfully investigated this crime.

The prosecution team, led by the indefatigable Susan Dannelly, combined their efforts with those of their police colleagues and carried the case through to its successful conclusion. Members of the Miami-Dade Coroner's office shared their professional analyses with my own, and, collectively, we were able to put a murderer behind bars.

This is and should be a particularly harsh punishment for an ex-policeman, since MacArthur will be serving his twenty-five-year sentence with many individuals he helped bring to justice.

Tragically, all of this will not restore Pilar Soles MacArthur to her children, other family members, and her loving friends. Just like the "Pilar" character in Ernest Hemingway's classic novel about the Spanish Civil War, *For Whom the Bell Tolls*, Pilar MacArthur was a heroine, one who stoically met a fate she never deserved. If the tragic murdering of a beautiful thirty-five-year-old victim can mean anything, Pilar's loss should underscore the terrible problem of spousal abuse, whether it is physical or psychological or both. Pilar MacArthur died more than twelve years ago, and our civilization has made some progress in dealing with cases of spousal abuse, especially in diagnosing and treating this menace in its earliest stages. But this progress will never be enough until this terrible problem, so indigenous to the American home, is completely eradicated.

EPILOGUE

It is a dangerous and untidy world.
President John F. Kennedy, Nov. 14, 1963

America seems to be in the process of rediscovering itself. These times prompt me to cite President Kennedy's words spoken at his last news conference. It also seems appropriate to quote an African American athlete, philosopher, and Muslim, as I end this book. Muhammad Ali said, "The truth shall set you free." I have been very fortunate that the nature of the work I do largely enables me to focus on the scientific pursuit of this liberating truth, even though dark human motives have caused a crime and, thus, the need for my skills as a forensic scientist.

As someone who was born and raised in China, please let me point out that there is a more introspective America emerging today. This is the America where more and more citizens are striving toward an individual peace each of us must try to find in life. This is, of course, a sharp contrast to the fate of the victims and the perpetrators of violent crimes who are put forth in this book. The five cases presented, with their cast of individuals who were citizens from all walks of life, involved men and women who, to the outside world, seemed successful and at peace. The truth, however, was far different. Even in the O. J. Simpson case, where the accused was acquitted of two murders, there had been a lengthy history of domestic conflict, a struggle for control, and even abuse. All five marriages were conflicted very deeply and in each instance ended up in tragedy.

Stepping into the crime scenes or looking through a microscope at what was the aftermath of these struggles is a very sobering experience. And these crimes are not isolated. Spousal abuse remains the number one unreported crime in America. The criminal investigator and forensic scientist are later responsible for scientifically finding the evidence which will clearly exhibit to a judge and jury just how a murder has been committed and by whom. Most ironically for myself, three of the five cases featured a husband who was also a police officer, though in one case that role was only at a part-time level. There does not seem to be any way to account for this. I say this since I have worked with, literally, thousands of wonderful men and women who have devoted their lives and talents to law enforcement.

In each of the troubled marriages covered in this book, there was a breakdown in the participants turning for help. Marriage counseling was at a minimum in all five situations. Family, friends, and society should work together to stop the inevitable slide to divorce and death. The first step for any battered and/or controlled woman to prevent any further physical and psychological abuse is to assess the problem and then to take action, action which will not slide back into ambivalence. I feel that it is important for me to express these facts as clearly as possible. Love, compassion, and mutual respect are all essentials of any successful marriage.

As I conclude this work, I hope that the reader has also been able to perceive aspects of the forensic expert's responsibilities and work. We must always struggle to establish the facts and truth in any investigation. How did a terrible crime occur? What were the means the perpetrator used? Were there any witnesses? What could they have been able to perceive? Has the crime scene been adequately preserved? Is forensic evidence present? Has all of the evidence been correctly collected and preserved? Have the detectives and forensic scientists established a chain of custody which will stand up to the glare of a courtroom proceeding? Has all the physical evidence been examined according to the highest scientific standards? Has all of the evidence been presented, whether it is incriminating or exculpatory in nature? In short, have the police and prosecution investigations been dedicated to finding the truth, the whole truth, and nothing but the truth?

Throughout this book I have endeavored to show how an investigation should be conducted and I have pointed out where the strict standards this goal requires have not been observed. As part of this, I have told how a forensic scientist works and the large number of hours we have to put into this profession. Now I am in my sixties and, as I look back at my life, I have decided to put forward the considerable energy this work requires. That's because I feel deeply that science, when given a fair chance, can define the truth in any case. That is my life's credo: Find the truth and bring it before the court, no matter where the facts lead us.

But, as I have pointed out in each of the five cases, I have not worked in a vacuum, off somewhere in a laboratory, and on my own. I have had the great opportunity of working with countless dedicated police officers, detectives, prosecutors, lawyers, and forensic scientists in this, my quest. Whether fellow forensic scientists, police officers, criminalists, detectives, or prosecutors, I will always consider myself very lucky for having worked with such highly talented and dedicated colleagues. Ultimately, any court decision which reflects this truth is the direct result of a great team effort. I am simply one member of that team, and I am proud to end this work on this note. I will always be grateful for the great teammates I have found throughout the world, individuals who have combined to find the truth and nothing but the truth.

NOTES

A PROLOGUE

1. *Webster's Third New International Dictionary of the English Language*, unabridged, s.v. "toxicology."
2. Ibid., s.v. "anthropometry."

CHAPTER ONE. THE MATHISON MURDER CASE

1. Crystal Kua, "Several Witnesses Testify at Hearing on Mathison Case," *Hawaii Tribune-Herald,* 17 December 1993.
2. Crystal Kua, "Blood in Van Not Consistent with Mathison's Explanation," *Hawaii Tribune-Herald*, 21 December 1993.
3. Dave Smith, "Key Blood Marks Not in Van," *Hawaii Tribune-Herald*, 15 November 1995.
4. Dave Smith, "Mathison Trial: Specialists Take Stand," *Hawaii Tribune-Herald,* 17 November 1995.
5. Dave Smith, "Mathison: Didn't Do It," *Hawaii Tribune-Herald,* 21 November 1995.
6. Dave Smith, "Jury May Get Case Today," *Hawaii Tribune-Herald,* 22 November 1995.
7. Rod Thompson, "Cop Guilty in Wife Murder," *Honolulu Star-Bulletin,* 23 November 1995.
8. Dave Smith, "Jury: Mathison Guilty," *Hawaii Tribune-Herald*, 23 November 1995.
9. Ibid.
10. Dave Smith, "A Happier Anniversary," *Hawaii Tribune-Herald,* 26 November 1995.

CHAPTER TWO. THE WOODCHIPPER MURDER

1. Arthur Herzog, *The Woodchipper Murder* (New York: Henry Holt, 1989), p.45.
2. Dr. Mel Goldstein, Phone interview by Tom O'Neil, 12 March 2001.
3. Herzog, *Woodchipper Murder,* p. 37.
4. Ibid., p. 32.
5. Ibid., p. 34.
6. Ibid., p. 51.
7. Ibid., pp. 127–29.
8. Ibid., p. 138.
9. Walter Flanagan, interview by Tom O'Neil, 30 March 2001.
10. Herzog, *Woodchipper Murder*, pp. 153–56.
11. Ibid., p. 154.
12. Ibid., p. 158
13. Ibid., p. 155.
14. Ibid., p. 161.
15. Ibid.. p. 221.

CHAPTER THREE. THE O. J. SIMPSON CASE

1. Based on a telephone interview in the summer of 1996 by Tom O'Neil with the juror in question.

CHAPTER FOUR. THE SHERMAN CASE

1. Roseanne Simborski, "Sherman to Stand Trial, Judge Rules," *Day of New London*, 1 September 1990.
2. Roseanne Simborski, "Attorney Says Sherman's Rights Violated by Delaying His Arrest," *Day of New London,* 11 October 1991.
3. Roseanne Simborski, "Phone Call Seen Key in Sherman Trial," *Day of New London,* 9 October 1991.
4. John Ruddy, "Sherman Guilty of Murder," *Day of New London*, 8 February 1992.

5. Roseanne Simborski, "Sherman Gets 50 Years for Murdering His Wife." *Day of New London,* 18 March 1992.

6. Ibid.

CHAPTER FIVE. THE MacARTHUR CASE

1. Meg Laughlin, "Pilar and (Mistress)," *Miami Herald*, 4 September 1994.

2. Ibid.

3. Ibid.

4. Ibid.

5. Dan Keating and Joan Fleischman, "Metro Sergeant's Wife Dies in Apparent Shooting Accident," *Miami Herald*, 2 August 1989

6. Ibid.

7. Joan Fleischman, "Lawyer: Officer's Wife Accidentally Shot Herself," *Miami Herald,* 11 August 1989.

8. John Lantigua, "Cop's Colleagues Cast Doubt on His Honesty," *Miami Herald*, 3 December 1993.

9. David, Lyons, "Ex-Detective's Wife Planned to Leave Him, Friend Says," *Miami Herald*, 4 December 1993.

BIBLIOGRAPHY

Alcamo, I. Edward. *Biology.* Lincoln, Nebr.: Cliff Notes, 1995.

Asimov, Isaac. *The Genetic Code.* New York: Orion, 1962.

Baden, Michael, and Marion Roach. *Dead Reckoning: The New Science of Catching Killers.* New York: Simon & Schuster, 2000.

Bolsover, Stehpen R., Jeremy S. Hyams, Steve Jones, Elisabeth A. Shepard, and Hugh A. White. *From Genes to Cells.* New York: Wiley Liss, 1997.

Bosco, Joseph A. *A Problem of Evidence: How the Prosecution Freed O. J. Simpson.* New York: William Morrow, 1996.

Connors, Edward, Thomas Lundegran, Neal Miller, and Tom McEwen. *Convicted by Juries, Exonerated by Science: Case Studies in the Use of DNA Evidence to Establish Innocence after Trial.* Washington, D.C.: U.S. Department of Justice, 1996.

DeForest, Peter R., Robert Gaensslen, and Henry C. Lee. *Forensic Science: An Introduction to Criminalistics.* New York: McGraw-Hill, 1983.

Dickens, Charles. *Oliver Twist.* 1838. Reprint, New York: Penguin, 1985.

DiMaio, Dominick J., and Vincent J. M. DiMaio. *Forensic Pathology.* Boca Raton, Fla.: CRC, 1999.

DiMaio, Vincent J. M. *Gunshot Wounds:* Practical Aspects of Firearms, Ballistics, Evidence, and Forensic Techniques. 2d ed. Boca Raton, Fla.: CRC, 1999.

Freed, Donald, and Raymond P. Briggs. *Killing Time: The First Full Investigation into the Unsolved Murders of Nicole Brown Simpson and Ronald Goldman.* New York: MacMillan, 1996.

Geberth, Vernon J. *Practical Homicide Investigation: Tactics, Procedures, and Forensic Techniques.* Boca Raton, Fla.: CRC, 1999.

Haglund, William D., and Marcella H. Sorg, eds. *Forensic Taphonomy: The Postmortem Fate of Human Remains*. Boca Raton, Fla.: CRC, 1997

Herzog, Arthur. *The Woodchipper Murder*. New York: Henry Holt, 1989.

Lee, Henry C., and Robert Gaensslen. *Advances in Fingerprint Technology*. 2d ed. Boca Raton, Fla.: CRC, 2001.

————. *DNA and Other Polymorphisms in Forensic Science*. Chicago: Yearbook Medical Publishers, 1990.

Lee, Henry C., and Howard A. Harris. *Physical Evidence in Forensic Science*. Tucson, Ariz.: Lawyers & Judges, 2000.

Lee, Henry C., and Jerry Labriola. *Famous Crimes Revisited: From Sacco-Vanzetti to O. J. Simpson*. Southbury, Conn.: Strong Books, 2001.

Lee, Henry C., Timothy Palmach, and Marilyn Miller. *Henry Lee's Crime Scene Handbook*. San Diego: Academic Press, 2001.

Toobin, Jeffrey. *The Run of His Life: The People v. O. J. Simpson*. New York: Random House, 1996.

Watson, James D. *The Double Helix: A Personal Account of the Discovery of the Structure of DNA*. New York: Atheneum, 1969.

Wecht, Cyril. *Grave Secrets: A Leading Forensic Expert Reveals the Startling Truth about O. J. Simpson, David Koresh, Vincent Foster, and Other Sensational Cases*. New York: Penguin, 1996.

INDEX